First Printing, November, 2018

ISBN 978-1-946032-20-1

Fascinating Womanhood
PO Box 3831
Springfield, MO 65808

Author: Dixie Andelin Forsyth
Cover Art: Shintayu Arifin
Interior Art: Shintayu Arifin and Emily Andelin Hicks

www.fascinatingwomanhood.com

Acknowledgements

I have many feelings of gratitude at the end of an over four year process as I write this tribute to all those who have helped me with the completion of this task and contributed in so many ways.

My husband Bob and son Richard have been irreplaceable in their daily help and devotion. Without them, I don't know how this ever could have been accomplished.

My daughters Melissa, Amanda, and Cherry have been with me from the beginning and have helped me in countless ways in outlining and through many reviews. There is no adequate way to thank them for all they have done.

In addition, my sisters Kristine, Ginny, and Merilee have all loved, encouraged, and supported me by helping with some of the initial edits and so much more. They too grew up with the original Fascinating Womanhood written by our mother. I appreciate their insights and wisdom.

A heartfelt thanks to Marta Carters, our Brazilian country director for all their kind and dedicated support and help.

I also appreciate the encouragement I regularly receive from the rest of my family; my other children Tiffany, John, and Gi na, as well as my brothers John and Paul.

And to you, the readers and online contributors, for your invaluable feedback and encouragement. You inspire me every day.

Table of Contents

Section 3 - Creating a Lifelong Love Affair

Fascinating Womanhood
For the Timeless Woman

The Purpose of this Book

*"Nothing feels better than when you love someone with your
whole heart and soul and they love you back even more"*
~ Karen Kostyla

My mother, Helen B. Andelin, published Fascinating Womanhood after four years of hard work when I was 13 years old. All of her 8 children were still at home; the youngest of my sisters, Merilee, was a baby. Mom would get up at 4:00 a.m. to write so she would not disrupt family life. I recall a few times when she went away for a week to do intense writing and to get a lot done in a relatively short amount of time. My grandmother, my father, and often I helped out at home. I loved to cook and take care of my younger siblings.

I was taught the principles of Fascinating Womanhood from my childhood before I even felt any attraction for boys. As a little girl, I thought boys were somewhat disgusting because they often smelled like sweaty, wet puppies. I was more interested in playing princess and pretending to be a mother to my baby dolls. But I witnessed the romantic marriage my parents had. I remember seeing them out the window, hand in hand, on their regular walks—they valued their alone time together. My three sisters and I were fortunate to have never had to unlearn bad habits related to femininity and how to understand, respect and treat men. We are all married to men we adore and have been for many years and are very grateful to both parents, but especially to Mom for teaching us timeless principles and being a great example of them.

When Fascinating Womanhood was published in 1963, my mother had no idea it would become a best seller. Its purpose was to teach women the secrets she had discovered to achieve a deeply romantic marriage. It had transformed her relationship with my father; she hoped it would do the same for many others.

The movement she started grew to involve about 1,500 teachers worldwide. She was on television and radio shows, and articles about her were in prominent newspapers and magazines. Her book was translated into 7 languages. She also wrote a bestselling book to single girls, entitled "The Fascinating Girl," and she wrote a book for mothers: "All About Raising Children." Dad wrote his book on inspiring masculinity called "Man of Steel and Velvet" during this period, and it has sold over a half million copies.

Mom was criticized when she wrote Fascinating Womanhood by many who embraced the second wave feminist movement. Perhaps they thought she was saying all women needed to read her book and practice its principles. She was just trying to reach those who wanted a fabulous marriage, and taught many timeless concepts in her original book.

Before she passed away, mom expressed to me a need to update old information and add exciting concepts we had learned. Cultures in every country alter somewhat with each generation but timeless principles are always true. Despite changes in the past 50 years, there is much of value to study in Vintage Fascinating Womanhood. I like to think of my mother's book and this new sequel as companions with a common purpose: the happiness of women and superb romantic marriages.

Some of the timeless principles my mom presented included the image of a divided woman; one with both angelic and human qualities.

The angelic focused on traits of character that are an essential part of a romance that actually lasts. She taught us some of the secrets of how to understand men and the importance of developing character, inner happiness, and becoming a "Domestic Goddess." Developing this part of you helps a man feel emotionally safe and awakens a feeling of near worship. It brings a deep peace and comfort to his soul, and to yours.

The human qualities help us become more fascinating, feminine, and charming. Men adore these characteristics in us and they make us feel womanlier.

Fascinating Womanhood for the Timeless Woman moves to a deeper level of integration, combining the essence of my mother's original teachings with new knowledge and skills that will assist you in gaining greater self-esteem and developing your marriage into a lifelong love affair. In addition to the bulk of the book that applies to both married and single women, I have also included a special chapter for singles who are looking for "The One."

These principles are needed now more than ever. Divorce and break-up rates are at an all-time high, leaving broken hearts everywhere. The many psychology and communication books which are available today that deal with marriage and relationships are helpful. But they focus very little on the importance of femininity and the unique influence women can have on relationships. For these reasons, I felt compelled to add my perspective in the hopes of helping you, my priceless sisters, re-learn this unique power to make a difference in our marriages and all our relationships.

Fascinating Womanhood for the Timeless Woman has three distinct purposes:

First: Reclaim Femininity. Learn more about how to become empowered in a way unique to our gender. Too many of us have abandoned our natural power base.

Femininity is a natural gift that brings great influence and power to the woman who masters it. In this book, you will learn the value and strength of being wholly female—distinct from a man. The fact that this statement is not boringly obvious is the point.

Second: Inspire Masculinity. Learn how to understand men on a deeper level and inspire masculinity in them, and not diminish it.

Women have a great influence on men. They are different from us, not only in their physical bodies but in their perspectives, the way they solve problems, and in their basic masculine needs.

You will also learn what makes you irresistible to them.

Many of these secrets used to be passed down from mother to daughter from generation to generation. Today most of us aren't taught these principals at all.

Third: Create your own lifelong love affair. If you desire a romantic marriage that lasts your whole life and if you are married to a basically good man, you have within your grasp the power to inspire and achieve this kind of love. Practice the principals in this book and you will be happier, and so will your beloved.

Fascinating Womanhood for the Timeless Woman will show you just how powerful your influence can be. The real magic in a relationship occurs when the change you earn for yourself has a powerful influence on others, perhaps even leading to their own embrace of change in themselves.

Applying the principles of Fascinating Womanhood for the Timeless Woman is a lifelong endeavor. You don't have to be perfect. I'm certainly not. Don't get discouraged. You will find that you will be rewarded when you show sincere effort in even small things—perhaps more positive results than you thought.

Many women have reported profound changes in the way their husbands treated them soon after applying just a few of these principles. I still make lots of mistakes and have to redirect myself. You probably will too but it's okay to be human. You can still be adored while you're learning.

Chapter 1
The Deepest Kind of Love

"It is love, not reason, that is stronger than death"
~ Thomas Mann

In ancient Greece, there were four words used to distinguish between the different forms love can take. Agápe referred to the love shared between God and man: charitable or pure love. Éros was known as the love of passion and beauty: a more physical and sometimes sexual love, appreciation or attraction. Philía designated a more platonic, equal type of love between friends, brothers or sisters, classmates, community or coworkers: the kind of love that enjoys doing things together and appreciating life and each other with a lot of loyalty attached. Storge, last of all, was about the forgiving type of love that parents often have for their children or a people might have for their country: a stubborn, enduring kind of love that looks past faults and goes to battle for its own.

In the English language, we simply use the single word "love" to describe many different levels of positive feeling about something or someone. There is love of God, love of friends and children, even books, pizza, movies... you name it. Sure, we have words "like," "adore," "esteem" and others, but we tend to stick to L-O-V-E and sprinkle the one word throughout our speech, hoping our meaning comes across based on context.

For example, if we say "I love spaghetti," what we really mean is we very much enjoy eating it—we don't want to marry it or build a shrine to it, and hopefully most people know that. We might say "I love my university professor," but would we really jump in front of them to take a bullet that's speeding towards them? We often use the word "love" in a way that actually defines lust, not the kind of feeling worth sacrificing for, and certainly not the kind of love you stay with through cancer and bankruptcy and sick children. Relationships where sex is the main ingredient don't actually need real love at all and are doomed to fade over time.

The kind of love I am focusing on in this book, and especially in this chapter, is the deepest kind a man and woman can share: incandescent and eternal romantic love that combines all four of the Greek definitions into one beautiful sphere. The romantic love I refer to is the kind that lasts not only a lifetime but beyond. It can endure separation, death, and all the hardships we face, and it brings joy, fulfillment and purpose to our lives while doing so.

"You know you're in love when you can't fall asleep because reality is finally better than your dreams"
~Dr. Seuss

So what is this kind of love? It is deep, faithful and true. It can lift you to emotional, spiritual and intellectual heights you never imagined. It is unconditional, cherishing, valuing, respecting; enjoying each other's company and friendship whether you are doing something special or nothing at all. It is honoring each other and combines deep emotional as well as physical intimacy. There is knowledge that you are each other's number one priority; each other's number one confidant. You know each other's deepest desires, fears, and dreams and still feel safe. You know each other's faults and still feel totally cherished. As stated above, this kind of love includes passion, but it doesn't feed on it. Its strongest attribute is care for the one loved. When you truly love, you feel alive as never before. I'm not talking about infatuation that contains the seeds of eternal love but is only its infant. Without maturity, infatuation will wither and die.

Infatuation feels great because it is a promise of real romantic love yet possible. Many people believe infatuation is all there is to love and when it fades, so does the relationship. They think love has died. They do not see the huge vista just beyond the horizon.

If you think real, enduring and satisfying romantic love sounds impossible to attain, you haven't yet learned everything about this most priceless human emotion.

Many people have enjoyed true romantic love, though most are not famous. These people usually don't broadcast their love for each other publicly because it's intensely private. We know some of these stories because of personal histories and others from people we have known. Some people have never witnessed such a relationship, but it is absolutely possible! It's just not as common as it could be.

You don't hold all the cards but you have access to enough. You can foster this love, to see that it can be planted and grow bottomless roots that will wind around both your hearts forever. If this sounds like a fantasy, rest assured it's not. I know because I have it, my parents had it and I know others who do too.

"Love is the most powerful magic, the most powerful emotion that there is"
~ Anonymous

What You Will Learn in this Book

- What deep romantic love is and how to attain it
- Men's and women's specific needs; the similarities and differences
- Understanding yourself and why you are so valuable
- What feminine power is and why we as women have so much influence
- Recognizing how some of your natural weaknesses can be strengths
- The biological differences between male and female brains and how understanding these differences will strengthen your relationships

- Femininity: what it is and why it's so vital to both our attraction and identity
- The appearance and mannerisms that fascinate men
- How to acquire real charm
- Why physical beauty is not necessary for a lasting, loving relationship
- The pros and cons of the Feminist Movement: how it has helped and hurt us
- How to bring out the best in him
- What a good man really wants in a woman
- Understanding masculine pride and how to help break through his wall of reserve
- The four levels of intimacy and why they should follow in order for a lasting relationship to be possible
- The importance of character and the part it plays in a long-term romantic relationship
- Understanding boundaries and the importance of them
- How to create atmosphere in your home that will help everyone feel relaxed and their best
- What to do when your man makes mistakes
- How to be attractive, even adorable when you are angry
- The kind of men to avoid and how to spot a rat
  And More!

"Love: The irresistible desire to be irresistibly desired."
~ Mark Twain

Section 1
Reclaiming Femininity

"Sometimes it is necessary to re-teach a thing its loveliness"
~ Galway Kinnell

This section is devoted to reawakening the native and unlimited power you were born with as a woman. We will get into more detail about your inherent worth, some of the physical properties that make you unique, how to deal with special issues you face as a woman, and how to cultivate charm and why it is one of the most effective tools in your arsenal. In all, I will be outlining the aspects of your feminine power and you will learn how to cultivate it to achieve love and happiness.

Femininity is inherent to women, but it must be reclaimed because it has been lost by far too many. Though there are many women in the world, feminine arts are no longer emphasized, encouraged, or even taught in most cultures. Instead, we are often taught that femininity and gender identity is a trivial or bad thing. We live in an age of so-called "toxic masculinity" and the notion that to be a woman equates to wearing women's clothes and makeup—that it is fundamentally a superficial and weak thing. Opposition to femininity is the new global norm, not the exception. There is a war on women, but it is mischaracterized as a struggle for more legal rights, more jobs, more money, and more political power. The real war is against our feminine identities and our role as the world's feminine women and mothers.

As I look around I see identity confusion: women don't seem to know what it means to be female or why it's valuable. Our gender has been seriously compromised to the detriment of our happiness. Femininity has been marginalized and our future diminished despite the gains made in the working world and with basic human rights. Too many women are unhappy, depressed, and disillusioned.

We need to return to femininity. How we look does matter, but femininity is much more about those traits which are natural to us and give us inherent power and value. We all have at least a latent form of femininity, and so we are all valuable. The only difference between women is the degree to which they access and cultivate what is theirs from birth. For women, being true to themselves is the only true path to happiness and fulfillment.

Chapter 2
Your Limitless Worth

"If women didn't exist, all the money in the world would have no meaning"
~Aristotle Onassis

When my mother finished writing Fascinating Womanhood in the early 60's, she didn't question that women were of great worth. She came from a traditional home with old world values and assumed women knew their worth because she knew her own. In her relatively sheltered world of friends and family, the question of woman's value didn't come up. She was close to her brothers, father, uncles, and husband. They all loved her and she felt treasured.

Many things are different today. Too many of us don't realize the value of being a woman. Today's media promotes gender fluidity, and the qualities which are unique and valuable to our gender are marginalized. Many people in modern society trivialize female qualities like gentleness or sensitivity, saying those traits are undesirable and suggest weakness. Even enjoying wearing the color pink has been mocked on television—remember the girl baby in the incubator raising a fist to protest her pink hospital bracelet? Somewhere along the road, being girly, being feminine, became a no-no in society.

We are different from men, we're uniquely female. Our bodies are dissimilar, and even our brains are different in important ways. We are so unique that there is a specialty of medicine entirely devoted to us and our diverse issues. Women as they are by nature are glorious creatures, as many men will admit. And there is so much joy for us in being who we are, in unlocking our true potential. In this book I want to help you realize how important and fulfilling it is to think and act female. As a woman, you are much more valuable than you realize. You need to expand your vision of yourself and your importance. Thinking and acting *female* is endlessly fulfilling, as you will see when you implement the timeless principles in this book.

Women are the Gatekeepers of Civilization

Masculine, moral men are wonderful. We need them. They are physically stronger than we are. They are courageous and perform dangerous tasks, and they provide a model of true masculinity for our children.

Without feminine women to temper and gentle them, men would be more war-like and aggressive than they naturally are. It is in their nature to be more aggressive, and this is in part due to their higher levels of testosterone. They have a greater sex drive, more competitive natures, and their masculine ambition sometimes leads them into trouble with other men. They are born this way and we should not judge them for this fact alone. Overcoming their basic nature is often challenging, and they need our womanly help to do this.

When men are at their best, they are the protectors, builders, and organizers of civilization, while we are the gatekeepers. But they are vulnerable where we are strong. They *need* us.

Men become more uncivilized when women are either absent, corrupt, or immoral. This is when we forget our feminine nature; we forget what fulfills our lives and gives it true enduring meaning. When women fall, men and families are doomed. Nations cannot stand for long without strong families. And in any civilization where women are largely corrupt, God help the men.

When women go wrong, men go right after them.
~ Mae West

Fascinating Womanhood teaches women to apply and nurture the power of femininity, inspire true and righteous masculinity, and to help build enduring love affairs with their men. Couples who have such love affairs are powerful because they combine masculine leadership and strength with feminine sensitivity, insight, and a relationship emphasis. This kind of "power couple" forms a strong foundation on which to build the kinds of families that are the true and lasting strength of nations.

Portrait of a Feminine Woman

Who are we at our best? What traits define us? Why are we so indispensable? We care about relationships, the ones closest to us, specifically family and friends. But we also care about entire groups of people we have never met. We care about the hungry and poor. Women often start and head humanitarian causes to ease suffering. It's not that men don't care. Most do. I'm emphasizing our specific strengths in areas where we excel.

Women have great power — feminine power. Most of us aren't even aware of it. Fewer understand it. Those who sense it and use it know what I'm talking about. Some apply it inappropriately, ultimately to their own detriment. When we learn to recognize it and use it wisely, we can have an effect that changes the world, even if it's only the small world of those we know and love.

We can be assertive and persistent in accomplishing our goals, whether in personal development or business. But feminine women don't typically start wars. Our concern for loved ones tends to play a more central role. This is one of the sources of our feminine power. We are protective of those we love. We sometimes neglect ourselves to go to the rescue, going without sleep or even food for the welfare of others.

As women, we are emotionally strong yet sensitive creatures, inclined to like pretty or artistic things. Because we appreciate beauty, we like to *feel* beautiful too. We often work diligently on our appearance. We experiment with our hair and makeup. The makeup and hair industry is dominated by women's products and services. We love to try on clothes and find something that makes us feel attractive. We believe in health and taking care of ourselves. Also, because we appreciate beauty, we are interested in making the world around us more attractive. We don't like to settle for the mundane or drab. You know the phrase "a woman's touch"? There's a long-held idea in society that, with a woman around, one's environment will look and feel better.

Feminine women dream of romantic love. We love to be in love and long to be adored. We enjoy the feeling of being protected. It helps us find security in a special way. We feel safer if we have someone we can count on. Of course we have the ability to provide for ourselves and our families when we need to, or when we want to develop a specific talent, but we appreciate if we don't have to do it *all*. When we have careers, we put our families first in our hearts and motives. We love our children and risk death to give them life, and have been doing this since time began.

There are more of us that possess traits of noble character than our masculine counterparts. We are more often interested in doing what's right: what is good, whether we receive any credit or not. More of us are content to remain in the shadows and out of history books if we are successful in helping others. We go to extraordinary lengths to make the ones we love happy. We often go out of our way for strangers. Being sensitive, we are sometimes hurt by others we love and serve; yet we do it anyway, expecting little in return.

Women can be strong, feminine leaders and great examples of courage and kindness, but our successful leadership differs from a man's in that it's feminine and has more power when used in this womanly way.

We don't tend to specialize in task leadership— focusing on tasks that need to be done to meet certain goals—as often as men, but we can do many jobs exceptionally well and can juggle several things at once. Due to differences in male and female brain structure, men tend to be more focused on one task at a time. Men can multi-task but women make it look easier. For example, we can make dinner, listen for the washer, hear the door bell and carry on a conversation all at once. My husband says: "When I am grilling, I'm grilling. Don't distract me." He loves to focus on one thing at a time without interruption. He can kind of do it, but too much multitasking frustrates him.

We are the gatekeepers of procreation because we are the world's mothers. To be a mother is the toughest, most thankless, time-consuming job in existence. It is also the most rewarding and requires skill, persistence, stamina, courage, patience, and love. Those of us who are mothers never retire from our career from the time we give birth to our deaths.

No matter what we do as women, we succeed best, fastest and more often when we implement our natural talents and gifts that are inherently female by nature. If you're not sure what some of these abilities are, you will know by the time you've finished this book.

A Woman's Value

As part of developing a romantic relationship, it is important to understand and believe in your value as a woman. This is foundational because your perception of your worth determines how you interact with others and what you can achieve. You can accomplish dreams you never thought possible if you first understand and believe in a greater vision of yourself.

Historically, there has been a spectacular disregard for women and our basic value. We have been treated like slaves, married off without consent, traded as property, mutilated, abused, and excluded. In some countries, when a girl is on her period she is considered unclean. Without adequate sanitary protection, she has no choice but to stay home from school during this time. That means she likely misses about a week of her education per month. This can significantly alter her ability to be educated, which can in turn can have an impact on the rest of her life. In some countries, a woman's grave is not marked or her birth recorded. The men who are supposed to love her, and protect her (her husband and male family members) have the power to kill her when they choose, and they sometimes do.

But our worth remains unaltered.

Women can contribute to society in similar ways to men. We are leaders, scientists, artists, musicians, poets, dancers, and heads of companies. But you are valuable as a woman in your own right, independent of any worldly acclaim. Your worth does not depend on your position, and it does not diminish a man's worth. Women and men are equally necessary and important.

All great individuals in history — the rulers, heroes, explorers, scientists, and inventors — all were born of a woman, carried and delivered with great pain. Nearly every person who has ever lived has been raised by a woman or a mother figure. The world's pre-school and elementary school teachers are predominantly women and they instruct the world's children who are not biologically theirs.[1]

It is likely that more women have died in childbirth than all the men who ever died in all wars in history.[2] They died as a direct result of giving life or from complications during pregnancy.[3]

Women have babies every day of the year but wars are sporadic. Historically, every pregnant woman has known she stood a chance of dying and had to prepare for that possibility. When women die this way, they leave behind devastation in their families with not only grief but the loss of a mother for any other offspring. They leave a higher rate of poverty and poorer nutrition for the remaining children.

It has been and will always be our task to give birth and to predominantly raise earth's children. Can you think of a greater contribution to the world than this?

---

[1] According to the most recent population survey released by the U.S. Bureau of Labor, male educators constitute just 2.3% of pre-K and kindergarten teachers, 18.3% of the elementary and middle school teacher population, and 42% of the high school level teaching staff in the United States.

[2] Until the advent of modern medicine, giving birth was a significant cause of death for women in all cultures. A conservative estimate still places it worldwide at about 1 death per 100 births. Today it is estimated that about 287,000 women die each year from either pregnancy or childbirth throughout the world; 99% of these in developing countries (Maternity Worldwide).

[3] Mahmoud Fathalla, Founder of Safe Motherhood Initiative.

Women Lead and Inspire

There have been female Nobel Prize winners, monarchs, heads of corporations, writers, artists, and more. There are many stories of courageous women who have risked and given their lives, who inspire and also raise other leaders.

Florence Nightingale, known as "The Lady with the Lamp," fought to improve civilian and Army health care throughout her life. She inspired the founding of the International Red Cross which still helps countless numbers of people. Lucien Baudens, a contemporary author said of her strength and courage, "This frail young woman... embraced in her solicitude the sick of three armies."

To get a better idea of what some of us have endured and also contributed, let's look at a tiny sampling of women who have used feminine influence to improve the world outside their homes.

1. *Adi Roche:* Founded an organization that helps orphans of nuclear disaster.

2. *Abigail Adams:* Mended the rift between two former U.S. presidents.

3. *Aung San Suu Kyi:* Dedicated her life to freeing Burma from an oppressive dictatorship and creating democracy without violence.

4. *Carrie M. Thomas:* Pioneer and model for women in education.

5. *Corrie Ten Boom:* Risked her life to help hundreds of Jews escape during WWII.

6. *Malala Yousafzai:* Pakistani activist for female education and the youngest Nobel Prize laureate.

7. *Visaka Dharmadasa:* Works to ease the horrors of war in Sri Lanka.

8. *Sacajawea:* Guided Lewis and Clark across the Northwest Territories of the United States.

9. *Robin Lim:* A midwife and founder of Yayasan Bumi Sehat health clinics, which offer free prenatal care, birthing services and medical aid to anyone who needs it.

10. *Queen Emma:* Left a legacy of hospitals and schools for the people of Hawaii.

11. *Harriet Tubman:* Organized the Underground Railroad and helped lead American slaves to freedom.

12. *Clara Barton and Florence Nightingale:* Red Cross founders.

13. *Chi Nguyen:* Honored for helping street children in Vietnam.

14. *Dr. Hawa Abdi:* A Somali doctor who built a hospital, risked her life to help others, and was nominated for the Nobel Peace Prize

15. *Dorothy Humbert:* Inspired many women when she went back to college in her 70's

16. *Immaculée Ilibagiza:* Inspires thousands of people around the world by teaching her experiences of discovering God

during the Rwandan holocaust and learning the power of forgiveness

17. *Katherine Johnson, Dorothy Vaughan, and Mary Jackson:* Mathematicians and engineers who worked at the National Aeronautic and Space Administration (NASA) during the space race. They calculated space trajectories for Project Mercury and other missions. Their calculations were critical to the success of many missions.

This list is small compared to the multitude of heroic women who are our fellow sisters. It does not include the millions who are not famous but who have risked their lives in defense of others and the ones they love, are loyal, hardworking and pillars of feminine strength. Perhaps you are one of them.

Most of us live ordinary lives but can still accomplish extraordinary things within our own personal spheres.

Women Are Homemakers

Women are the most adapted to the art and skill of being homemakers—the bedrock of home and society. Our natural talents involve all the arts of being a mother and creating and maintaining a comfortable atmosphere in our dwellings. This atmosphere encourages all who visit or live within the home to feel warm, nurtured, fed, and loved. In turn, these consistent positive feelings have an enormous influence in the mature development of strong adults and productive members of society, and ultimately nations.

We Are the World's Mothers

The word mother doesn't have to apply in a literal sense because women have the capacity and power to be mothers to everyone in need. The value of a woman isn't diminished if, for any reason, she is unable to have children of her own. And she is capable of filling the role of mother for countless people in her capacity for kindness, nurturing, and service.

When we become mothers in the literal sense, we have the ability to feed infants from our breasts. Human milk is better for babies in the first year of life than anything man-made. Formula doesn't come close to the real thing. Our milk provides antibodies, is always sterile and the perfect temperature, and it's free. The natural formula of your breast milk is unique and customized for each baby.

Whether literal or figurative, mothering comes naturally to most of us. It's a hard job and relatively thankless, and the direct financial compensation is usually... well, zero. Our ability to multi-task is perfect for this occupation. Most of us are willing to do mundane tasks day after day for the benefit of those we love, like cleaning, preparing food, mending clothes, first aid, and more.

Consider the following job description:

Help Wanted

This job will take all the creativity you possess. You will need to have some elementary knowledge in the medical field.

Cooking skills are important. Sewing is an advantage, at least the ability to sew on buttons and repair hems. You must have some expertise in teaching, philosophy, bookkeeping, nutrition, counseling, interior decorating, and time management. There will be a need for skill in negotiation, general repair, and cleaning, such as removing unknown tough stains from many surfaces and fabrics. Knowledge of gardening and plants, as well as food preservation, is advised. Since help is needed in all countries, driving may be a necessity as well as the ability to chauffeur, shop and run a basic budget.

You must work 365 days a year with little to no time off, including nighttime. Quitting will not be tolerated. You will also be expected to love the people you serve to the point where you are willing to sacrifice your own health and maybe even your life for them. You will need to pray for, worry about, and sacrifice for these people and their spouses, even when you are not sure they love you back. To be successful, you must love their children and grandchildren and take an active part wherever possible in their lives.

There will be no paycheck.

You have no doubt guessed this is the job description of a mother.

Why is it, despite the complexity of this career, so much of the world considers motherhood and homemaking beneath the dignity of an educated, intelligent woman? A mother's credibility is even suspect much of the time, though it is the most important and demanding job ever. Your compensation will consist of the quality of the relationships you build with those you serve, your own strength and character that will increase because of this service, and the love of generations who follow after you.

The job you do as a mother will have repercussions for generations, unlike most careers.

Why Do We Do It?

A woman who hasn't had children yet might reasonably ask, "With such a job description, why would any rational person take on such a task?"

The simplest explanation is because it's worth it! We do it because it plays to our core strengths, so we're good at it. And the human race couldn't survive without us. Nothing produces more meaning and satisfaction for women than to be the best they can be. So, in summary, we do it because we were meant to have the greatest joy possible.

Nothing produces more meaning and satisfaction for women than to be the best they can be. So, in summary, we do it because we were meant to have the greatest joy possible.

Not all of us are able to bear children. We usually see this as a tragedy or a dream unfulfilled, but adoption is sometimes a noble option. Others express their natural maternal instincts through helping others, building relationships, and in doing good. Those of us who have raised children to adulthood have experienced a lifetime of work, heartache and love, knowing what it means to be a mother, would never trade it for anything else the world has to offer. The experience of loving our children, and then grandchildren, is enormously rewarding, satisfying, and soul-building.

A Mother's Instinct

Even when we get older, we tend to never lose our maternal instincts and sensitivity. I recently went with my daughter Gina and her baby to visit her former workplace, an assisted living facility. She had promised some of the residents they could meet her newborn son. When she came in, it was touching to see how these women, some in their 90's, reached out to touch the baby. Their eyes were tender and lit up instantly. You could see the deep emotion that just seeing an infant brought out in them.

Even though my children are grown, I have noticed whenever I am in a store and hear even the distant cry of a baby, my maternal antennas are instantly up. That means immediate concern kicks in and I instinctively look around for the source of the cry. I can't help it. The younger the baby, the more anxiety I feel. I'm sure you feel the same. We care about children, even ones we don't see.

There are charities whose goal is to help newborns in need: those whose mothers are so poor they don't even have a blanket or a diaper to bring their baby home from the hospital. This service is almost entirely done by women who care about other women and their infants. One group acquires used wedding dresses and makes burial clothes for little ones who are born premature and don't survive. Another makes blankets or newborn kits that include basics for the first days of life. Nurturing is an area where we excel, and it has diverse application.

Men Need Us

Emotionally healthy men recognize our value and seek the often elusive yet deeply satisfying relationships we can build together. They hope to find a woman who loves them and whom they can serve and protect in return. We have the innate temperament to provide the best atmosphere for a lasting romance to occur.

A man I know said, "You tame us. You gentle us, and yes, teach and inspire us."

You have the power to use femininity and the charms you were born with to influence people and the world for the better, whether in an official position or behind the scenes.

In Summary:

- You are of great and limitless worth.
- The contributions women add to the world are so valuable as to be beyond calculation.
- Women are essential. We are the world's mothers, homemakers, and leaders. Men need us.
- Never underestimate your value as a feminine woman.

"A woman has more facets than a cut diamond. The brilliance seen from one angle is not diminished because a flaw is seen from another."
~ Merilee Andelin Saunders, The Queen's Dagger

"Women really do rule the world. They just haven't figured it out yet. When they do, and they will, we're all in big trouble."
~ Anonymous

In 48 BC, Cleopatra was queen of Egypt. A rising Roman Empire under the soon-to-be Emperor of Rome, Julius Ceasar, dominated the Mediterranean and all nations who bordered it. Ceasar sought to control Egypt's grain supply by meddling in local politics, and his machinations soon threatened Cleopatra's life and the independence of her nation. Through nothing but feminine power, because she lacked any other resources to bargain with, Cleopatra not only convinced Ceasar to support her status as queen and her nation's semi-independence, but she formed a powerful personal bond with him and was to live by his side until his assassination in Rome years later. She would then convince his successor, Marc Antony, to continue support of her status and privileges and to eventually marry her. Her unique sense of fashion dominated all Rome for centuries to come. It is often said that she was not beautiful, but that she was captivating in her presentation and demeanor, and the most powerful men of her time desired her favor. Many more served her willingly without obligation, even until death. Though she did not embody all the virtues Fascinating Womanhood espouses, Cleopatra lived in a barbaric age and thrived in it because she knew her natural strengths. She remains a shining example in many respects of the latent feminine power that all women have, no matter their station or physical gifts.

However, feminine power is something that not all women use or even know they possess. The word "power" in this phrase is not exaggeration. With it, women have unlimited potential for influencing the world, for good or evil, or for selfish purposes. But it is most potent as a force for good. To learn more about feminine power, we must take a look at power in general and its two types.

Masculine Power

Webster's Dictionary defines power as: "Ability to act or produce an effect; possession of control, authority, or influence over others." There are approaches to power that work best for both genders, and control is best suited to men. They are more aggressive and competitive than women, practically radiating testosterone and masculinity.

Men are happiest, and indeed thrive best, in an adversarial world of struggle for limited resources, reputation, and control. They crave the fight for survival, whether literal or in the abstract, and they revel in their hard-fought victories.

The main way men exert their power is through the use of:

- *Authority:* granted by station and sometimes just presentation
- *Persuasion:* good sales tactics or psychology
- *Money:* to negotiate or buy
- *Brute Force:* use of direct physical force

The masculine approach is mainly task-oriented. This means they objectify goals and approach them with little emotion, forgetting often how their pursuit may affect feelings or personal connections between people involved. Relationships often don't factor in to this task-orientation, but rather a narrow focus on the goal itself, as if it were a singular prize to be won.

Masculine power is not only the use of brute force but the talent to exert male power to reach a desired goal. It can be used for both good and evil. The assertiveness that is inherent to this type of power is absolutely essential to the world. Men are the main ones who have built cities, explored new frontiers, and defended our homes. The world needs mature masculine accomplishment and leadership. Such strength is sorely needed now as much as ever. Good strong men help make our world a safer, better place. Masculine power can seem somewhat brutal at times, but it can also be quite refined.

George Washington is an example of masculine power, but in a more cultivated form. During America's war for independence from Britain, the Continental Congress lacked adequate resources to fully confront England, and so he was forced to conduct a war of tactical retreats and indecisive actions to buy time and discourage the enemy. Though he won very few battles and was not considered a great military tactician, Washington inspired loyalty and morale through character: most importantly, a willingness to risk physical and financial hardship alongside his men. He showed that great authority and persuasion can be exerted through courageous and humble bearing, and he ultimately won one of the most lopsided conflicts in military history, and formed a nation.

Men are generally better at using masculine power and women are better at using feminine influence. As women, we have found other ways to influence people around us and the world we live in. Men are bigger and physically stronger, and they have put more effort over the centuries into developing and using control. Women often attempt to exert a type of masculine power, but they pay a heavy price and can't pull it off as well as men. This is because when women try to be men, they are not playing to their strengths but rather to their weaknesses. Women are at their best when they practice feminine power—a power that easily matches the native power of men. Yet it's a different kind of power.

In fact, this is almost always where our greatest impact resides. But dictionaries don't recognize the difference between masculine and feminine power. This is a measure of how great a secret it has become, and why femininity is so hard to find or recognize anymore.

Women Make Poor Men

When women practice masculine power, they naturally become less feminine and more masculine. But women are not good at being men, and so it puts us at a disadvantage. Yet much of society teaches this is the only way women can be validated. In accepting this betrayal of our natural femininity, we lose part of ourselves in the process and we are kept low and weak— kept separated from our native source of power. Even more, this betrayal undermines our relationships because there is no balance between the masculine and the feminine. We can become perpetual victims. Men are left unsatisfied, disappointed, and sometimes repelled: they instinctively reject us or seek other sources of fulfillment.

The control and conflict that radical feminists promote is *not* the answer. They would have us approximate men but only ever as much as a twisted caricature of them, and we end up invalidated even more: our femininity diminishes and we betray ourselves in the process. The result is frustration, perhaps anger, and sometimes distrust for men. The self-defeating part of this often blocks us from having the enduring romantic relationship we desire.

Have you ever stopped to realize that copying men is an admission that, as women, we aren't good enough, maybe even inferior? Is it preferable to be a man? No. There is everything right with being a feminine, fascinating woman. We don't have to betray our own sex in any way to be loved, treasured, or even to be professional.

You might think you only need to be charming around the man you are in love with. Being a feminine woman should be who you are with all men, including male relatives, co-workers, and strangers. Men love being around a fascinating woman even if there is nothing romantic involved. It makes them feel good and it makes you feel good.

The Intimidating Boss

Eva felt lucky to be working for a high-powered but demanding executive at a Fortune 500 company. She was his personal assistant and often made reservations of various kinds for him. She learned quickly that he could be very intimidating and hard to please — and when not satisfied — look out, world. He let everyone know not to displease him, especially those under him, which was almost everyone. Before Eva was hired, there had been a string of about 7-8 assistants who had quit because this man was so difficult and demanding.

Once, Eva was asked to arrange to have a car pick her boss and several other executives up for an important board meeting in Europe. She quickly calculated that he would need to arrive at the airport at least 2 hours early for the international flight and it would take about a half hour to drive there. So, to be safe, she tacked on another half hour just to be sure there were no unexpected delays such as traffic jams, an accident, or even unexpected nasty weather.

Her boss marched into the office the next day demanding, "Who the hell gave me this itinerary? I hate wasting time! Why am I scheduled to arrive at the airport so early?"

Eva quickly responded, "Oh, it was me. I am so sorry! I got worried that you might miss your flight! I'd feel so terrible if you missed that flight. I know how important it is for you to be there."

To everyone's surprise, the boss softened and said, "Well, it's not that big of a deal." Then he said: "Would you please check and see when everyone else is leaving? Thank you." Everyone around who heard him was shocked because he said 'please' and 'thank you' in the same sentence!

In what way might Eva have handled her boss that, no doubt, wouldn't have had such a favorable outcome? She might have gotten defensive saying something snarky like, "If you want to be late, that's your problem." Or she might have told him off. Eva realized that her boss was a very high-powered man, used to not only getting his way but detesting what he saw as any waste of time. Her innate femininity along with her knowledge of understanding men is always her best option. Instead of either quitting or losing her job, her relationship with her boss became better and she found herself more trusted than before.

Your Feminine Power Base

Our feminine perspective gives us a unique advantage that makes up the essentials of our power base. These qualities include:

Our capacity to love: Our relationship perspective and the way we love is different. Here I'm talking about the love that exhibits caring and respect for others and acceptance of our own humanity and human life. It is patient, long-suffering, and seeks the benefit and good in people. It is not self-centered. It accepts people for who and where they are. Our love promotes reaching out and communicating to find ways to improve our relationships. Women are more willing to talk, reason, and find common ground.

Princess Diana is known around the world for her capacity to love not only those close to her but countless others she had never met through her many humanitarian projects. She became known as "The People's Princess" because of this great quality she possessed. She was the first royal to physically touch people without gloves. She held sick children on her lap and hugged people who suffered from AIDS. She adored her two sons and taught them to follow in her footsteps.

Spirituality: Women are naturally interested in learning about spiritual things.[4] We are often drawn toward finding and understanding the meaning of life and our relationship to the Creator of that life. Of course, there are men of incredible spiritual strength, but we seem to have more natural spiritual energy, interest, and intuition. It is a feminine divine adornment of mankind. Spirituality promotes humility, gratitude, patience, and a drive for service.

---

4   Zuckerman, Phil, Ph.D. (2014, September 26). Why Are Women More Religious Than Men? Retrieved from https://www.psychologytoday.com/us/blog/the-secular-life/201409/why-are-women-more-religious-men

Mother Teresa was a woman who devoted herself to doing what she felt strongly God wanted her to do. She was an example of compassion, untiring work with the poorest of the poor, and the forgotten. Too few dedicate their whole lives to such a noble and spiritual cause as Mother Teresa did.

Delicacy: Being delicate is not necessarily a weakness. The opposite of delicate is coarse, hard, or crude. Delicacy can also be a strength. It means to be very fine in texture or quality. Consider an egg with its fragile shell. Though it is thin, it's still strong enough to hold its precious contents and even resist breaking when held tight in the hand, but still easy to open. Like the shell of an egg, a woman's delicate strength is in her determination to hold precious things together, like relationships. Keeping relationships together isn't always something you can control, but living the timeless principles of Fascinating Womanhood will give you the best chance of doing so.

Men like this quality in us. Being delicate means to possess an exquisite trait, to be graceful, dainty, and fine. We can be delicate and emotionally strong at the same time, and should feel free to embrace our finer nature. It becomes part of our irresistible charm.

Men don't usually like to be described as delicate. It sounds unmanly to them, but it's part of our feminine source of power. It's completely appropriate and natural. When we allow our delicate natures to show, a man's feeling of strength and protectiveness is awakened. It provides a contrast to masculine coarseness and insensitivity. Men feel needed around such a woman.

Audrey Hepburn is a woman who possessed delicacy. It's not just that she looked physically delicate. She also seemed to be self-aware, easily wounded, and did not try to cover up her vulnerability. She presented a great contrast to male coarseness. It was said that all of her co-stars and directors were enchanted by her.

Sensitivity: Women naturally care about others and have a heightened awareness of feelings. Women are sensitive and attentive to other's needs and pain. Our emotions are closer to the surface. We cry. For women, it's okay to cry over even small things like a movie, a novel, or a dead bird. It's our prerogative. If anyone calls you a "sissy" for crying over something sentimental, you can just tell them, "I have a right to cry. I'm a woman."

Far too many women are afraid to be seen as sensitive in a world that demands we act like men, and either hide or cease to have strong emotions concerning events and relationships around us. Women are now taught the same things that men learn in boot camp or spring training for professional sports teams: "There's no crying in the Army, soldier!" Or, "Stop being a wimp!" Men are expected to be stoic and emotionally tough, it's part of their job and many prefer it that way. We are women and our role is different. It may mean we're more vulnerable to emotional bullies, but sensitivity is actually a source of strength for us.

Helen Keller's significant trials not only helped her become physically sensitive to everything she touched, but she was also known for being emotionally sensitive to others. She is a wonderful example of overcoming trials few would be willing to handle, but doing it with such feminine sensitivity and also grace.

Dignity: Dignity is an inherent attitude of self-worth. To avoid the appearance of arrogance, it requires the addition of character, resulting in the ability to be aware of and set appropriate boundaries in relationships. Dignity is always attractive. It also is essential in any kind of balanced romantic relationship.

Queen Elizabeth II is a woman I think of when I contemplate dignity. She has been queen of Great Britain for over 65 years. Throughout all those years, she has always shown regal dignity in her presentation in spite of the many trials and disasters she has endured during her life. From World War II to her personal family concerns, she has never appeared angry, defensive, shocked, or even fatigued when she appears in public. She is always a poised and self-possessed woman.

Graciousness: This strength is characterized by kindness, warm courtesy and tact. Our gender doesn't have a monopoly on being gracious but more of us invest in it and hold it as valuable. This is because we don't tend to be as coldly objective as men. Graciousness promotes acceptance of humanity and elevates us and everyone we interact with. When you are gracious, people recognize it immediately and feel safer around you. It often brings out the best in others as well.

Queen Noor is known for her characteristic grace and courage in a complex world. When her husband King Hussein of Jordan died, she consoled a distraught nation. She has been involved in many humanitarian programs and continues to exert a gracious influence on the world.

Gentleness: This is a hallmark of our sex. It can be beautiful and inspiring. It involves the actions we often take to uplift and preserve others' feelings. This is not an adjective men usually aspire to in describing themselves. Have you ever heard a man bragging to another: "Oh yeah? I'm much more gentle than you, bro!" We sometimes refer to a man as being a "gentleman," but today that describes someone who is polite and has good manners, not necessarily one who is a gentle person.

Maya Angelou: No matter what I have read or seen in her videos, Maya Angelou always strikes me as a very sincere and gentle woman. She was a famous writer, poet, singer, memoirist, and civil rights activist.

Melanie Wilkes, from the novel Gone With The Wind: This iconic character, beautifully played by actress Olivia de Havilland in the film adaptation, is a wonderful example of a gentle yet strong soul. Though she was not physically strong, she did what had to be done without complaint. She is a fictional character but is a great example of a woman who is tender and kind while also being true to her convictions. She was a real hero of both the book and film.

Quiet Strength: This is a quality of maturity and emotional intelligence. Quiet strength is being able to stay the course without much entitlement or complaint. It's humility in the face of trial. Many men also have this quality but when we exercise it in a feminine way it's very attractive and exhibits a silent influence, different from a man's. Women tend to implement quiet strength daily as we are often called on to practice it.

Jacqueline Kennedy: Few would deny the amazing quiet strength Jackie Kennedy displayed during the funeral of her assassinated husband, President John F. Kennedy. She quietly stood with her two small children as her husband's casket passed her and captured the hearts and admiration of a grieving nation.

Rosa Parks: She became well-known for refusing to give up her seat (in the "colored passenger" section of a bus) to a white traveler, after the white section was filled. After this incident she was fired from her job as a seamstress at a local department store and received death threats for years afterwards. She patiently endured a subsequent arrest and was willing to become a controversial but influential figure in the civil rights' movement of the 1950's. She became an international icon of resistance to racial segregation. Later, she wrote a book entitled, "Quiet Strength."

Charm: To possess feminine charm is to fascinate, attract, and please people. It is one of the most powerful qualities we can possess. That's why an entire chapter of this book is devoted to the subject. Charm affects all we come in contact with. It validates everyone with whom it comes in contact. Men have a type of charm, but feminine charm has a magic all its own. Though manifested differently in each woman, all of us possess it at least in latent form if we choose to develop it. It is part of our inner beauty.

I can't resist telling you about two of the most charming women I know:

Minnie and Audrey: Minnie and Audrey both genuinely show their delight whenever they greet people. If you are fortunate to be in their company, they are always interested in you, how you feel, and what you think. You leave feeling better about yourself. When either speaks to you, they touch your arm or hand gently, showing affection and a sense of closeness to you. Their many friends flock to them. Being invited to lunch with either one is always a wonderful experience. But that's how they are with everyone who knows them.

Julie Andrews: She has been described frequently as charming and gracious—always sharing the spotlight with others. She is known to be warm and personable to people she meets in her private life, no matter their station.

Understanding Men: Our ability to understand men can give us tremendous power. When you study the timeless principles of Fascinating Womanhood, you gain the skills to influence men at a different level than women whose feminine power lies more dormant. You have the same stuff that Cleopatra, Princess Diana, or Audrey Hepburn had.

A whole section in this book is devoted to understanding men. Your life will change as you achieve a greater comprehension of men's sensitive pride, and their vulnerabilities and strengths. When a man begins to truly trust you and feels safe, you can accomplish more together than you ever knew possible.

Martha Washington: She was the wife of George Washington. She adored her husband, traveling hundreds of miles to be near him during the war for American independence, always dressed well, entertained difficult political guests, and brought cheer to the degraded troops. Not only did her husband George love her, but the soldiers did as well. He always did better when she was around to listen to him, console him, and support him. She organized parties and dances. Many women got together with her and chatted while they repaired and sewed uniforms and knitted socks. In a very real sense, the American Revolutionary war could not have been won without her constant support and understanding of her husband.

Yoko Ono: People sometimes resent Yoko, but John Lennon found what he needed amongst the many women he could have chosen. His famous song "Woman" shows what he valued in her. He penned these lyrics:

Woman, I can hardly express,

My mixed emotions at my thoughtlessness,

After all, I'm forever in your debt.

And Woman, I will try to express

My inner feelings and thankfulness,

For showing me the meaning of success,

Woman, please let me explain,

I never meant to cause you sorrow and pain,

So let me tell you again and again and again.

I love you.

Femininity: Femininity is at the heart of your power base. It's who you are, all day, every day. Its influence has more power than you can imagine. This is the subject of an entire chapter of this book.

"One of the best things that ever happened to me is that I'm a woman. That is the way all females should feel."
~ Marilyn Monroe

Nicole Kidman is a famous Australian actress who personifies femininity in my opinion. She is womanly in the way she dresses, speaks, walks, and moves. No one would ever mistake her for a man no matter the setting.

Understanding and Cultivating Feminine Power

Feminine power can begin with simple things like the way you say something, how you move, your tone of voice, your general presentation, and non-verbal things like facial expressions. It is reflected in the way you treat others, whether and how you serve, and the degree to which you develop your own personal character.

Feminine power is influential with both genders. The combination of femininity and positive character traits will make you irresistible. Using womanly power enhances our femininity just as men become more masculine by exercising masculine power.

After awhile, men grow tired of their own kind, who are often insensitive and competitive with each other. If we try to act like one of the guys in order to get close to a man we adore, then we become like another man to them. What do they want with one more guy? Why would we want to be thought of as just another man in his life? What makes us different from men is what attracts them to us. Our feminine nature brings out the best in men and in ourselves. This is why and how in many cases opposites attract.

You will find you have influence and power with men you know and even with some you have just met by developing your femininity, character, and by accentuating the differences between you and them. Don't just play the people management game, which involves being manipulative, self-serving, and insincere with the sole goal of controlling others. This rarely ends well. Your greatest power is in using your feminine influence for good — for serving others. It can do more than you might think. You might even change the world, it's that powerful.

Feminine power is the ability or skill to inspire the world to want to change, rather than the masculine approach of force or leverage. Our perspective is nurturing, empathetic, supportive, and bonding. We are more open to reaching out and talking, even getting help with what we are trying to do. Instead of crashing through doors, we encourage doors to be opened for us. We can excel at this.

The Wind and the Sun — Aesop's Fables

The Wind and the Sun were disputing which was the stronger. Suddenly, they saw a traveler coming down the road and the Sun said: "I see a way to decide our dispute. Whichever of us can cause that traveler to take off his cloak shall be regarded as the stronger. You begin."

So, the Sun retired behind a cloud, and the Wind began to blow as hard as it could upon the traveler. But the harder he blew, the more closely did the traveler wrap his cloak around him, till at last the Wind had to give up in despair. Then the Sun came out and shone in all her glory upon the traveler, who soon found it too hot to walk with his cloak on.

The sun's gentle rays didn't need to work hard upon the traveler and were much more powerful than the force of the wind. Its influence caused the traveler to remove his own coat freely and without resentment. Feminine power is similar to this.

Feminine influence is long-lasting. Consider the lasting influence the loving mother of George Washington had on him. He gave her credit for having a powerful and positive impact in his life. That influence endured long past her death and radiated to affect an entire nation. Our power might take time to produce results, but it is enduring. Our tendency towards gentle influence produces loyalty and minimizes resistance. Feminine influence encourages personal growth in others and energizes the agency of another person to improve.

What influence did Mother Teresa's kindness and charity have on the world? Did she control armies, guns, or laws to promote her work? Did she command a huge salary? Of course not. But her influence is felt widely despite her humble beginnings. Just her name evokes the greatest in human goodness. She won the Nobel Peace Prize. She spoke to world leaders and was greatly revered. Her selfless work with the poorest of the poor continues years after her death.

Though Princess Diana was born with title and wealth, what she is remembered for most is her feminine influence as a mother, humanitarian, and a caring compassionate woman.

And then there is Mumtaz, the most beloved wife of Shah Jahan of India. In a world where women didn't have position or control over their lives, her influence on the monarch and the people was immense. The Shah took her with him on his military tours and even sought her advice in running the country. And he built the world-famous Taj Mahal for Mumtaz — an enduring symbol of the loving devotion she inspired in her husband.

Feminine power has been understood and practiced by countless women throughout the ages. There are millions who are not famous but who have risked their lives in defense of others and the ones they love, were loyal, hardworking, and pillars of feminine strength. And today, there are others who quietly go beyond any call of duty for those they love. Perhaps you are one of them. Like Coco.

Coco

When Coco met her husband John, his dream was to be a rock star. He was a very good musician. She pledged to support his dream.

They made an agreement that he would pursue a music career until he was 35 years old. It was a promise of specific support for over a decade. Coco and John had 4 children during this time. John made money but never quite got to the level in the music business he had hoped. He realized few musicians, even very good ones, ever got the break they needed to get to the top of this competitive industry.

When John turned 35, he kept his side of the bargain and decided on a career as a pharmacist. This required a lot of schooling and demanding work. While he got his education, Coco ran a daycare in her home to help with finances. She not only had her 4 children to care for but several other children at the same time. It was hard, but she never complained.

Today, they have a lovely home, their children are married and have families of their own. John has a wonderful career and is appreciative of the support Coco has given him over the years. She has had a profound positive influence on him and their family. They've earned their great relationship, but Coco's support and patience is legendary. What a fascinating woman!

You Don't Have to Go Down in History to Be Great

Some people do the extraordinary or even the remarkable and get written up in history. But most great people never become famous. True greatness is in our willingness to serve and sacrifice for others.

You are in a unique position as a woman to be important, whether you are in the history books or not. You will be remembered by those upon whom you had an influence. They will tell your story to those who follow, and they will have largely forgotten your imperfections. When you put yourself forward willingly in the noble service of others, regardless of whether you think you've succeeded or failed at the tasks you've chosen, you achieve true greatness.

Feminine Influence is Real Power

Women have special powers when they use their femininity. Men are usually at a loss to explain it but are mesmerized. I have heard it called "magic" by men who are powerful, intelligent, and successful. A woman can be like a beautiful melody, singing in joyful vibrations that calm and strengthen. This enchantment delights and inspires men. It satisfies them and makes them feel more masculine.

Feminine power will help you become happier and more successful as a woman, and it will permeate all areas of your life. Femininity is a beauty drawn from the deep wells of love: it is the power of being a woman. Being a feminine woman is who you really are, at your core.

Why Do We Need Power?

Women balance men and bring out the best in them, especially in our personal relationships. We need them as they need us, but civilization is ultimately in our hands. Feminine power brings out the best in women and has a far-reaching influence on the world for good. As a united womanly force, we can change this world for the better.

It All Begins with Feminine Power

Feminine qualities make life fascinating and more beautiful. They also contribute to a romantic marriage. We possess these powers in abundance and we have them by instinct, or by learning we can re-awaken what lies dormant in each of us.

In a way, women enter this world with a great advantage of built-in sense of purpose because of our nature. As a consequence, women are naturally less susceptible to the baser temptations of life. Men derive their power and meaning from competition, strength, and action, and they pay a terrible toll for the vital role they play: they often fall prey to the temptations their type of power can bring. So, they stumble often and need our gentling influence to be their best.

As women, we get our natural power from tuning in to our innate goodness and tendency to think selflessly for the greater good, our humility, and our core strength in nurturing. Have you ever noticed in Disney animated movies, the most frightening and powerful evil characters are often women: Maleficent, Cruella de Vil, the wicked stepmother in Cinderella, and the evil queen in Snow White? When a woman is bad, it's so contrary to our nature that it seems the more wicked for it. In contrast, Princess Aurora in Sleeping Beauty, Snow White, and Cinderella are what inspires the male characters in their stories to heroism, and the context of their romance is what brings meaning.

You have the power to make the world more beautiful with your feminine influence, your softer gentler ways, your peaceful way of looking at things.

It's Already Within You

Don't let this talk of inner change intimidate you. This is like the red ruby slippers from the Wizard of Oz. This power to reach your destination has always been with you. You just need to learn how to awaken it. Studying the timeless principles of Fascinating Womanhood will help open a new way of seeing yourself and the world.

In Summary:

- Feminine power is different than masculine power but is every bit as influential.
- Your feminine power is your natural collection of core strengths that differentiate you from men, and these are:
    - your capacity to love,
    - your spirituality,
    - delicacy,
    - sensitivity,
    - dignity,
    - graciousness,
    - quiet strength,
    - charm,
    - ability to understand men,
    - and your natural feminine nature.

Though women do not have a monopoly on these traits, they tend to be more natural for us to access and develop than for men. We have more native capacity and potential for growth in these areas. They are a woman's power base.

- As you learn and practice your feminine power base, you will more fully understand the true power you have.
- As you apply this knowledge wisely, it will give you, as well as others, indescribable joy.
- Your behavior as a charming woman will delight others who assist you. It will make them feel good.
- We usually underestimate our feminine impact. Human beings would cease to exist without us. And men need us.

*"Women are never stronger than when they
arm themselves with their weakness."*
~ *Marie de Vichy-Chamrond,*
Marquise du Deffand, Letters to Voltaire

Women are often in a position of vulnerability with men because of their relative size. But our vulnerability doesn't have to put us at a disadvantage in all areas of our lives. We are just as valuable and intelligent as men. In fact, in some capacities it is we who are the stronger ones. What we often don't realize is that some of our greatest strengths lie in the very things that make us feel vulnerable. Understanding how your vulnerabilities can work for you will further deepen your potential for a lifelong love affair with the man you love.

Physical: Females learn that males carry an overwhelming physical advantage from an early age. We are exposed to play with other children where this point is made constantly in order to create and maintain pecking order, and the physical differences between the genders only increase towards adulthood. The average adult comparison in physical strength wouldn't even be close in most cases, assuming similar height, age, and health. Today, science and training can make the average woman a closer physical match to her average male counterpart. But we must cross a great span and expend enormous effort to approach this muscular level. Even then it would be difficult for us to equal a man's native strength due to their greater levels of not only testosterone but also upper body muscular mass. Few females take up the challenge because it is simply not the natural order of things. We would do better to rely on our native strengths rather than play a game where the balance is tipped in favor of the other side. We don't need to because we have our own power. Brute force is not the only power that makes a difference. In fact, it is a somewhat crude form of power that isn't nearly as advanced as feminine charm and influence.

Vulnerability: The vulnerability that our comparative weaknesses give us also brings certain advantages if we understand how to use them. Chief among them are our natural inclinations towards self-awareness and humility. These are powerful concepts for individual development for what they contribute to intelligence. Plato famously stated that the unexamined life is not worth living.

Humility promotes clearness of thought, and there is nothing more dangerous to intelligence than arrogance. Don't underestimate the power of these relative advantages.

Popular opinion might say that having humility means having low self-esteem, but the opposite is true. It implies we recognize the power of self-restraint and the need to be teachable and free from excessive vanity. Why is vanity bad? It promotes a desire for control and encourages competition. It makes us more blind to personal danger. Recognizing our susceptibility brings out men's desire to protect. Denying it makes us seem phony and out-of-touch.

Self-awareness can make you more vulnerable to criticism, doubt, and lowered self-esteem. This is why some might consider it a weakness. You may take on more personal responsibility for problems than is necessary. However, self-awareness can increase your ability to be understanding—not only of yourself, but of the man you love, your family, and others. It is a type of two-edged sword that could be seen as a flaw when we judge and expect perfection, but it is also a great strength which is vital in building and maintaining quality relationships. Being aware helps you achieve a better appreciation for the struggles others have in their daily lives.

In summary, vulnerability can be an asset because it increases your self-awareness and sensitivity to others.

Our Surprising Strengths

The uterus is powerful and is the strongest muscle by weight for either gender. This muscle belongs exclusively to us as women. It takes a lot of strength to give birth.

Also, we tend to be more physically flexible than men. For example, have you ever noticed how many women can do the splits compared to men? If you ever go to a yoga class you will see plenty of evidence.

Our Special Strengths Which Some Think are Weaknesses

These qualities are mentioned in other places in this book, but I want to emphasize how they are potential areas of strength for a woman:

Femininity: When we are girly around men, they feel more masculine and it brings out their best qualities. *Girly* doesn't mean childish. It involves the way we move, sit, talk, dress, speak, and all things female. Femininity makes us feel good about ourselves even when we are totally alone.

Though femininity is sometimes thought of as weakness, when it is directed toward masculinity, the slightest brush with it tends to make a man feel more vulnerable.

"If I asked you about love, you'd probably quote me a sonnet But you've never looked at a woman and been totally vulnerable; known someone that could level you with her eyes, feeling like God put an angel on earth just for you who could rescue you from the depths of hell."
~ Robin Williams,
Good Will Hunting

Men recognize feminine influence more than they might admit. They have mixed feelings about it. Part of it delights them but another part scares them because they feel defenseless. It disarms them. But they will enjoy it immensely when you have their trust.

Your Feminine Mind: We have greater and easier access to our feelings and can put them into words more quickly than men. We'll talk more about this in chapter 9, Brain Matters.

Feminine Courage: Feminine courage is more often expressed in our patience and perseverance in the face of suffering, while men tend to show courage in conflict and competition. Courage is not the absence of fear. It's doing the right thing in spite of being afraid. Some view women's courage as a weakness compared to masculine courage. Men are not the only ones who are brave. Many women exhibit spectacular courage, and this is true in business and other occupations, but most especially in our homes. Many of us endure physical and emotional stress and take on daunting challenges, sometimes for years at a time. Women often find themselves triangulated in the context of family. They face a husband who is often more insensitive and rigid, and less willing to compromise and be concerned about the emotional requirements of a family. The children are incredibly dependent and sensitive. And then there are the wants and needs of the mother herself: she often comes last in the revolving demands and pressures of the whole.

Having a baby and raising a child takes a lot of bravery. It involves frequent challenges like loss of sleep and personal freedom, constantly carrying our children in our arms while multitasking household responsibilities, and chasing our children around and wrestling with them throughout every stage of their development. No mother escapes motherhood without natural cuts and bruises, sometimes a broken heart. And there is the added challenge of protecting children in public and while our men are away. It can be difficult to defend your kids from bullies and from their own doubts and fears, and many of us are called upon to care for kids with special needs. We are up to the challenge, but loving and caring for a child in a vulnerable environment takes all kinds of courage. There is nothing more courageous than a mother protecting her young. It brings out the "mother bear" in us.

Your Feminine Perspective: We have a unique feminine view on things, less tinged with thoughts of power and control than men, and this makes us more agreeable. More women are content with a personal sense of peace than men. We tend to be more relationship-oriented: more focused on connections with others than getting our way or being number one. Our talent with relationships gives us social advantage.

Part of understanding how your weaknesses can become strengths lies in a recognition of your basic needs and wants.

What Makes Women Tick?

Most important to women are:

1. *To feel loved and adored.* There is nothing more wonderful than feeling the love of a good man, the deep and eternal kind of love that lasts forever. Men sometimes misunderstand a woman's

basic need for love as being motivated primarily by libido. We are looking for romantic love more than sexual satisfaction. Love for us has more to do with trust, feeling protected, and feeling cherished.

2. *Most women have the inborn need to nurture, whether we have our own children or not.* We support each other, men, children and beloved pets. This is a great strength of women. The world needs us.

3. *To feel secure and safe: physically, financially, and emotionally.* It is frightening for us to feel unsafe or that our marriage is not stable. Safety is a strong need in us. Our need for security extends to safety for our children — that they have the necessities of life. This drive is deep in healthy women and this is where the "mother bear" analogy comes from. We would leap into fire for our children without thought for our own safety, even if they are adults.

Unfortunately, we sometimes make foolish decisions in this regard. Women are occasionally tempted to seek financial and even emotional security by becoming the mistress or wife of a wealthy man — one they believe can take care of them. It is a testament to how important feeling secure means to us, but we almost always seek love in these relationships. When a woman marries for security, most still wish for and need romantic love, even if that relationship doesn't provide it. When a woman gets into any relationship for money, she becomes a user of men.

This is beneath us. It also puts us at risk for abuse and resulting unhappiness.

4. *We want to feel attractive no matter our age.* Feeling attractive is important to our self-esteem and confidence. Some of us believe we can only be beautiful while we're young. This isn't true. Never give up on taking care of yourself. There are several fashion models still working into their eighties who remain gorgeous. Carmen Dell'Orefice, China Machado, and Daphne Selfe are all great examples.

When I was first married, there was a beautiful woman in our church congregation who I admired. She was in her 80s and always came to meetings dressed in such pretty clothes. She had beautiful silver hair done in a French twist, wore false eyelashes and sat with her hands gently folded in her lap—always a classy lady. She had impeccable manners and was soft-spoken. I thought she was so beautiful and I wanted to be like her. I never forgot her and have always tried to emulate her. You can be beautiful as you age.

5. *We need to feel understood and respected for who we are and who we may become.* We need validation, reassurance at times, as well as affection, good conversation, and family commitment. We need men to encourage and value our feminine uniqueness, to honor it, even when it is inconvenient or illogical to them at times. We appreciate when a man will listen to us and try to understand our point of view. If he does, it encourages us to do better and try to accomplish more.

6. *We want to be free to pursue our dreams.* We need to feel successful at our work, raising a family, or playing in an orchestra, competing in the Olympics, or wherever else our talents may lead us.

7. *The need to have joy.* To feel happy means that despite what happens to us, whether it is positive or negative, we carry a constant understanding of our personal worth and also faith that most people mean well. Happiness comes from gratitude and the belief that all will be well in the end; it comes from emotional stability and recognizing the quality of our relationships.

Happiness flourishes in positive relationships, but it must come from inside each of us. The core of this latter principle is mental and emotional management. We are the inventors of our own happiness. We must craft it. It starts as an idea, a concept. We must first deal with the unknown, and we do this with our imagination. We fashion happiness from what we may obtain, but this mostly depends on what we can conceive. We perfect our vision over time, and it eventually becomes reality.

In Summary:

- Though we are generally smaller and not as strong as men, our vulnerabilities grant us compensating strengths.
- Some of these strengths that many consider weaknesses are: femininity, the feminine mind, your feminine perspective, bearing children, humility, and being teachable.
- Your feminine needs beyond basic survival are: to be loved and adored, to nurture, to feel secure and safe physically, financially and emotionally, safety for our children, to feel attractive, to feel understood and respected, to be free to pursue our dreams, and to have joy.
- Understanding this chapter and applying its timeless principles will greatly enhance your romantic relationship or marriage.

"God made man stronger but not necessarily more intelligent. He gave women intuition and femininity. And, used properly, that combination easily jumbles the brain of any man I've ever met."
~Farrah Fawcett

"Those of us who embrace the feminine know its strength."
~ Betsy Cornwell

What are the first things that come to mind when you hear someone use the word feminine? Do you think pretty? Sweet? Graceful? Unfortunately, many people today associate femininity with weakness or manipulation. Ironically, it is in forgetting the true character of femininity that women become weak. Femininity is the core of your strength as a woman.

What is Femininity?

All human life starts with women and we are our species' primary nurturers. We fill this role because we have the capacity and strength for it. The talents we are inclined to, that support us in this role, define femininity and must be cultivated to achieve their full potential.

Femininity is both a physical and mental state.

Physically, it includes our ability to bear and feed children from our bodies, but this is not all. It also includes a special fortitude and endurance in the promotion of family and relationships and is sometimes expressed in a brave and selfless stance in defense of loved ones—especially children. It is also exhibited in our capacity for hard work over long hours in often thankless service to others. It may additionally be seen in our physical grace: our display of dignity and self-respect, our graceful bearing and movement. Femininity is most often appreciated in our beautiful appearance that comes from natural gifts and self-care. And it is evident in our delicacy, our softness, our quality of fineness, and our vulnerability to injury.

Mentally, it covers our limitless aptitude for leadership in the role of exemplar and nurturer of relationships. When we pursue the most natural application of this skill set, we are called mothers, and this is a title that is at least equal to any that humans may lay claim to. As mothers in any context, we excel at guiding and developing both individuals and groups towards excellence. We have these talents partly because we can multitask and because we have a conspicuous gift for charm. We often enjoy a heightened awareness of others' emotional states and needs, and this gives us the ability to react quickly; but this ability also gives us insight to provide comfort, encouragement, de-escalation, and fortification. And our heightened understanding of others makes us naturally more flexible and willing to cooperate to find mutually beneficial solutions to problems.

Femininity is Your Source of Power

Femininity and masculinity have been with us from humanity's origins. The partnership between these powerful forces brings out the best in us. Trying to change centuries of the fundamental and complimentary way civilization has progressed is not only fruitless but doomed to failure.

For at least a hundred years, the Western world has been on a crusade to establish equality of the sexes before the law, and this has mostly been a good thing. But it is plain to see that while equality or fairness ought to exist between us, there are significant differences between our genders. Equality is not necessarily sameness, and we wouldn't want it to be in all cases. Our differences can be crucial to happiness, especially if you have an interest in a relationship with a man. If you want to be your best self, and if you want to be enchanting to the opposite sex, you need to draw attention to what makes you *different* from them. The greatest contrast between the genders is femininity and masculinity. To appeal to men, you must emphasize your feminine features, like your higher voice, the way you move, your appearance, your tenderness, and your delicacy. These things compliment and highlight his natural masculine strength, deeper voice, and his manly courage.

Femininity carries great power. Combined with character and charm, it's an unbeatable combination. You may be beautiful, smart, and accomplished, but you won't be completely fulfilled as a woman without cultivating femininity. And it will be the key to your success in a romantic union with a man. He is more interested in being with a real woman than a genderless someone.

We are female and should be proud of it. We don't need to act like, look like, or be like men to be extraordinary and strong in our own way. We don't esteem ourselves above men, but neither are we beneath them. Our femaleness is unique, beautiful, and priceless. We need to rediscover it. It is who we *are*. Femininity belongs to women, so let's take it back along with any other words that used to be ideally female like dainty, gentle, delicate, sweet, and demure. In no way do these adjectives diminish us; they make us more valuable; we can now view them as a badge of honor. Deep down we want to be our genuine selves. So, go ahead. Be as girly as you want!

Our Costly Blunder

Dictionaries often define femininity like this: "pertaining to a woman or girl: feminine beauty and dress; having qualities traditionally ascribed to women, such as sensitivity or gentleness." It's never very specific. And dictionaries often reflect prevailing views in culture around the world. Much of our sense of gender is vague or a long-forgotten notion. And many of us are guilty of inadvertently undermining our own sex by the way we walk, talk, and present ourselves; by the ease with which we accept anti-feminine propaganda and social re-engineering. We sometimes do this without even realizing it.

Too many people today see femininity as weak, insipid, or even unintelligent. One woman told me she thought femininity meant manipulation. We contribute to these false notions when we devalue the contribution we make as feminine mothers and homemakers, insisting that all stay-at-home mothers are unemployed, unambitious, unaccomplished, unglamorous, or just unimportant. We inadvertently give the impression we actually believe men are better than we are in the way we emulate and seek to copy them. Some of us appear to seek validation by wearing masculine-inspired clothes. We sometimes copy the way men talk, walk, and move, and we learn to be aggressive. Do we believe they will treat us with more respect if we act like them? Maybe we'll be more valued?

We will never be men and we'll never be totally convincing at pretending to be them. We can't succeed on their terms as well as they do, but we can succeed beautifully on our own. We have plenty of influence and feminine power just being us. We are lucky to be women. Femininity is at the core of who we are: our perspective, thoughts, values, feelings, and character. We are at least as powerful in our own sphere as men are in theirs.

Femininity: Hardwired from Birth or Learned?

Femininity is an attribute that is both innate and learned. We are born with female bodies and brains. Traits like basic intelligence, personality style, and talents may be biologically programmed to a certain degree, and these natural attributes include many of your feminine inclinations. Other parts of your identity are more trainable or negotiable, such as acquired education and skill. They are affected by the culture in which you are raised, choices you make, and the way you spend your time and energy.

These days, feminine skills are rarely ever taught to young women. It's not reasonable to expect that we are born with all the charms, mannerisms, and social skills we need.

I suffered as a child with shyness. I constantly heard adults say, "She's bashful, isn't she?" I still struggle with it to some degree, but through hard work and the repeated confrontation of my fears, and with the support of my husband, I have come a long way. I have proven to myself that I am not only what I was born to be, and I have learned this is true of everyone. We all have potential in the fluid portion of ourselves to become the best person we can be. Femininity and charm, along with character and mature behavior, are skills that can be learned and cultivated.

In Summary

- All human life starts with women and we are our species' primary nurturers.
- Femininity is both a physical and mental state
- Femininity is our greatest source of power. It is your key to success in a romantic union with a man.
- Femininity is both hard-wired and learned. By understanding the timeless principles of Fascinating Womanhood you can achieve your full potential.

Chapter 6
Feminine Appearance

I've heard women ask about having a more feminine appearance. They sometimes say things like: "Why do I have to be something I'm not? I just want to be myself." Your appearance can be a fluid concept. Have you ever considered that your self-perception may have been influenced more by others than by you? People tend to outsource their sanity and expectations of themselves.

Some of us have parents who validate our natural feminine nature and some do not. I've known girls whose parents only seem pleased when they act like boys, especially fathers who wish they'd had a son. They don't like the whole idea of girly things or femininity. Girls in this position often try to conform for acceptance and love. Some girls never own a dress and have no idea what it's like to look in the mirror and feel pretty, confused with the idea of what it means to be female and perhaps afraid of perceived consequences like teasing or standing out too much.

"There is no such thing as an ugly woman"
~ Vincent Van Gogh

Does Appearance Matter?

How we look isn't everything, but of course it matters. Appearance includes how you present yourself physically: how you move, walk, and talk, your style (which includes your hair and clothes), and even how you interact with others. It includes what radiates behind the clothes, from your soul. Please don't be tempted to think you are doomed if you weren't born with classic beauty. Every woman is beautiful in her own way, she just needs to learn how to identify and express it.

First Impressions

Perhaps the most important way that appearance impacts relationships is with first impressions. Don't underestimate its influence. Unless you're in an emergency situation, don't even consider going out of the house without looking like a feminine woman. It would be an injustice to yourself to diminish your own feminine power. This doesn't mean you always have to wear a dress. But you don't ever want anyone to wonder if you're male or female. You never know who you will meet, and dressing in an attractive way feels good. It's part of self-care and reflects high confidence and respect for everyone you meet. Looking feminine is always a good idea.

Clothing

There are some who believe that to have credibility in a world of men, we must not only act like men, but look and dress like them too. Sometimes we cut our hair like men, walk like men, and move like men. We become aggressive and competitive, even with a man we want to attract. We don't seem to realize we are sacrificing part of our femininity to be accepted. Men's clothing tends to hide our feminine nature. This deception has crept up on us so gradually that we have hardly noticed. To be considered professional, we often dress and act like men in business, in sports, and even in personal relationships. Don't resort to wearing men's clothes unless you can wear them adorably. The key is to *accentuate the differences.*

An interesting exception to the use of masculine inspired clothing is pairing an item which is traditionally masculine, such as a suit coat, with a skirt or pants that are decidedly feminine. When you do that, your whole ensemble accentuates the differences. It can actually make you look more female. Another exception is when a very elegant woman wears masculine inspired clothes but accentuates her female figure, makeup, hair and shoes. This combination of highlighting, in one look, both masculine and feminine, can be stunning.

Personality and Your Clothing Style

There are many types of women, and some clothing suits certain individuals more than it does others.

Sporty

This style emphasizes comfort: cotton pants and shirts, relaxed styles, even in dresses. A woman can be feminine and wear these types of soft, comfortable clothes. She wears garments she can play in and enjoys being natural and casual. I think of singers Taylor Swift and Gwen Stefani, actresses Gwyneth Paltrow, Lupita Nyong'o, Gal Gadot, or Kim Yoo Jung.

Classic

This is a woman who tends to focus on dressing for a career or status and usually chooses the perfect business attire. She prefers quality. This is a style made famous by women like Princess Kate or Audrey Hepburn: classic lines, sophisticated and elegant—not a lot of ruffles but feminine to the core.

Dramatic

This style is all about glamour. When she enters a room, she likes to make a big entrance, to be noticed. She is drawn to bold colors, "bling" and expensive fabrics. Omotola Jalade Ekeinde, Jennifer Lopez, and Elizabeth Taylor come to mind.

Romantic

Women who prefer this style often love ruffles, lace, flowers, and ribbons; anything that inspires romance. The British actress Jane Seymour is famous for this style, as are Zooey Deschanel, Tonto Dikeh, and Zhang Zivi.

There are feminine clothes that fit each of these types. Be true to your style and to your mood. You may even feel attracted to more than one of these styles on different occasions. Your job may require you to dress in an understated way, and classic might fit the bill there. At other times, you might feel dramatic or romantic. Enjoy looking like a woman, no matter your style.

Androgyny

In fashion, androgyny is an attempt to look neither male nor female. It seems to be mostly an endeavor for women to look more like men, and seems to imply that male identity is superior to female, or at least somehow a human "generic look."

Some extremist types act like all people should be androgynous, claiming there is no significant difference between the sexes; that the differences are learned and not truly part of us. The truth is, aspects of gender identity have cultural roots, and so they are learned, but most of what makes us male or female comes from birth and is not chosen. It is biological fact, part of our DNA, and does not belong in political debate. Women around the globe identify with each other because the core of what makes us feminine is the same. We are all sisters.

So why would anyone go for the androgynous look? There are many potential reasons but they all point to a lack of female identity. Some women seek to be invisible to men—perhaps because of past trauma, but also because of depression, a lack of education, or the wrong kind of education. Deep down, almost any woman will admit that she wants to look beautiful. We yearn to be noticed and respected as feminine women.

Diminishing the differences between men and women ultimately diminishes both sexes and leads to a more confused individual, and an even more confused society.

Pizza Clothes

This is a term coined by my daughters and our family has been using it for years. It is the clothing you wear — usually old sloppy pajama bottoms, sweatpants or jeans, and an oversized, stretched out t-shirt — when you're tired of trying, and so you order a big pizza and eat the whole thing right before downing a quart of ice cream. It could also include anything that is undignified, or which signals you've given up. You might be discouraged or unhappy, but please avoid wearing pizza clothes. Dressing like this undermines self-esteem and encourages unfeminine mannerisms. It fosters an attitude of depression and discouragement.

The differing reactions from others to your appearance may make you feel invisible or, on the other hand, add to your feeling of worth. Put some effort into your presentation. It will make a huge difference in your day and your attitude. Don't lose your influence or give away any of your feminine power. Keep it, because it's valuable and belongs to you.

Little Girl in the Red Dress

I was waiting in the car on one occasion and I saw a playground filled with children, out for recess. I noticed a small girl who looked to be about 4 years old. She was wearing a bright red dress with three tiers of ruffles. The other children, many of whom were girls too, wore the typical shorts or jeans and ran about playing happily, as did the little girl in the red dress. But I noticed immediately how very feminine and dainty this child was when she moved. She would pick up the sides of her dress as though she was about to curtsy when she sat down on a log. And she ran in such a charming way. She acted like a princess, and I believe it was at least partly because of the dress.

You don't have to wear frilly dresses every day to be a thoroughly feminine woman, but consider how different clothes make you feel when you are in them. This doesn't mean you shouldn't wear pants — most of us do. But we should pay attention to how we act in everything we wear, whether it's a ball gown or jeans we save for working on the house or in the yard. The way we dress can have a dramatic effect on how we see ourselves and how we behave towards others.

Hair

The key to success with your hair is to distinguish yourself as a woman — to highlight the natural differences between the genders. A clean head of hair is a necessity. Greasy or dirty hair is never attractive on anyone, man or woman. Brushed hair is also essential.

Experiment with what looks good on you. For most of history women wore their hair in specific styles, sometimes elaborate. Many women today have the attitude that the easier, the better.

You may have gorgeous hair without doing much, but most of us would benefit from taking a bit of time with it.

In the first three quarters of the 20th century, women often got up an hour early just to do their hair and makeup before going out. They went to bed nightly with curlers or rags in place. Women worked more at their appearance, and we should bring this back. There are so many creative things that can be done with hair. Some women look great with short and relatively care-free hair. Others like longer hair that sometimes needs more time to arrange. Just keep it feminine. The results will boost your self-esteem and make you feel prettier and more confident.

What do you do if you don't have great hair? There are perms, wigs, hair add-ons, and great cuts that can make you look dazzling. There is also hair color. If you want beautiful hair, there are so many ways to have it. Emphasize the differences!

Make-Up

Some women don't like makeup and some men discourage it. This is a personal choice. But it should be noted that make-up was created to make us look better, not worse. It can be applied too thickly or inexpertly. It can also be minimal and can give us a look that would make one think we are not wearing makeup at all. Or it can be dramatic and emphasize our eyes, cheeks, and lips. Well-applied makeup can make us look younger and less tired. As a woman ages however, makeup becomes even more of a friend. There are excellent books on makeup application and also free advice on the internet, in stores, and in magazines.

Facial Expressions

Everyone has difficult days when they get angry or fearful. We have our time of the month, pregnancy, and later, menopause. You can guard against harsh or hard expressions that are unattractive. These expressions don't advance your goals or make you feel better. Some people seem to have an unconscious frown even when they don't feel angry or even sad. This is one of those fluid parts of your presentation that can be changed if you are willing to practice. Look in the mirror sometime when you are particularly angry. I did that once when I was mad and got a shock. Then I had a shocked expression that also wasn't my favorite. Some expressions are not attractive, and this is usually when they are inspired by negative emotions. There are times you won't want to show your feelings to just anyone. It's wiser to keep some things to yourself until you are ready to share them.

On the other hand, notice how you look when you smile. Think of someone you love or something you like. Look in the mirror when you are happy, when you have done something nice for someone, or are excited, and see what that looks like. This will help you learn to adopt your best facial expressions. Actors use techniques like this. It will take time and consistency, but it will change you.

Character Affects Appearance

Character is so important that there is a whole chapter in this book dedicated to it. Character, or lack of it, affects appearance. The man you love will notice the way you treat others; he will either be enchanted or repelled. Your treatment of others reflects the way you will treat him, and he will take note. A girl with shallow character has a hard time keeping the love of a good man. Men and women with little or no character seldom stay together for the long-term; their selfishness tends to destroy the relationship sooner or later.

Physical Reflection of Character

Marie was a woman born innocent like all children. She was selfish and stubborn as a child, and at times cruel and dishonest. But she was also charming and popular at school. She once said, "I do nice things for people so they will be in my debt. Then I can collect." Those close to her didn't take it seriously at the time. They thought she was kidding. Unfortunately, it was how she lived her life. She used people and never really cared about anyone but herself. This was made clearer as the years went on. She grew in to a beautiful young woman and many desired her. She graduated from college and married, but she was cruel to her husband and her marriage ended in divorce. She hurt people wherever she went. As her bad choices multiplied, her eyes seemed to narrow, and she began to look cruel as she aged. Like the classic book, "The Picture of Dorian Gray," her physical appearance began to reflect her inner identity. As she got older, people commented that something was strange about her and kind of scary. Her character was reflected in her appearance.

Seductive or Feminine?

"Your clothes should be tight enough to show you're a woman but loose enough to show you're a lady."
~ Marilyn Monroe

Being feminine and being seductive are two different concepts. Some girls dress and behave as though their goal is seduction and that their main interest is sex. But this might not be their true intent. They may just want masculine attention and romance, but the impression they are unconsciously giving to men must also be viewed through a man's perspective. Men notice a seductive woman. They are wired to notice! The problem is that there are a lot of men who are only interested in sex, not long-term attachments. Is this what you want? In addition, a good, moral man might see such a woman as shallow or untrustworthy. While attracting a man romantically will tend to involve sex at some point if the relationship develops, it will not be the main purpose of being feminine.

It's a bit like going fishing. If you're not careful when it comes to men, you might end up with something you don't want—someone even emotionally or physically dangerous. You need to use the right bait so you don't end up catching a shark. He might fool you into thinking he's a great catch at first, and it could become difficult to throw him back. Sorting the good guys from the bad can be challenging because it takes time to get to know a person's true character. There is a chance you might develop feelings for him during this time of discovery, and it is a complicated thing to be in love with a bad man. Some of you are nodding your heads as you read this, because you know it's true.

Even when you use the right bait, you still aren't sure of what you will catch so be careful. Know the type of man you want. Get to know him well enough to make the best decision you can. You don't want to get a shark or a jellyfish.

When it comes to presentation, it's always better to leave something to the imagination. They say: "If you've got it, flaunt it." But I say reserve it for special and private occasions and it will be more valuable. You can be feminine, charming and have sex appeal while being modest and dignified.

The Right Time for Seduction

Being seductive is best when you are married to a man you love and who loves you. Anything short of that is high-risk behavior and could potentially hurt you in the long-term. You might get away with it, but you might not.

It puts you in a vulnerable position that could lead to deep and lasting hurt, and it could blunt your ability to trust or feel intimacy with others in future.

Drinking, Smoking, Feminine Health, and Appearance

There are some habits that compromise health and, therefore, feminine appearance. Smoking, poor eating habits, excessive alcohol consumption and drug abuse are major culprits. You might escape apparent consequences with bad routines for years, but it always catches up. Smoking ruins your skin and hair, deepens your voice, darkens your teeth, can cause premature wrinkles and potential life-threatening side effects. Excessive drinking causes heart and liver problems, brain damage, weight gain, hair loss, and sometimes addiction, which can change personalities for the worse and harm relationships.

Obesity

Obesity is an issue in a lot of societies. Many women worry about weight throughout their adult lives. Excessive weight can ruin your health and contributes to heart problems, diabetes, high blood pressure, and lowered self-esteem. Your belief in yourself will absolutely change when you take charge of your weight. Doing that can be hard, but it's worth it. Even moderate success can make you feel so much more beautiful if you've been feeling too heavy. Get the body that makes you feel like a goddess, whatever that body is. Your whole life will be transformed when you do.

Exercise

Exercise is very important for your body and your mental health. It's an excellent way to counter the physical effects of stress and depression. This is because regular exercise produces hormonal activity in the brain that stimulates neuron growth and repair. It also provides naturally for your brain what antidepressant medications provide artificially. There are so many ways to exercise too! You can be a regular walker or jogger, swimmer, dancer, or you could lift weights and practice yoga. Stay active. Yoga has an added advantage of helping us become more graceful. It helps with flexibility, balance, and mental focus.

Posture

Walk with a straight back. There is nothing better to help improve posture than looking at yourself in a mirror. Some women find good posture difficult because of the heaviness of their breasts. But even if this is your case, you can build core strength through exercise and posture correctors. In time and with training, you can teach yourself to walk and sit with shoulders back. You'll be surprised. Your body will remember once you've practiced it enough. Good posture makes you look and appear more confident. It can actually give the impression that you've lost weight. We talked earlier about first impressions, and your posture is something everyone notices. You want that impression to be good, especially if you're looking for a man.

Conclusion

Some women may reject femininity because of societal pressures, fear of attracting too much attention, and sometimes from a desire to hide due to past trauma. It's not easy out there. But don't lose hope. Femininity is your true nature. It is your identity and your birthright. It is the source of your personal power and the thing that will propel you farthest in life. Abandon it, and you only weaken yourself. Turn your back on it and you betray yourself. Don't be afraid. You have the tools that you need. You only need to embrace them and fight for yourself and others.

In Summary:

- As Van Gogh said, "There is no such thing as an ugly woman". You are already beautiful.
- Your appearance and first impressions matter. Everyone has some control over this.
- Your clothing makes a statement and communicates a lot about you.
- Your character and health influence your appearance.
- You don't have to be seductive to be feminine and wanted.
- Femininity is most fascinating when you save the most personal parts of you to be appreciated by the man you love.
- You don't have to compete with or look like a man to be valuable.
- There is power in femininity which is different from men. Don't reject it. Embrace it. It will change your life for the better.

"It seems to be the fashion nowadays for a girl to behave as much like a man as possible. Well, I won't! I'll make the best of being a girl and be as nice a specimen as I can: sweet and modest, a dear, dainty thing with clothes smelling all sweet and violety, a soft voice, and pretty, womanly ways. Since I'm a girl, I prefer to be a real one!"
~ Mrs. George de Horne Vaizey

Chapter 7
Charm

Charm is more valuable than beauty. You can
resist beauty, but you can't resist charm.
~ Audrey Tautou

While it is important to present yourself as well as you can, it will come to very little without feminine charm. You could think of physical appearance and charm as two sides of the same womanly coin. Without the one, the other is incomplete. Both are essential to femininity, but charm is by far the more powerful.

Everyone loves to be around a charming person. They validate us, and this helps us to feel good about ourselves. Charm is pleasing, motivating, and uplifting. There are those who practice a kind of superficial charm, but they can't fool very many for long. True charm reflects inner character. When you are charming, men will be attracted to you and everyone will want to be around you.

Not everyone is born with it, but you can learn it. Let's start with the way you move.

Physical Grace

Becoming graceful involves learning how to walk, move, sit, and stand. It includes gestures of your head and hands and displays a pleasing, fluid motion.

Men love a graceful woman. Women also love grace because it is beautiful to watch. Grace can be practiced and mastered. You just need to be aware of some of the principles and add them to your feminine repertoire. It's already latent inside and will become a part of you. It feels good to be graceful!

Sitting

As you sit, be aware of what your body is doing no matter where you are. Never sit down into a chair heavily. Sit in a calculated fluid motion like a dance routine. Don't spread your legs out after sitting; cross your legs or feet daintily. Try not to cross your legs like men sometimes do, with one leg horizontal across the other, the sole of your foot or shoe pointing outward. This is not charming at all. Practice in front of a mirror a few times if you need to. Start with how you normally sit and notice if it is charming. If your technique needs work, practice makes perfect.

Walk Like a Celebrity

Pretend you are a celebrity and paparazzi are waiting around the corner to take your picture. Notice how you walk in a mirror or store window. Do you walk like a man? Masculine men walk with their hips straight and feet slightly apart. Men march and lumber, and they like to swagger: they move with a gait that is heavy and meant to express formidability. This looks aggressive. Feminine women stroll, and they sometimes strut when they have a lot of confidence. They walk with arms slightly swinging and shoulders straight, putting one foot in line with the other; this will cause your hips to naturally sway. You can walk like this whether wearing heels or flats. Walk with confidence and an erect back. Avoid walking like a duck with feet turned out or with legs apart like a soldier storming the enemy. Move with grace, whether you're running or walking. Never be tempted to drag or shuffle your feet. Create curves as you walk — we're made for it because of our bone structure in our hips. It's natural and beautiful. Remember with every step that you are important and valuable, and keep your chin up as you practice.

Find a role model, whether it's a real person or a character in a book or on film and emulate them. Model how they walk and talk, move their hands and speak.

Sometimes the best examples are in movies though they may be in literature. Find an actress, celebrity or character from a novel who expresses herself the most like you want to be; study the way she moves and communicates with people. A personal favorite of mine is Jeanette MacDonald. Look her up, she was famous in Hollywood in the 1930s. She was so feminine and dainty. I love the way she moved and laughed. Or find a role model that fits with you. A more modern example might be Nicole Kidman or Gal Gadot.

Don't underestimate the importance of your walk. It isn't everything, but it can make a significant difference. Your goal of being a charming feminine woman is amplified by the way you move.

Hands

The way you move your hands can greatly emphasize your charm and femininity. Always try to use graceful, feminine hand movements to express yourself. The way your hands move can make you mesmerizing. It's not important if you were born with naturally beautiful hands. How you use them will more than make up for any perceived personal defects you may have.

My husband remembers a Sunday school teacher from his childhood days who lead children in singing. He remembers how she moved her hands; that they were so graceful and mesmerizing he couldn't take his eyes off them. This impression is strong enough for him to remember it to this day.

Have you ever watched a skilled female hula dancer? This is a Polynesian dance accompanied by music and hand movements. The way hula dancers use their hands to tell a story is fascinating and hypnotic; their hands move like rippling water.

Eva

Eva was celebrating her one-year birthday. Her parents sat her on the floor with a piece of chocolate cake on a plate, expecting her to make a mess of it as many one year olds do. However, she looked at the cake and then with both tiny hands, carefully moved toward the treat, daintily picking up a small piece that had broken off and putting it in her mouth. Then she went back to the larger piece and delicately picked it up with two little fingers on each hand like a Duchess with a tea cup. She held it with gentle hands and didn't stuff it in her mouth but took small, careful bites. Her parents were charmed and couldn't wait to tell the whole family.

The Feminine Handshake

Shaking hands is a standard greeting and it's hard to avoid in social situations, especially professional ones. Cultures have different standards, but there is no where on earth where a woman can offer a manly grip and make a good impression. When you must shake hands, do it in a feminine manner. Don't squeeze hard like a man trying to bring a victim to his knees, but don't offer the limp "dead fish" handshake either. There is no charm in this. You want to communicate warmth and friendliness without challenging the other person to a duel of strength.

It's easy to give a feminine handshake. When you have developed your womanly side, which includes charm and girlishness, you will naturally offer your hand in a confident and light grip. This means that you will not hesitate or be nervous about it, but you will not show aggression either. A feminine handshake expresses a sense of self-worth as well as tenderness for others.

What Does a Feminine Woman Sound Like?

It's the gentle sounds, feminine laughter, sighing, cooing, and secret whispering that we make when addressing the man we love or when we are pleased with something, that are naturally girly and enchanting. This seems instinctual in some women but can be learned. Your voice, including pitch and tone, can be distinctly feminine, even if you feel it hasn't been up until now.

The best example of cooing might be when we are around babies or small children. We often make soft noises with those we love or have tender feelings toward. This is both attractive and charming. It is a style of communication that is in sharp contrast to a masculine man's.

Seek to comfort others in the sounds you make and the way you speak. Speak gently, but with enough volume to be heard by those intended. Don't yell or use crude gestures or mannerisms. Don't whistle loudly or use profane language. Dirty jokes and foul language are not feminine, and there is never a real need for it. Good manners are feminine in women as well as masculine in men. A charming voice is polite and genteel. It works in any society or culture, in any situation. Remember, you are a great lady.

Blushing

Most men find blushing when smiling to be charming. It signals to them a charming vulnerability and encourages their masculinity. Blushing is charming because it means a degree of personal guard is down. It is involuntary and difficult to fake, and so it is a mark of sincerity. For a man, it is inviting and endearing to be around a woman who responds to his efforts at charm with vulnerability, which is never threatening and calms his guard dog. Vulnerability is a necessary ingredient to bonding and intimacy. If you can't blush, you can't do much about it. Just don't feel embarrassed if you blush around a man you find attractive. It's delightful to him.

How You Treat Others

Men notice the way you treat people. A good man will either be enchanted or repelled, depending on what he sees you do. Your attitude and approach towards other people is a reflection of the way you will treat him, and he will sense it. This is especially true with strangers or those who serve you, such as a waiter or housekeeper. A woman who is shallow will have a hard time keeping the love of a good man. How you treat others is a hallmark of charm.

Tenderness

To be tender means: "Marked by, responding to, or expressing the softer emotions; being considerate, showing care. To be loving and gentle, showing affection and love for someone or something." Rather than being a mark of weakness, it is a mark of character. Let's celebrate being tender. It's clearly a timeless positive attribute in women.

I will never forget seeing Princess Diana sitting with patients who had contracted the AIDS virus in the 80s. This was a time when it was commonly supposed that the disease could be transmitted by touch, and it was considered inappropriate for a person of her high standing to touch a commoner with bare hands. She held children with the disease on her lap, hugging and touching them gently. She held the hands of adults who were too weak to stand, motivated from a deep desire to comfort those who suffered. Princess Diana became even more famous for her tenderness than for her birthright or privileges from marriage.

When a woman reflects this aspect of timeless charm, she is a princess to all who behold her, regardless of where she comes from.

"There's a difference between beauty and charm. A beautiful woman is one I notice. A charming woman is one who notices me."
~ John Erskine

Smile

Scientists have identified more than 50 types of smiles. Research has indicated the sincerest smile of all is the Duchenne smile, or genuine smile—a grin that pushes up into the eyes. You can smile with your eyes, but the muscles needed to do this are involuntary. If you look at someone and then genuinely smile, it will instantly be charming.

No matter how much classic beauty you were born with, it's always enchanting when you smile genuinely. You will smile most naturally when your mental focus is elevated. Smiles can also originate from baser instinct, but they tend to look more mischievous or sinister. Practice smiling by filling your mind with delightful thoughts, and do it is often as you can. Think of things which you are grateful for, or contemplate beauty and humor, and you will find it hard not to smile. Happiness is attractive and contagious, and people will want to be around you.

Refinement

The essence of refinement is good manners. As stated earlier, manners are feminine in women and masculine in men. When a woman applies good manners, she naturally tends to apply it in a feminine way.

It's time to bring back the skill of good manners and refinement, which are charming and make us nobler in bearing, counteracting a society functioning at its lowest level by inspiring a higher level of behavior. It honors us as women to exercise good manners wherever we go.

Refinement can include writing thank you notes, remembering social invitations, and being courteous to everyone around you, no matter their social status, age, or financial situation.

When you are in the home of another, always remember to compliment your host or hostess on their generosity for having you. If you stay the night as a guest, make your bed in the morning and keep the room or place you are given to sleep tidy. I was always taught to leave any room I have been in a bit neater than when I entered it, if possible.

Sometimes being invited to dinner can be tricky. If you have a food allergy, politely let your host know in advance. Your host will surely appreciate finding out before dinner that you are deathly allergic to shellfish. If you have a food aversion, don't distress your host by giving him/her a list of your dislikes. You will sound picky, which is rude. It's better just to deal with it politely unless you are asked for personal preferences.

Showing sincere gratitude is also a mark of refinement. Never engage in heated arguments while someone's guest, or with your own guests. Show genuine interest in what other people are saying.

You will inadvertently hurt people at times. When you do, as soon as you are aware, apologize and let the person know you would never do anything to hurt them on purpose. Then forgive yourself and try to consider the feelings of others more in future.

Ladylike Behavior

"Being born a woman doesn't automatically make one a lady."
~ Anonymous

Having the manners and character of a lady is essential for us to have good self-esteem. It involves treating yourself kindly, but it also concerns how you treat others and is an essential part of charm. Being a lady means being polite and having honest regard for other's feelings.

To be ladylike, you should always be looking for a way to be kind and generous, as well as learning the skills necessary to rise above challenges. Some of the main points to remember are:

A lady…

- is on time, if not a little early.
- values others as well as herself.
- is disciplined in mind and heart.
- takes care in her appearance with posture and poise, and dresses appropriately.
- has a good work ethic.
- has a balanced life with values intact.
- loves with her whole heart.
- is gracious.
- is authentic and never puts on pretenses.
- is graceful and generous in giving as well as receiving.
- is loyal and only gives up on someone if they insist on burning bridges.
- is a good conversationalist.

On Being a Good Conversationalist

Being good at conversing with others is important in every context of social life. Here are some tips:

Be interested in the other person. Be attentive. Listen to them. No one likes speaking to someone while they are distracted with cell phone texting or looking at something which is apparently more interesting.

Teach yourself to remember others' names. Dale Carnegie said, "Remember that a person's name is to that person the sweetest and most important sound in any language." You might think you aren't good at remembering people, but you can learn a few techniques that make it much easier.

When someone gives you their name, repeat it back.

Make sure of the name by asking them to spell it. This will be helpful if you have a visual memory as it creates a mental picture of the person's name. Hearing yourself say someone's name will help you remember it. Then, during the course of conversation, say their name periodically as you talk. It will help the person feel more connected as well.

Associate the person's name with something or someone else. Picture images that sound like the person's name. For example, if you meet a woman named Ann, you might think of Anne of Green Gables when you see her. If you meet a man from Ecuador named Gabriel, you might picture or think of the Angel Gabriel. It really doesn't have to make sense how you remember it. The quirkier the easier.

Make a connection between the person you're talking to and someone else you know with the same name, like a celebrity. For example, if you meet a woman named Emily, you could think of the film star Emily Blunt or maybe the writer, Emily Post.

Ask questions, but not meaningless ones like, "How are you?" and, "Is it cold enough for you?" Ask more open-ended conversation starters, if there's time, like, "What kind of work do you do?" And, "What are you passionate about?" Remember to listen after you ask!

Always be pleasant. Personal anecdotes often go over well. Don't force these into conversations, but wait till they naturally fit in. Beware of smutty or offensive stories in mixed company. Be sincere and sensitive to others' feelings.

Look for visual signs and notice body language. For example, if you see eye rolling, clock watching, foot tapping, or looking around the room, you've overstepped your bounds and more than likely your time limit. Pay attention to subtle expressions: the quick smile or frown, or a slight sadness in the eyes, a nervous hand, or foot movements.

Don't lecture or take yourself too seriously.

You don't have to be right all the time!

A conversation is not a monologue. Don't talk too long at one stretch. Give the other person a chance to jump in. This won't be hard if you are interested in them, and in what they think and feel.

Don't offer unsolicited advice. People don't tend to listen to advice they didn't ask for.

Try not to interrupt. This might be difficult if the other person is totally monopolizing the conversation. It will be much easier to stay interested if you focus on what they are saying.

Smile. People who smile during conversation give the impression they care about what others are saying, what they are interested in and what they enjoy. When you smile while speaking, you add even more charm to your conversation.

Don't exaggerate, except with tasteful humor. No one really likes to be deceived, or for things to be overly embellished.

Issue compliments generously. Compliments help raise self-esteem and encourage feelings of fondness, provided they are sincere. Look for things you notice about a person that are genuinely good from your perspective. Tell them and be specific.

Be gracious in accepting compliments. Even if a person pays you a sarcastic compliment, there is often a germ of jealous truth hiding behind it. Look for and accept the compliment. Go beyond a mere "thank you" and add something like, "I'm glad you liked it," "It's so kind of you to have noticed" or, "Thanks for your interest."

Subjects to avoid unless you know a person well and are of the same mind:

1. Money
2. Religion
3. Politics
4. Race
5. Sexual Orientation
6. Gender

A Tip for Talking

Most men's favorite subject is themselves. It's actually most people's favorite, but we are focusing on our relationships with men. If you want to keep a man interested in talking to you, be interested in him, his dreams and passions. Most people feel ignored and misunderstood. Someone who is genuinely interested in listening to them will draw their attention.

Women Who Lack Feminine Charm

When you are a charming feminine woman, you radiate beauty in a natural way. Even an average looking woman is more attractive when she adds charm and femininity. She can also seem unattractive no matter how beautiful she may be if charm isn't one of her attributes. Women who lack charm don't have as many friends, don't tend to keep mature relationships, and aren't as successful long-term in anything they try to accomplish.

Natural beauty is a blessing but not a necessity for love and happiness. The majority of men marry women who are not especially beautiful. Most people don't look like super models and don't undergo a lot of cosmetic surgery to enhance natural loveliness or to stay youthful. On the other hand, classically beautiful women are not guaranteed to be adored by the men who marry them. Age catches up with everyone, but charm is eternal.

In Summary:

- Being charming is attractive to both men and women. It can help you to be more successful in your relationships and whatever you do.
- As a woman, your feminine charm is unique and has influence that masculine charm does not.

- Being charming involves caring about others and the way you treat and communicate with them.
- Some of the skills that complete your charm include the way you present yourself: the way you move, sit and speak, your feminine skill as a hostess, as well as your own personal refinement.

"Charm—which means the power to affect work without employing brute force, is indispensable to women. Charm is a woman's strength, as strength is a man's charm."
~ Havelock Ellis,
English Physician, Writer

Chapter 8
Thanks for the Pants

"We have to be careful in this era of radical feminism, not to emphasize an equality of the sexes that leads women to imitate men to prove their equality. To be equal does not mean you have to be the same."
~ Eva Burrows,
13th General of the Salvation Army

Do you consider yourself a feminist on some level? How many of your friends identify themselves as feminists? Have you ever wondered why some feminists have agendas full of anger while others seem more peaceable? Are they all standing for the same cause?

Understanding feminism necessarily requires a look at history, especially how legal and social change have gotten us to where we are today. Feminism has changed the world in powerful ways over the last 100 years. It has been liberating in some ways, but it has also produced distinct negative consequences.

First-Wave Feminism

First-wave feminism refers to a global movement for women's suffrage that took place between the mid-19th and 20th centuries. The term "women's suffrage" means the right to vote.

Simone de Beauvoir, a French writer (1908-1986), wrote that the first feminist to "take up her pen in defense of her sex" was Christine de Pizan (1364-1430). She served as a court scribe for several dukes and the French royal court during the reign of Charles VI.

Mary Wollstonecraft (the "Grandmother of British Feminism") published one of the first feminist treaties: "A Vindication of the Rights of Women" in 1792 and advocated social and moral equality of the sexes.

In the United States, early suffragettes included Lucretia Coffin Mott, Elizabeth Stanton, Lucy Stone, Susan B. Anthony and many others.

Feminism began because women resented their lack of freedom and the abuse they received as second-class citizens. Men like Ernest Belfort Bax were typical of many 19th century pseudo-intellectuals who made ridiculous arguments about the inferiority of our gender. He made the case that relative body and brain sizes proved female inferiority. Though this does not even deserve a rebuttal, to dispel any false notions that may persist, body size does not always equate to the ability to defend or assert oneself, especially given modern technology, and brain size has nothing to do with intelligence.

Another influential voice who was characteristic of his time, Otto Weininger, an Austrian philosopher, stated: "No man who really thinks deeply about women retains a high opinion of them." Unacceptable and wholly ignorant statements like this marginalized women during this time and helped give birth to the feminist movement.

First-wave feminism has a good image in the United States mainly because it helped women get the right to vote. It also brought reforms in higher education, in the workplace, property rights, and in health care.

But it led to some unintended consequences such as increased rates of women working outside their homes, which amplified the workload for mothers of young children; and a lingering spirit of resentment towards men, which became thematic of the movement to come and helped promote a sense of victimhood that pervades to this day.

Second-Wave Feminism

It is generally agreed that second-wave feminism, which started in the United States but eventually spread throughout the world, began in the early 1960's and lasted until the early 1980's. Betty Friedan is widely credited with the beginning of second-wave feminism with her book, "The Feminine Mystique" in 1963. Helen Andelin also published "Fascinating Womanhood" in 1963, promoting traditional feminine values and romantic marriages. Neither author knew of the other until years later.

They both recognized similar problems but approached them in different ways.

Second-wave feminism broadened the debate to include sexuality, fairness in the workplace, reproductive rights, and other issues. It brought increased attention to domestic violence, stalking, and marital rape; and it lead to the establishment of rape crisis centers and battered women's shelters. It also addressed and brought about changes in custody and divorce laws. Second-wave feminism was in some ways an immense success, but it led to some seriously negative consequences.

Abortion remains a troublesome issue from this era. In the US, the highest court backed the ability of a woman to end the life of a fetus in her womb during a period of non-viability — a complicated phrase that is still fought over. A study in early 2018 determined that since this government action, over 60 million abortions have been performed in America alone. First wave feminists didn't support the idea of elective abortions, or the notion that it could be considered a sort of late-stage contraceptive. They were ardent supporters of marriage, family, and personal accountability. Elizabeth Cady Stanton, an early suffragette, referred to abortion as "infanticide" and wrote: "When we consider that women are treated as property, it is degrading to women that we should treat our children as property to be disposed of as we see fit."

Of Fish and Bicycles

By its second-wave, the feminist movement had lost much of its original bearings. And to this day, some of the biggest leaders of the feminist movement seem to truly hate men. They have spread an attitude among many women that men are bad and can't be trusted. They assert that there are few or no significant differences between the genders and that women don't need men, as in the now famous statement by Australian Feminist Irina Dunn in 1970: "A woman without a man is like a fish without a bicycle."

They sincerely seem to believe in a literal type of equality, where men and women are considered the same in physicality, in agenda, in thought, even in dress. In this brand of equality, women are encouraged to emulate men in order to find validation. But the emphasis on equality of outcome, or sameness, can't work. Successful marriages and families are much stronger where there is a division of labor between husband and wife, and responsibilities are borne according to core strengths, all to encourage excellence through specialization and to avoid costly duplication of effort. Modern feminists would frustrate this efficient system in the name of fairness, but all it gets us is exhaustion, confusion, frustration, and often increased tension with our men.

The toll that the feminist version of equality has taken on families, marital relations, and subsequently nations is a tragedy. Women are the gatekeepers of civilization. The blurring of male and female roles as well as our lack of understanding and practice of our greatest source of power decreases emphasis on home and family, the loss of feminine pride, and invalidation of both sexes.

Second-wave feminism is where things started getting dark for women, so let's review the benefits and misfortunes of this movement:

Positive Consequences of Second-Wave Feminism

- An increased recognition of the value and contribution of women in the workplace.
- Improved laws regarding fairness in the workplace and at home in personal and family life.
- Improved property rights.
- Better education opportunities for women of all classes.
- Improved legal protection of women in domestic and personal safety issues such as domestic violence and stalking.

Negative Consequences of Second-Wave Feminism

- A notable contribution to identity confusion: a loss of the sense of true femininity and masculinity; pressure on women to be less female and on men to be less masculine.
- Widespread animosity for men.
- The pressure to be both mother and breadwinner; in this latter position women may now be pressed to pay alimony and child support on top of everything.

- An undermined concept of marriage, family, and interdependence. It is now common to hear sentiments from women like: "Who needs men?" or "I can have a child with a 'sperm donor' and raise it without a father." This puts children in the position of being possessions, rather than a human being who thrives best with both a father and mother.
- The widespread, cultural acceptance of abortion.
- The general diminishment of women as victims. Blaming masculinity for all our problems and supposing that the fight is against men for greater rights or access is to assume they are the sole guardians of such things—that we cannot achieve enhanced rights without their approval. Weak or corrupt men may attempt to stand in our way, just as their female counterparts may try to do, but they are incapable of providing serious obstacles to Fascinating Women.

Third-Wave Feminism

Third-wave feminism is generally thought to have started in the early 1990's and by some accounts may be considered active in the present day. What is new mainly focuses on gender identity issues. On the upside, feminists are still concerned with defending women by seeking to abolish things like female genital mutilation, sexual predation by power figures, and so-called 'honor killing laws' where the head of a family is permitted to kill its female members for breaking social or religious rules. However, these issues are rarely at the forefront of most feminist discussions today.

New language has been invented in this era to redefine traditional sexual and gender identity in terms of binary (two choices) and non-binary constructs (more than two choices). As the new logic goes, having more than two gender choices is a way for everyone to liberate themselves from oppressive social norms, including so-called 'toxic masculinity.' A pseudo-science has arisen that attempts to differentiate gender from biological sex, with gender being only a psychological state of mind, and therefore fluid. We are in the midst of a "gender revolution."

Defining gender as a state of mind is entirely new to the human race and has deep philosophical and political roots in socialism—specifically identity politics. Such notions are being forced on societies in order to effect social change, and they leave many with feelings of disorientation and fear. These mass attempts at mental reprogramming defy science and common sense and contribute to the erosion of relationships and the traditional family.

Notions that promote victimhood degrade all humans and benefit no one. The only way to help women is for each gender to understand and respect and appreciate our respective differences. To empower ourselves as women, we need to appreciate the profound influence of feminine power—the real source of our personal success and happiness.

The feminist movement started with mostly good intentions and has accomplished some welcome things for women—thanks for the pants! But it has now become part of the problem because it actively opposes gender distinction, customary male-female relationships, and the traditional family. It has billed itself as the only women's movement, but it actively works against female identity and values. What we seem to have accomplished to this point is the permission to have a career while raising our kids and taking care of our homes. We now have to do it all, and women have never felt more pressure or dissatisfaction. Feminism has gotten some good laws passed but its track record with making women happy is abysmal.

"It is a naive sort of feminism that insists that women prove their ability to do all the things that men do. This is a distortion and a travesty. Men have never sought to prove that they can do all the things women do. Why subject women to purely masculine criteria? Women can and ought to be judged by the criteria of femininity, for it is in their femininity hat they participate in the human race."
~ Elisabeth Elliot

4th Wave Feminism and Beyond?

There have been numerous attempts to coin a new generation of feminism, some citing technology concerns, but nothing serious has emerged and one might suspect most fledgling movements are marketing schemes to advance private agendas.

Equality Versus Sameness

Feminist women often claim they want equality. What do they mean by equality? Literal sameness? Obviously, men and women are not the same. No decent person opposes the concept of legal equality of the sexes. Radical feminists suggest equality means everyone should *be* the same, which is ridiculous.

We have monthly periods, men do not. We can bear children, men can't. One scientific study found over 6,500 genetic differences between boys and girls that relate not only to the sexual organs, but also to the brain, skin, and heart.[5]

But in free societies, feminism has created a culture of some of the weakest women in history. Our grandmothers were far stronger and not so easily offended or victimized than women today. The more ardent the feminist, the weaker she is.

When angry women demonstrate their displeasure at what they perceive as unfair treatment or laws by marching, waving signs, and screaming foul sentiments, they do far less than they could by practicing femininity, and learning what it takes to build strong relationships and solid families — things that bring about real and positive change. Victim mentality has been undermining our gender and invalidating us for decades.

Modern feminists are threatened by traditional feminine women and differences of opinion. Recently, a female Olympic athlete, Kerry Walsh, said she valued her role as wife and mother

5   Borkhataria, Cecile. (2017, May 4). The REAL difference between men and women: Researchers find 6,500 genes differ between the sexes. Retrieved from http://www.dailymail.co.uk/sciencetech/article-4475252/There-6-500-genetic-differences-men-women.html

more than her career. She bravely stated, "I was born to have babies." She was severely criticized by feminists who didn't approve of what they saw as a reduction of female identity, rather than the enlargement of womanhood that Walsh intended. They used words like *sexist* and *misogyny* to describe her priorities; words that reinforce the false notion that women are inherently weak. Walsh responded that being with her children was more important and brought more joy to her than any of the awards of her sport. Fascinating Womanhood commends Kerry Walsh for her courageous and inspired stance.

Fascinating Womanhood in the Modern Era

Today's fascinating women boldly announce that we are not afraid to say what we want or to marry a good man and raise a family. It's sad that we are required to stand up to those of our own gender who would belittle us for choosing to cultivate femininity, marry instead of merely co-habit, and dedicate ourselves full-time to motherhood rather than seek a career. Motherhood and homemaking are among the most difficult of all professions, and those who travel this road deserve the greatest respect.

We desperately need to return to our core strengths and identities. If we as women want to attain the things we have always longed for — personal happiness and a lifelong relationship with a man who will adore us forever — we need to embrace our natural femininity. Feminine women value themselves and their families. They possess the greatest measure of feminine strength. They embrace gender differences and, even when ridiculed for it, they bear themselves up with their feminine power and don't identify themselves as victims when they are free to choose and act. They understand that to be a woman is validation in itself.

In Summary:

- First-wave feminism started for good reasons and accomplished important things but began a trend of anger towards men and unintended consequences for women.
- From the second-wave to the modern day, feminism has focused more on anger and distrust of men, along with the ongoing attempt to masculinize women while feminizing men.
- The emphasis on abortion rights today leads many to treat babies as personal property, to trivialize infanticide, to avoid personal accountability, and to erode the value of family and motherhood.
- There is a real attempt at legitimizing gender sameness as well as gender fluidity, which is neither scientific nor sound; both are destructive.
- We need to understand and appreciate the value of our beautiful and unique sex. We need to reclaim femininity. We are engaged in a world-wide crusade that unites women of all ages, races, cultures and religions. The more successful we are, the stronger our marriages, families, and nations will be.
- You can help with this change of attitude by understanding your value as a woman, the importance of your femininity and the impact it can have on the world.

Chapter 9
Brain Matters

You may wonder why I have included a chapter about the brain. What I have learned about it and how it affects our relationships has been life-altering for me in understanding myself and also men—especially my husband. When he is in a good mood, it's so easy. Okay, he's in a good mood most of the time. But there are times when he is tired, hungry, sick, frustrated, or maybe just overwhelmed. With the insights in this chapter, I know much more about what's going on inside his head and I understand better what it takes to help him get back to his normal happy self. Moreover, I can more easily do the same for myself, which makes an enormous difference.

It is helpful that so many of the differences between men and women are obvious, but some escape notice. A study of the brain reveals much about men and women that might otherwise be overlooked, including gender differences. Our brains are hard-wired differently in some respects and this can affect personality, preference, priority, and need. It brings to light our sometimes-different approaches to happiness and fulfillment, and it confirms that the vast majority of men and women have gender-related strengths and weaknesses which can be attributed to brain and body architecture and function.

Brain science is complicated stuff. I am not a doctor, but my husband is. He is a Neuropsychologist and has taught me as much as I can learn in an informal setting through the course of our marriage. This information has enriched our relationship and helped me in many ways, so I want to share the most valuable concepts with you.

Brain Basics

Your upper brain can be viewed as divided between two major parts: left and right. Discussing the brain in these terms is user-friendly, but it has certain limitations. In reality, brain architecture is more complex. But thinking of the brain as featuring a rough division of labor can still be very useful to the layperson.

The upper *left* side of your brain may be thought of as the *rational side*, mainly because it is key for speech. It is also a center for logical problem-solving and anything to do with analysis and reason. The upper *right* side of your brain may be thought of as the *intuitive center* and is known for things like creativity, inspiration, and idealism. Those of us who didn't specifically study the brain in college are often aware of about this much.

But there is also the lower portion of your brain, the part that develops first when you're a baby. It's an area that most people disregard because it's thought of as being entirely reflexive and not really trainable, kind of like a wild animal. Any understanding of basic brain functioning must include a discussion on this subject. In fact, the lower brain is vital to understand because we all deal with its complications and benefits every day, and each of us must learn to domesticate it, using the animal example, because it is key to making the most of our rational and intuitive areas.

Upstairs and Downstairs

It helps me to think of the brain, in simple terms, as consisting of an "upstairs" and a "downstairs." The upstairs portion of the brain includes the left and right sides that were earlier described as rational and intuitive, respectively.

The downstairs is a collection of parts in charge of survival, our sense of pleasure, and most of our automatic processes like hunger, thirst, breathing, heartbeat, and digestion, among other things. Our primary memory center is located here because it has so much to do with what will keep us safe and what is dangerous. In fact, most of our memories have to do with survival, staying far away from danger, and feeling as good as possible. So, this downstairs is all about staying alive, and that is why it gets to manage basic living functions.

Our sense of pleasure comes from this area because most things that feel good have something to do with survival or our sense of safety and well-being. Take for example: food. Eating good food feels great. It's reassuring and satisfying. It's comforting. The downstairs loves to give us high-fives for feeding our body so it has plenty of fuel. Anything that makes us feel calm, relaxed, or even excited because it is pleasurable, and equally, anything that makes us feel fear or anxiety, has to do with the downstairs portion of our brain.

Your Three Personalities

Your brain constantly presents you with choices. When all three perspectives are available, you will get two from your upstairs brain, one part rational and another intuitive, and then there will be your downstairs point of view.

My husband Bob likes to say he grew up thinking he was an individual, but in time he learned that he was more of a group. He realized that his brain was a collective of distinct parts trying to work together, though occasionally in competition and sometimes even outright conflict with each other.

This group concept was portrayed with comic effect in the Pixar film, "Inside Out." The story is about a young girl named Riley who is uprooted from her Midwestern town and moves to busy and chaotic San Francisco. Her emotions: Anger, Sadness, Disgust, Fear, and her most important emotion Joy, start to disagree on how to deal with this dramatic change, sometimes fighting each other for control of Riley's thoughts and feelings, other times simply collapsing or running around her brain's headquarters in panicked circles. In time, these facets of her brain learn to work more in harmony and Riley grows and adapts to her life changes.

Life constantly presents challenges to us, and we must learn to coordinate our different brain perspectives to make the most of them, like Riley does. The toughest part is reigning-in but maintaining an appropriate working relationship with your sense of anger, sadness, disgust, and fear: essentially your downstairs.

There may be some temptation, as the only main "upstairs" character Joy does in the movie, to dismiss the downstairs as a problem, but its functions are important to survival. When events come at us fast and we have to react quickly, the downstairs almost always takes over and gives us the resources we need to make it through.

If you were at home reading a book and suddenly heard an explosion that shattered your living room window, you wouldn't just sit there and keep reading. When we face sudden and perceived danger, we react first and then process later, so you would react before your upstairs brain had a chance to thoroughly process the event. Your heart would beat faster, your adrenaline would pump to give you a short burst of energy. You first actions might be to take cover or run. If you just continued to sit there and read, your life might be in danger.

When life affords us the chance to think a little before choosing, we tend to get a variety of answers on how to deal with a problem from a combination of the two-part upstairs perspectives, in addition to the automatic downstairs reaction. This can sometimes feel like different voices in our heads, or separate aspects of our personality. We are effectively presented with three perspectives. The first is what I have referred to as the downstairs with a safety and pleasure perspective. The second is from the rational, logical, and verbal processing mind. The third perspective is inspiration and creativity.

People often say things like: "There is a part of me that wants to ... but another part that doesn't." Or you might have heard something like: "Sometimes I think I'm my own worst enemy." Have you ever said: "My mind is playing tricks on me," or, "I'm a fool for doing that, I know better"? Almost like there is a part of you that is on your side, and another part that is trying to undermine you. This is inner conflict and is common to everyone who has ever lived. It happens when the upstairs left wants something that makes sense, but the upstairs right wants something a bit more experimental and full of unknown possibilities, all while the downstairs thinks everyone should just stay in bed and play it safe, and none of them can quite come to a compromise. We spend our lives balancing these voices and trying to get them into harmony as much as possible.

The Guard Dog

I sometimes like to refer to the downstairs as "the guard dog." This makes sense after you realize how it behaves. Earlier, I compared the lower portion of the brain to an animal. You could also think of it like a pet you just brought home who badly needs to be housebroken.

The guard dog is a fairly simple part of us that wants to protect us and wants to feel good. It loves food and will pretty much eat until it bursts, if allowed, unless an adult human comes along to stop it. It likes to play and have fun and is driven by impulse and appetite. Its motto is: "If it *feels good*, do it." But it's a nervous creature, constantly thinking about keeping itself and others safe. And so, perhaps its other motto is: "If it might be *dangerous*, it is." When it's scared, it generally has three solutions: fight, run away, or freeze.

The guard dog is quite reactive and doesn't really plan things out. It's fast, but primitive. This is why many people think it can't be trained. Its potential for evolution is limited, but like with a dog, training can help a lot.

People's guard dogs can be different, but what we feed grows stronger. If we make the untrained guard dog the most important part of the household, its rather barbaric agenda will dominate, and it will be hard to get it to obey commands once it gets used to being in charge. But if you balance it with the agendas of the upstairs, it can be a great friend and ally.

In the end, survival is the most important thing for the downstairs brain. Anytime you experience something in life, your brain receives it like it's a person coming over for a visit. The guard dog is going to bark if it doesn't either know or like the visitor. Everything that wants to come through *must* pass by your guard dog first.

As I've said, this dog is not sophisticated. But it can get better at correctly perceiving threats and controlling appetite with time and training. With help from the upstairs, it can be fashioned into something like a domesticated pet: still simple, still quite reactive, but better at its job and more controllable; a friend and ally rather than an enemy.

In life, we are constantly engaging our downstairs to first make sure that a person, a situation, object, or an idea is safe. Once we are satisfied that it is, the data can pass by initial entry to our brain and on to the higher functions — the upstairs portions where reason and creativity get things done with high level skills and technique. This is where we are at our best.

Remember that with communication and any sort of attempt to connect with another human being, you have *got* to get past that guard dog. If you scold or ignore it, it's all you're going to deal with until you calm it down again. So, when you're dealing with human beings, the person you're talking to needs to be relaxed before they can think about more complicated ideas. If the person is being difficult, look to the satisfaction of basic needs before pressing forward.

In relationship terms: if your man is being defensive, combative or avoidant, consider that there is probably some survival or comfort element at play and it needs to be addressed before much else can be accomplished. Or, if *your* guard dog is barking, you have to deal with it first before you can effectively deal with anything else.

The Meat Locker

Not long ago, I went into a building for a meeting and the conference room was freezing. The heating system was broken and it was winter. It felt like a meat locker. I found it difficult to tap into my upstairs brain, whether rational or intuitive. My guard dog was barking about the temperature not being acceptable. It was hard to concentrate and the meeting required upper brain planning and creative thinking. We were all so cold we couldn't even take off our coats or gloves. There were four of us at the meeting and their guard dogs were all barking too. We cut the meeting short and went home.

Will You Please Go to Sleep!

Matt was a good man. He was kind, mature, and supportive. However, when he was sleepy he would sometimes get grumpy and short-tempered. The next day he would say he didn't mean it or didn't remember it.

In one instance, his wife Sarah was feeling affectionate when they got into bed for the night. She leaned over and kissed him on the cheek. He rolled over and said, "Will you *please* go to sleep!" He dozed off while Sarah cried herself to sleep.

In the morning, Matt claimed he didn't remember a thing about the encounter. Sarah realized that when Matt was very tired, he was downstairs — reacting and not really thinking. In the future, she was more aware of when he was in this mood. Understanding this helped her to not take it personally.

Realizing when a person is downstairs and how to address the fact is key to understanding human behavior and better navigating social and domestic situations. It's important for dealing with people, especially the man in your life, and for being an effective communicator as well as an effective influence for good.

Your Guard Dog is Important

You may get the impression from reading about your guard dog that it is somehow your enemy. It isn't. It must be put in perspective and recognized for its value, but managed in regard to its weaknesses. Your downstairs brain is meant to help you survive, not build a successful life. If it ends up running your life, the guard dog could ruin it. But you don't have to allow that to happen.

The truly integrated and successful person relies upon a strong and active partnership between their upstairs and downstairs brains. The downstairs is only a problem when given free reign and no training. At its best, the downstairs is part of a reward loop between the downstairs and upstairs because of its role in reward and motivation. Remember, the overly repressed downstairs gets wild and will eventually act out.

There is much more knowledge, light, and creativity upstairs to enrich your life. The highest level of brain functioning is when you combine intuition — or the big picture — with logic and order. A decision or concept must make sense and feel right, but not just for the moment. When all of this is aligned, you can feel it. This describes the "ah-ha!" moments when you have a flash of inspiration and a clear sense of what to do about it. You feel both excitement and confidence. In these situations, your guard dog is calm and your mind is at its best.

When my mother decided she wanted a deeper romantic marriage, she engaged her rational and intuitive minds to finding solutions. She searched libraries and spoke with experts, and eventually came across some inspirational pamphlets. These things provided increased understanding in time, which lit a creative fire in her mind. She gradually began to comprehend the potential impact of what she was discovering on her marriage and others'.

When she applied the principles of femininity and understanding men, my father confirmed her intuition by being much more romantic towards her. With time, her dream of a fabulous marriage was realized. It comforted her downstairs, leaving her guard dog consistently happy.

The combination of the upstairs and downstairs parts of her brain working together was the unbeatable combination that created Fascinating Womanhood.

The Rational Mind

If there was a motto for this part of your brain it would be, "I do what needs to be done when it needs to be done, whether I like it or not."

Your upper left brain is essentially the rational part of you. Its objective is to verbally process and help other parts of your brain as needed. At best, it is a servant or sometimes a tour guide, but it often tries to take control and credit. It approaches everything in a logical, step by step fashion, loves order, routine and detail, making sense, doing things right.

This logical network houses the verbal part of your brain for right-handed and most left-handed people. The most important speech centers are here and therefore it is considered by many to be the dominant hemisphere. It is often thought of as the "conscious mind" and functions through observing. It is self-critical, analytical, and helps in choosing and decision-making tasks. The upper left brain is also organizational and focuses on planning, boundaries, and a sense of time. Executive functioning skills, attention, social abilities, self-awareness, judgment, planning, and the will to do things occur here, often with the help of the intuitive or right mind.

The main goal and purpose of the upstairs left is rational, orderly thinking.

The Intuitive Mind

The motto of the intuitive mind might be something like: "I know in my heart what to do."

When detectives are solving a crime, they sometimes follow a hunch. Many times, their instincts are right. This gut feeling has nothing go do with your actual gut or digestive tract. Your figurative heart, or intuitive mind, doesn't have anything to do with the muscle pumping blood in your chest. The reason you have a sense that intuition comes from your gut or heart is because cranial nerves connect your brain to internal organs and you sometimes feel sensations there when you feel things out.

When we are young, most of us are not used to listening to our intuitive minds. With time and experience, you can learn to trust your intuition.

Have you ever gotten a bad feeling about something? You may have felt uncomfortable, like something didn't fit, or that there was some present danger, or perhaps simply that you needed to leave a place. This is your intuitive brain sensing things it can't prove.

Gut instincts are not always right. If you sense danger, investigating the person or situation further often helps. It is usually beneficial to consult the perspectives of your upstairs brain and take them in to consideration with your more immediate downstairs reaction. This sort of mindful approach to life is vital to forming and strengthening relationships.

Your intuitive mind is also more connected to the spiritual. It sees things in pictures and feelings. That's where your impressions come from, the ones that tell you what you *feel* you know more than what you can logically understand and prove. These functions need to be appreciated and developed.

Some people reject the whole idea of intuition and believe the rational mind is the most important. Albert Einstein once said: "The intuitive mind is a sacred gift; the rational mind its servant. We live in a culture that honors the servant and has forgotten the gift." If you honor the servant over the gift, you are deterred from developing and integrating your mind. We need to treasure this gift. It's your listening post to the universe.

You'll also find that this gift will become more helpful to you when you learn to balance it with your sense of reason and logic. The key is, you should want things to make sense and feel right.

Male and female brains are far more alike than they are different, but these few differences are significant and are important to understand.

Two Sides of a Coin

The difference between male and female brains is mostly a matter of how the upstairs brain is connected. For the female brain, research has shown that there is more of a connection between the upper right and left portions, allowing for them to work together in a more natural and efficient way. Men tend to enjoy greater connectivity within each side of the upper brain, especially from the front to the back. This means that men are inclined to be more visual, non-verbal, and action-oriented; and it indicates that women tend towards a comparatively easier time with communication. With greater connections between left and right, or side-to-side, the female brain has an easier time with upstairs left-right integration, and this has many potential implications. As women, we can talk about how we feel or verbalize ideas faster and easier than a man, and we are better suited to combine analytical with intuitive thinking in what is often referred to as "women's intuition."

Not long ago, after my daughter and infant granddaughter visited home, I took them to the airport in a nearby town. I'd never been to it before so I plugged the address into my GPS. We arrived at what we thought was our destination but it was an old airport. They had recently relocated but my GPS hadn't yet received the updated information. There were cars around so I thought we were at the right place.

We unloaded her luggage and the baby stroller. We said goodbye and then they disappeared into the building. For some reason, I just had a feeling I shouldn't leave yet so I sat in my car checking emails. A moment later, Gina came rushing out thinking I had already left. She said, "I'm so glad you didn't leave! This is the wrong airport!" She probably would have missed her plane, even if she had called me on her phone to come back, the timing was that close.

It didn't make logical sense to stay, but somehow, I just knew in my *heart* that something wasn't quite right. I'm glad I acted on my intuition. Later, I asked my husband Bob how he would have reacted in this same scenario. He told me that the minute he dropped her off he would have gone on to his next task, assuming he had finished his mission. Men and women are both capable of objective and intuitive thought, but men tend to exhibit more of the former than the latter. My husband Bob sometimes works from intuition but tends to be logical because it plays more to his strengths. I am very capable of focus, but my tendency is to feel things out because I am more sensitive to vulnerabilities and relationships.

It's important to understand mental differences between men and women because it's key to communication. Have you ever asked a man how he feels about something only to have him not respond or say something like, "I have to think about it"? And then much later he may suddenly be able to put his feelings into words? He may not be as fast at this process as you are because his left and right upstairs brains aren't quite as connected. Women often think or say to men: "Just say it!" We get impatient because men are not like us but we think they should be, as if they have a choice and they're just being difficult. They really can't help it. They often process in a different way and it's sometimes hard for them to quickly verbalize thoughts and feelings—especially the latter. This can be frustrating for women, but the disconnection

133

gives a lot of men the advantage of being less dramatic. They can often keep things inside better. For most women, if we can't talk about how we feel, it's torture, while men are often quite good at putting thoughts and feelings away until they are needed later.

When it comes to relationships, women tend to be better caretakers because they are so naturally focused on it. This is directly related to their greater left-right connections. It does *not* mean that men aren't relationship-oriented or that they can't be good caretakers. Some men are quite focused on relationships, but we usually outpace them in this area. Men tend to use one hemisphere at a time while women generally use both at the same time.

Men's brains are slightly larger than women's, but only because they usually have more body mass. This does *not* mean they have more capacity for intelligence. We typically have the same average number of neurons, and so our brains can hold similar amounts of information and can do similar types of tasks. Women's brains are often just packed tighter in to a more compact space.

Men have strength in other areas. They tend to have more connections within their left or their right upper brains, but quite often the left side. They tend to be more specialized in their focus and abilities, inclined to being "an inch wide and a mile deep." That's why men often become great experts, and this may result in them exceeding women in some areas. Though more women cook and are good at it than men, the best chefs in the world are usually men. The world's best at many things are often men, but this doesn't reflect poorly on women. Men can afford to focus more on specialized knowledge and skills because they don't bear the complication of such an integrated brain. Men end up with less drive to create and foster relationships in exchange for their focus, while women can be quite skilled at many things and are usually better at multitasking.

His Guard Dog

The trick to getting on the good side with a person is to learn the ins and outs of their guard dog, what makes them feel good and what makes them anxious. When you get good at calming the guard dog of a particular person, you get better access to the richer parts of their personality; in the case of your man, him at his best.

When the guard dog of a man is understood and comforted in a healthy way, it can have a deep calming effect on him. And when a woman takes care of a man and understands his basic needs, she truly becomes irresistible.

The Hollywood film star, Robert Downey, Jr. has given a lot of credit to his wife, Susan, for his ability to stay off drugs and become a mega star. She seems to understand him and his needs. It has been said by those who know them: "It's as if she has some calming effect on him." She has no doubt discovered the secret to helping manage his guard dog. Robert calls the decade they've been together his "Great Transition," and he credits Susan with being its architect. "She is the font of all good things," he says.

135

Recognizing a man's basic needs for food, shelter, and safety is a beginning. This book will also teach you about his manly pride, Pandora's box, and accepting him. When you understand these things, you will more quickly and accurately anticipate his needs. And when his downstairs is activated, you will know how to give him more time or room to get back upstairs. If he is hungry, you will know not to get into deep discussions before he has eaten something (and if you go a step further, you will know to perhaps cook something delicious for him to calm his guard dog). If he is tired, you will give him space to rest. If he is overwhelmed, you can get him to exercise with you, to laugh, or to do something fun that demands his attention. You'll soon get good at understanding him and it will become easy. You'll be able to tell how he's feeling by how he responds to different approaches. He may prefer time with you or time alone. It depends on the man. Some like physical affection and touch, like back rubs. Others prefer nurturing acts or caring words.

As children, boys are less inhibited in their aggression. Adult men have strong emotional reactions but tend to suppress them once they become aware. They learn to hide their emotions to protect themselves. Invalidating their emotions tends to stimulate a downstairs fight, flight, or freeze response.

When a man has strong feelings and doesn't quickly process them in a verbal way, he is more prone to fighting or getting physically or verbally aggressive. This can be seen in sports, performing music, in art, or other healthy activities and is not always inappropriate. Maybe this is why men like sports so much:

they can get some of their emotional feelings out in a socially acceptable, nonverbal way. They also tend to like war or action movies that have a lot of aggression in them.

Men focus more on solving a problem with the ability to limit concern for feelings and relationships while reaching their goal. I have worked with my husband Bob in some of his clinics for several years. I discovered very quickly that when he is at work, he is very task-oriented and is not as affectionate or personal as he otherwise is with me. At first, my feelings were often hurt. Compared to the private Bob I knew, he sounded and acted reserved, even aloof. It felt weird and impersonal. I didn't understand what was going on. Then he explained how he feels a need to compartmentalize his feelings and not allow himself to feel or express his personal side while at work. It helps him stay focused and get his job done. I don't know how he does it. For me, many things are often interconnected and it is difficult to put away my relationship focus.

Remember that men have six times the testosterone surging through their veins than women have. Testosterone tends to weaken impulse control in the brain. What that means is the "defend my turf" response is greater in males than in females, and men are much more likely to become aggressive when faced with a threat to their territory or a loved one. This comes in handy when women need to be protected, but it can also be misdirected.

Younger men with higher testosterone levels are better at face-to-face competition. Structures such as the military or similar work settings help to manage testosterone and curb male aggression because men are required to control themselves. An unstable environment where things are changing constantly causes a man considerable anxiety and will increase aggression and impulsivity. Evidence of this is seen in dangerous jobs like logging, oil rigging, the military, police, and firefighting, among others. Testosterone usually declines as a man ages and results in more willingness to be a team player—less need to be the "top dog" all the time.

Being aware of these things will arm you with the ability to help him find his equilibrium again. He will achieve his highest state of being when his guard dog is well-managed, and his sense of intuition and logic is balanced.

In Summary:

- The human brain is complex and is often thought of as comprising two major areas: left and right. The left is commonly thought of as the rational center, while the right is more intuitive. In this chapter, we call these parts of the brain "the upstairs."

- In this chapter, we have introduced the idea of the "downstairs" part of the brain and the guard dog, and the notion that we can train this part of our lower brains to be more in harmony with the upstairs.

- The guard dog is an analogy for certain aspects of the downstairs brain. It is responsible for safety and our sense of pleasure. Every sensation that seeks to enter the brain must pass by the guard dog before it can proceed to higher areas.

- The guard dog's main job is to keep us alive and feeling good, and this is the key to connecting with another individual. If you can learn how to pacify their guard dogs, you can reach the deeper, more genuine person within.

- Happiness, or staying upstairs, is a skill. It is something that you must practice, but you can become happy and influential with time and determination.

- Learning the skills of getting and staying upstairs is key to improving yourself and your relationships. When you learn the art of upstairs living, you make the world a better place. But more importantly, you and your loved one can understand each other on a deeper level and the relationship you build can last forever.

Chapter 10
Battling Your Inner Demons

ife is naturally stressful. When we experience something new or demanding, our guard dogs can sometimes get caught off balance. It tends to assume the worst with unexpected or challenging situations. Our stomachs might tighten up, we may sweat, our hearts pump faster and breathing often becomes shallow. While many situations resolve themselves fairly quickly, we sometimes have to deal with prolonged exposure to stress; this can become exhausting and it can take a toll on our entire lifestyle.

Women are especially sensitive to vulnerability and negative emotion. This is partly because we are wired to be protective of ourselves, our children, and all loved ones. We also feel vulnerability because of our relatively smaller stature and because our brains are so integrated, and this latter issue can often result in sensory overload. While our sensitivities have distinct benefits, we can become overwhelmed.

Years ago, Bob wanted to invite three couples who didn't know each other well to our place for dinner. For him, this was a very simple process: they come over, sit down, eat dinner, and we all have a good time. For me, it was much more complicated, and many dots started connecting to each other. Three couples? Would they all get along with each other? Did any of them have food allergies or major dislikes? Were any vegetarians, diabetics, or lactose intolerant? What should I cook for that particular group? Should I cook light food for dieters or a richer meal? What time would be best considering each person's schedule? Should we have soft music in the background for a romantic atmosphere, or should we go for something a little more light-hearted like jazz? Would our guests like to play games, or perhaps watch a movie? All of these details needed to be thought-out. Bob's minimal plan of hanging out and hoping for the best was not acceptable.

My view of things gave me more stress than my husband, who felt none at all. He sometimes helps me with meal preparation and related tasks, but I still take the major responsibility and feel more anxiety.

This example is not so much about who is right. We both were, in our own ways. It's good that I am sensitive about the needs of our guests but it's also good that he is relaxed and focused. Otherwise, he might not want to invite anyone over. We both bring important perspectives to the experience.

The story illustrates how we, as women, tend to connect everything, and how it can become stressful to us. Some of this comes down to personality style. In reality, some men are quite anxious and oriented to detail, while some women are rather laid back about life. What you will find, however, is that many male-female relationships share a similar dynamic: the woman is more attuned to relationship needs than her man and she often sees connections between variables where he simply does not. This can be a benefit, but it can also be a great challenge.

Stress, especially when it is prolonged, can contribute to tension in a marriage. When our nerves are strained, we are less patient and more prone to say things we don't mean. Learning how to deal with and manage stress is key to achieving a romantic marriage.

This is not an exhaustive study of stress and its management. There are books devoted entirely to this subject. We can experience worry in different ways: in our minds and in our bodies. Body stress responds extremely well to proper nutrition, exercise, adequate sleep, and other types of physical self-care.

Psychological stress is a little more complicated. But in the context of your brain and femininity, there are a few things that may help you with the mental and emotional experience of worry. I'll use myself as an example of how worry affects me and how I tend to deal with it.

What If?

One of the typical things I worry a lot about is if Bob will come home safely, especially when he's been working out of town in a nearby city. It means he must drive on the highways where people drive faster and are sometimes drunk. To me, it seems more dangerous. My scenario might go something like the following:

Bob will call me from the hospital 45 minutes away and say he's about to leave and will be home soon. I calculate it will take him no more than an hour, given traffic. Great. I'll start dinner now. Time flies. I look at the clock and it's been a little over an hour and he's not home. What happened? I try calling him. His phone goes straight to voicemail. I start to think: did he mute his phone? He often does when he's in the hospital. Even if he did he should feel it vibrate, shouldn't he? But if he has the radio on, he might not even feel the vibration. A few more minutes pass. Is he okay? Maybe he had to stop for gas? What if he got into an accident and that's why he didn't answer his phone? Surely, he's fine. A few more minutes pass and it's now twenty minutes after the time he said he should be home.

Oh no. I pray. It wouldn't have taken that long to get fuel. What happened? Is he okay? What if he stopped off and picked up the dry cleaning? Am I making phony excuses now and he's really hurt? What would I do if the police showed up at my door and said something awful had happened to him? Or maybe a phone call? Oh no, again! This could be really bad. I pray again. If he's okay, why doesn't he call me? He knows how I am, I worry so much about him. What would I ever do without him? I sweat. My hands and feet are cold. More minutes pass. My stomach has

143

a knot in it. I feel nauseated. By this time, I can only pace and look out the window every 30 seconds or so. I call again. Nothing.

Then his car turns into our driveway a full 45 minutes later than expected and I hear the garage door go up. I am so relieved I feel almost heady. When he comes in I throw my arms around him and ask, "What happened? I'm so glad you're safe. I was getting so scared something had happened to you! Didn't you say you were just leaving and would be home within the hour?" He tells me that just as he was leaving the hospital, a doctor stopped him in the hall and wanted to talk about a patient and he is sorry for losing track of time.

I have done this sort of thing too many times. It wears me out. I had to finally have a talk with him about how to manage this sort of stress. You may think I'm prone to stressing out and you'd be mostly right. But I bet some of you can relate. And I was right about his phone being muted.

What Just Happened?

If you look at this scenario based on what we've learned about the brain, it will help. The first issue to consider is the barrage of incoming negative sensory information.

In the example, I perceived a potential danger that triggered an automatic response from my guard dog. I went into "red alert mode." I felt vulnerable when Bob wasn't home at the time I expected him. "This could be life threatening," I thought. In real life though, the chances were pretty small that he was in danger.

Nothing terrible happened before. Why do I still experience the same reaction?

The reason is because the downstairs anxiety response happens before I can think it through. It involved pumping negative chemicals into my system. They focused all my energies on a potential fast response. When this occurred, my downstairs brain went into a sort of automatic pilot, and my upstairs mind was in the back seat. It couldn't respond fast enough.

In the initial moments of crisis, I don't think rationally about the situation. I just react to the emotional and sensory information overload. I may try several times to go upstairs. I may look at the clock and hope for good news, but that tends to trigger a further stress response that gets me sliding back downstairs again. It's like a feedback loop between stress and attempts at rationalizing or justifying what is happening. It feels like a sort of mental fog where I forget the upstairs portion of my mind, with all its resources and capacity for creativity and problem-solving. It's exhausting. As my fears grow, I become even more desperate with the thought the police might call or show up at my door and tell me he's been hurt or worse. Then I think: "How could I live without him?" I'm pretty sure I can't.

I really needed a better approach.

I've had the mistaken belief that I need to try to eliminate stress from my life. In fact, stress management is more about increasing my ability to handle stress than to eradicate it—which is impossible anyway. I need to look at stress from a different perspective. It can be a positive learning experience and a chance to become stronger. Our life experiences can help us build up a massive amount of emotional strength. It's like your immune system: you can't eliminate disease, but you can build your body's ability to fight it.

The Basement and Chemistry

The most stressful place to stay for lengthy periods of time is your downstairs. You could think of it a bit like the basement of a house. It's often dark down there, which means it offers limited perspective. When you spend too much time in the downstairs — scared, stressed, hungry, tired, jealous — it's a hard way to live and wears you out. And it's pretty much the same if your man is spending too much time down there.

Feeling low generates what we might call "negative chemistry." The most important negative chemical the brain and body produce in this state is called cortisol. This stuff gives you quick energy for a tough situation, so it's not always bad. But it's released when the guard dog perceives a dangerous situation and is only optimal for short bursts so you can get out of trouble. When you get too much of it over an extended period of time, like when you feel oppressed or unable to escape a bad situation, it can weaken the immune system and contribute to weight gain, fertility problems, insomnia, depression, and other undesirable health issues. Cortisol also often comes together with adrenaline, and things can get powerfully dark when they're combined. When you get too much of this stuff for too long, you can feel like you're mentally and physically broken — and this could be a state called "adrenal fatigue."

However, when you're feeling up, your brain and body produce a more positive set of chemicals, including dopamine and oxytocin. The beneficial functions of naturally occurring dopamine are too many to count, but to name a few: it is responsible in part or whole for our senses of pleasure, happiness, reward, focus and attention, the formation of memories, and resolving pain. Oxytocin promotes emotional attachment, eases stress, crystalizes emotional memories, facilitates childbirth and lactation in women, and much more. Mix these with adrenaline and you're going to feel like skipping around with a big grin on your face.

Ultimately, thinking impacts brain chemistry. So, changing your thinking, or helping someone change theirs, can change your emotional/chemical experience. Any of the following techniques should work equally well for both of you.

The Dopamine Shower

Whenever you feel good, you're probably feeling increased levels of dopamine. A dopamine shower is any healthy effort that seeks to naturally and safely stimulate dopamine production in your brain and body. This includes mental or physical efforts that will encourage the body to produce more of this feel-good substance.

The most effective way I have found is to quietly think of things for which I am sincerely grateful; to list what is going well in my life or to relive wonderful experiences in my past. If you allow yourself to dwell on these things, to increase feelings of gratitude for them, your body will trigger an increased production of dopamine. You can do this pretty much anytime you like. It's a matter of mental focus, and it's a skill that you get better at with practice. I try to do it every day.

If you are really down and having trouble thinking of things to be grateful for, consider some of the following which you may presently enjoy or with which you have had particularly good experiences in the past:

- Your body and parts that serve you well,
- Your magnificent and complex brain,
- Your sense of touch, sight, or smell,
- Your health,
- Spiritual and emotional support,
- Your husband,
- Your children,
- Family and friends,
- Humor,
- Food,
- Home,
- Work,
- Hobbies,
- The country you live in,
- And so on.

There are so many blessings you can be grateful for. You may have to power through some pretty thick darkness sometimes, but it's worth the extra mental energy. If you need to see physical evidence of your blessings, try writing your own list down and then reading through it any time you need to increase your positivity. You might be surprised at how good it makes you feel, and how quickly your practice pays off. Try doing it for only about 10 minutes and notice how your body feels. Bob and I like to have a Dopamine shower every morning before we get out of bed and take a water shower. It's exhilarating and sets up our entire day.

Other Ways to Get Upstairs and Stay There

Gratitude is just one of many ways to get out of the downstairs and stay upstairs. Try some of the following activities when you're having trouble:

Breathing

Your brain's breathing center is located right next to your guard dog, and the proximity has an impact on stress. When you're anxious, you might not realize it but your breathing becomes shallow and you take short breaths that are not from your diaphragm. This increases your anxiety. Deep slow breathing not only expands your diaphragm but helps get oxygen to your brain and can decrease some of your immediate anxiety. This strategy is one of the easiest things you can do quickly to get upstairs and it facilitates the dopamine shower. It's relaxing, and when you're relaxed you begin to feel more positive   emotions.

Humor

Humor is an amazing way to immediately relieve your more negative feelings. It's often said, "humor is the best medicine." There is a lot of truth to that. Laughing and seeing the lighter side of any situation helps you have more perspective. Notice how good you feel after you've been laughing.

Norman Cousins, an editor emeritus for Saturday Review, spoke often of the beneficial effects of humor. He said that although diagnosed with an incurable disease, one that would make him an invalid, he was able to laugh himself back into health by watching Marx Brothers movies and episodes of the TV show, "Candid Camera."

Creativity

Another way to get back upstairs is to do something creative or to use imaginative thinking. This will engage the intuitive portion of your brain and can include anything from gardening to decorating a room — whatever engages problem solving or using imagination. It could also include art, cooking, sewing, flower arranging, or playing music. None of this requires any real talent. Just engaging in any of these activities can get you upstairs.

Spirituality

Focusing on higher things, inspirational thoughts and prayer can help put problems in better perspective. This might include reading inspirational books, listening to music, or engaging in philosophical discussions with wise people. Spirituality can be religious, or it can simply be your pursuit of higher meaning for yourself and the world you live in. It's about connecting to something greater than you.

Service

There is so much suffering in the world. Do something for another person with no strings attached. In other words, think of someone who might be in need, lonely, sad, or scared, and go out of your way to lift them up. Expect nothing in return. By nothing I mean literally not even a thank-you. You will be amazed at how effectively this gets you out of the limited downstairs and into an upstairs mentality.

Years ago, I heard some news about a business friend who was in trouble. His wife had been unkind to me, but I had wanted to be friends. I told Bob I was going to make some bread and take it to them as a gift. He cautioned me to not expect a positive response from this woman. It was hard for me at first, but I realized he was right. When I took the bread over, I felt totally free because whatever happened, my gift was truly from my heart. I got no thank you, but it was okay. I felt very uplifted, so the act was at least good for my state of mind.

Acts of Kindness

Even small kindnesses towards others will help you get or stay upstairs. A smile or a compliment to another person, whether you know them or not, will do wonders to help you climb those basement stairs. Befriend someone who is going through a great trial and invite them to dinner or bring them something to eat. Find a way to help a neighbor. Most people are suffering in some way. Be aware. The possibilities are endless. Serving will not only lighten another's load but will produce some great chemistry for you.

"Kindness has converted more people than zeal, science or eloquence"
~ Mother Teresa

Exercise

Exercise is like "Miracle Grow" for your brain. Nothing compares to brisk activity for raising your heart rate and stimulating mental regeneration. We usually think of exercise being good for our hearts, muscles, and lungs, but one of the greatest benefits is improved mental functioning and stress levels. Even moderate physical activity has great health benefits and gets you into your upstairs mind quickly.

Physical Touch

I don't know how many times I've had someone give me a hug just when I needed it and it felt really good. I can still remember the first time Bob held my hand. That most significant of events triggered not only dopamine but also the bonding chemistry oxytocin for me. People thrive on affectionate physical touch. There are those who say we all need eight hugs a day to thrive and four to survive. Just remember, you tend to get as many hugs as you give. You don't have to wait for this gift.

I had a dear friend who was a naturally loving person. She had a habit of touching people lightly on the arm or hand as she talked. It was endearing. I can still remember how her eyes sparkled when she talked to me. She loved everyone. It's great to hear verbal messages of affection but the simple sincerity of a warm touch is unforgettable and also raises very pleasant body chemistry quickly.

Distraction

When I find I have plummeted into my downstairs, sometimes it's hard to conjure a dopamine shower or engage in some of these other activities that get me upstairs. This only happens when I'm so anxious that it's like I am in a mental fog and have no perspective. The answer is usually to do something that takes my entire attention: a distraction of one sort or another for just long enough to get a grip so I can then practice one of the techniques listed above. Action is a great distraction and might include some of our suggestions above like exercise. I also like to watch shows, listen to music, do something creative, or help someone in need. The important thing is activity that requires focus away from what is bothering me. And sometimes talking to someone

I trust can help me process my thoughts and get out of a cycle of unproductive thinking.

When Something Seriously Bad Does Happen

Most of what we fret about never happens. We spend a great deal of energy going over all the possibilities and trying to anticipate or avoid imagined catastrophe. However, sometimes calamity strikes. How we handle it makes all the difference. Sometimes people die in accidents and have unexpected financial or health problems. Divorce or other major life trauma becomes real. We can't eliminate stress, but we can learn to face it with courage, dignity and faith, which are upstairs coping skills. When you view stress as an opportunity for growth rather than something to either avoid or escape, you'll live more in your upstairs where all the positive emotions, hope, and meaning in life develop.

In Summary:

- Stress is a normal part of life, but you can learn to manage it.
- Most of what we all worry about never happens.
- When you do experience stress, there are things you can do to cope more effectively. Attend first to physical stress symptoms and you will be better able to tap in to your upstairs. With practice, you will get better at getting upstairs more quickly.
- View stress more as a positive that helps develop resilience.
- One of the most powerful techniques is learning to use gratitude and something we call the dopamine shower, but

there are other techniques like breathing, exercise, humor, creativity, service, spirituality, acts of kindness, and physical touch which help us to tap into and stay in our higher identities.

"Stress is an ignorant state. It believes that everything is an emergency"
~ Natalie Goldberg

We don't need to reinvent manliness. We only need to will
ourselves to wake up from the bad dream of the last few
generations and reclaim it, in order to extend and enrich that
tradition under the formidable demands of the present."
~ Waller R. Newell

Men and women have misunderstood each other's differences since the beginning of time, though they often expect each other to act like they are the same. It seems to be common in both men and women to accept differences intellectually, but we are continually surprised on an emotional and behavioral level. Women face a challenge of understanding men because we think and act differently in so many ways. We must learn to speak a new language, to think in a different way.

To achieve a lifelong love affair, we must learn to understand the special men in our lives so we can inspire the best in them. The core strength of women comes from femininity. Men derive their power from masculinity. The more you understand and help to inspire masculinity in him, the better your potential to create an enduring romance.

To inspire masculinity, we must first understand it.

Men are the builders, protectors, and organizers of civilization

To have someone understand your mind
is a different kind of intimacy."
~ Anonymous

Masculinity can be defined in many ways, but in its most ideal form, it is complimentary to femininity and never competitive with it. It is something that only the best men have to offer. Defining masculinity narrowly as "brutish" is just an attempt to tear men down, and describing the enlightened man as passive or weak is just as destructive. Though men are indeed more inclined to action and aggression than women, they also have infinite potential for creation, renewal, and heroism. True masculinity could be better defined as *managed strength*: the potential for both hell and heaven within, but choosing the latter.

We lie to ourselves when we pretend that there are no good men, or that there is not nobility in masculinity. Men and women need each other, and it is our better qualities that we seek to inspire. True masculinity has plenty to offer the world. Together, masculinity and femininity are the foundations of families, and therefore civilization.

Masculinity is at the same time physical, social, emotional, and relational. Truly masculine men can both contrast with and complement a feminine woman, but it is women who hold the keys to this dynamic. Without a woman as a counterpoint, masculinity lacks perspective and purpose, and cannot therefore endure — cannot exist really, except as a theory. So as a woman, you have a great power and responsibility to inspire masculinity with every man in your life. Women are the gatekeepers of civilization, while men are ideally its builders, protectors, and organizers.

To Become Their Best Selves, Men Need Women

Biologically speaking, women have a higher purpose in life other than simply surviving and maximizing their own pleasure. We have access to greater meaning by being born female because, in the bearing of children, we are thrust in to the soul-refining responsibility of motherhood. Though we may not succeed in having children, or may be unable to, we are emotionally and physically predisposed to the role of mother — whether it is with our own kids or surrogates. We benefit enormously from the experience. It helps us to grow personally in ways that men don't have natural access to. We must share this civilizing effect with men to ennoble them from their baser natures. Mothers are the original adults in human society — in the sense that they are compelled to take responsibility where others may more easily avoid. No truly masculine man ever lacked a refining mother figure in his early life.

Men play a vital role in procreation, but they don't have to be involved for long. They can run off and avoid responsibility, and the bad ones often do. This is a challenge for men in their personal development because they can pretend to be children their whole lives if they run fast enough. Men, without embracing a civilizing influence, will tend to seek pleasure over responsibility forever.

This is why women are the gatekeepers of civilization. Women hold the keys to unlocking true masculinity. Without us, boys don't become men. They stay lost, forever seeking pleasure that does not fulfill, and taking their aggression out on whoever or whatever is convenient. Lack of good women leaves men miserable and confused, and at a loss for constructive motivation.

"I'm a bit of a stray dog. I would not have been in the queue to get married, had I not met someone as extraordinary as Ali. I always felt more myself with her than with anybody."
~ Bono (U2 front man), speaking of his wife Ali Hewson

"I could be bussing tables at the Daily Grill if not for her."
~ Robert Downey, Jr., said of his wife Susan

When a man is raised with the influence of a good woman, he will tend to embrace and cultivate his natural masculinity. He will eventually find its culmination in a committed relationship with a truly feminine woman. When he finds the right woman, he will be willing to risk anything to protect and provide for her. It is the immense joy of a masculine man to fulfill this role. Women inspire masculinity through femininity and by being the ones who are the most focused on building and maintaining relationships.

The Truly Masculine Man

When we discuss masculinity in higher terms, we contemplate something which is actually lasting and constructive, and in my opinion, more genuine. Men who are crass and brutal are actually quite weak and live in constant fear. They are only remembered as the subjects of cautionary tales. While they may sometimes have lasting impact, they are objects of pity and ridicule through the lens of history. They neither build, organize, nor protect. While these men certainly exist, and we could fairly say in numbers which are far too great, they do not make up the majority; and to insinuate such a weak profile on men in general would do no good to anyone. We aspire and inspire by celebrating the qualities of our best men. So, I intend to use the word 'masculinity' in an ideal form throughout this book.

Men are not all the same, but all truly masculine men are both strong and caring. They balance their commitments to work and external responsibilities with the love of the women in their lives and their families. They happily embrace their roles as fathers and husbands. They are courageous and chivalrous and have a deep respect for all life. Their self-esteem is healthy enough to show tenderness and mercy, and they are willing to protect the lives of those they love and those who depend on them.

The masculine man takes care of his health and uses his superior physical strength for good. He has a deep inner spiritual core, which is a keen sense of identity and purpose. He is moral, humble, and strives to balance what is right with what he wants. He is not perfect but constantly tries to improve, and you encourage this through your loyalty and reluctance to believe anything ill of him.

A masculine man provides and is economical with what he has. Wealth may be a sign of virility in this world to some, but is not always acquired through, or a sign of, true masculinity. He doesn't have to be rich to be a real man.

And finally, a masculine man will tend to be attractive to you. He does not necessarily embody all that is physically ideal where society is concerned, but he will inspire and excite you with his presentation. Masculine men take care of themselves as much as they take care of others because they have high self-regard. They love and appreciate themselves without being overly egotistical or vain, and so their self-care includes not only their own interests but those of others.

In Summary:

- True masculinity could be better defined as managed strength: the potential for both hell and heaven within, but choosing the latter.
- Men need us as women to become the best we can be. No truly masculine man ever lacked a refining mother figure in his early life.
- Truly masculine men are both strong and caring. They balance their commitments to work and other responsibilities with the love of the women in their lives and their families. They happily embrace their roles as fathers and husbands.
- A masculine man will tend to be attractive to you.

There have always been a lot of males in my life. I have had brothers, uncles, grandfathers, sons, nephews, and grandsons, not to mention my father and my husband. I have learned that males have some things in common, and one of these things is masculine pride.

A man's masculine pride comes from his sensitivity to feeling vulnerable. It is a consequence of his biological role as protector and provider. Men are biologically more alert to present and potential danger, and they are better suited to dealing with these things in many ways. They tend to be more well equipped physically, and they are gifted with a greater amount of aggression and even an interest in conflict. Masculine pride is his instinctive sense of delight and fulfillment in being a competent man—in overcoming vulnerability, his awareness of his nature and his identity as a man, and his embracing of it for his personal fulfillment and the benefit of those he loves.

Masculinity is often ridiculed in modern society, but it is something a man holds to dearly because he knows, at least on an intuitive level, that his happiness lies in cultivating it, not suppressing it. Which is to say that men face a particular challenge in becoming civilized. And the world today would often have him believe that his masculinity is somehow a toxic thing which can only hold him back from evolving as an individual and a productive member of society. Just as femininity is our core strength, men need masculinity in its refined form. They need to work on it and not abandon it. His masculine pride gives him a sense that he can't walk away from his male identity — that he needs to be a man in order to be happy, and he needs you to understand that and appreciate it. Pride, in this sense, is a feeling of deep pleasure or satisfaction in some quality or achievement.

Men naturally feel a sense of pride in being the male they are or aspire to be, and this pride can quite easily be wounded. Anything that invalidates his physicality, his social role, or his role in a relationship, can injure his sense of masculine pride.

A lack of understanding of this concept is often a major blind spot for women. We receive our own satisfaction from being feminine, and many qualities of being female are quite different from being male. It can be hard to understand a man's interest in conflict and his objective views of the world. We may accept that men are different, but then we suppose our way is superior and they should act like us in every way we see fit. We wish they could be as aware of relationship issues, or the nuances of communication, or emotional cues. We try to train them to be as sensitive and intuitive as we are, and some men are quite talented at these things, just as some women can compete with some men.

But we make a mistake when we do not accept and allow for his masculine differences; when we try to change rather than understand and encourage what is different but good about him.

We easily wound a man's pride when we invalidate his masculinity, and this has hurt many relationships. It undermines trust and puts emotional distance between men and women. This section will help you to understand your man so that you'll minimize the pain that comes from wounding his masculine pride and maximize the influence you may have to inspire what is best in him.

Gym Membership

Ben and Holly were newly married. They liked to exercise together sometimes. One time, while out on a run, they encountered another runner who was a younger man than Ben and had quite an impressive physique. Holly stared as the man passed and then spent some time verbally praising the young man's appearance before remarking off-hand to Ben that he really needed to get a gym membership.

Holly didn't mean anything hurtful by what she said to Ben and she still loved him. But her comment was insensitive because it drew a comparison between Ben and what she characterized as a physically ideal man, insinuating Ben's inferiority. She hurt Ben's masculine pride in that moment.

She could have approached this situation in a more careful way by not only saying nothing about the younger man, but taking the opportunity to notice all the positive physical attributes of her husband along with his desire to exercise and stay in shape. She could reaffirm her own acceptance of him at face value while assessing herself and taking note of where she might want to become more physically fit. By doing this, she could defocus from his flaws and work on her own, making her less inclined to be critical of him.

A woman can similarly attack a man's social identity without realizing it:

You'll Never Succeed

David expressed his desire to become a lawyer to his friends and family. He was excited about the possibilities and he believed in himself. He was a college student and studying hard to qualify for law school, dreaming of a successful career, perhaps as a judge. His mother Carol criticized his dreams and ambitions, saying all lawyers are dishonest and take advantage of people. She also cast doubt on his character being up to the challenge. Further, she commented on the amount of education required to become an attorney being more than anyone in the family had ever achieved, and this seemed to indicate to her that David thought he was better than everyone else. These comments made David think he wasn't good enough to achieve his dreams, and his masculine pride was severely wounded. He stopped sharing any of his dreams or plans with his mother, and Carol never understood why there was so much emotional distance thereafter.

Carol loved her son. She was just trying to protect David and help him find the right career in life. She didn't see how she put him down or wounded him because that wasn't her intent. But she needed to be aware of how David's independence and belief in his own abilities mattered to his masculine pride in order to cultivate her relationship and trust with him. Instead, she unwittingly damaged them.

Women need to reward men's attempts at personal growth, even when they might disagree with their vision for it.

A man's pride that comes from his role in a relationship can also be wounded:

Rude Remarks

Anne and Brian were in a nice restaurant on a date. Everything was going well until they, and everyone else near them, heard a rude comment from a big man at a nearby table about how sexy Anne was and what he'd like to do with her in private. Both Anne and Brian were shocked by the loud comments of this man who seemed to have had too much to drink. Brian felt like he needed to defend Anne's honor by confronting the man verbally. As Brian stared at the offender, Anne seemed to read his mind and put a restraining hand on his. She said to him: "Let's just go. He's drunk and he looks much bigger and stronger than you. He'd probably beat you up." Brian took this to mean that his wife saw him as weak and was offended.

The story may have continued with the couple going home in tense silence, as Brian first contemplated his intuitive sense of injury, and then later as he felt resentment at not being taken seriously as a protector. Anne may also have been confused by this tension because she was only trying to protect him.

Anne could have said something like: "I think I know what you're contemplating, and I love that you are willing to defend me in this situation. But you know, that guy just isn't worth it. Let's not let him spoil our evening. Do you mind if we just leave?" She could have validated his intentions and, even though the jerk might have been tough for Brian to handle, she could have recognized and shown appreciation that he was willing to try, and even take some lumps for her. Brian didn't have to literally be big enough to take all comers in a bare-knuckle fight in order to be a real man; his willingness to sacrifice his bodily safety for her and her appreciation of it is what should have mattered.

Trust

Trust is a belief in another person's good intentions and the willingness to expose vulnerabilities to that person's free will. Never is vulnerability more evident than in an intimate partnership between a man and a woman.

A Man's Need for Trust

Men long to feel trust for the woman they love. It is vital that she is worthy of his trust and avoids betraying it, though she will make mistakes and will also need to occasionally restore it.

Most men have what in Fascinating Womanhood we call a wall of reserve before the relationship even starts. By nature, they tend to protect themselves first and trust when it is more convenient. A man will subdue every impulse to seek sympathy or appreciation from you unless he feels absolutely certain his feelings will be safeguarded. When he doesn't feel safe, he builds up or reinforces his secret wall of reserve.

Women face the challenge of convincing a man who is naturally on guard to take down his wall and let her in. Once this is accomplished, we should be wary of having to fight that battle again. It can take time for a man to trust his girlfriend or wife if his walls are thick enough. It can take years. When he does let her in, it most likely will be a gradual thing, not all at once. It's crucial to take his trust seriously and be patient with this process.

Deep trust is essential in maintaining a lasting romantic relationship. This doesn't mean you will ever be married to a perfect man. Trust can allow for human error and flaws. Hurt feelings and misunderstandings can be repaired with little or no damage to the relationship when both parties want the best for each other. In fact, occasional conflict in a relationship can strengthen intimacy when the repair process is effective and reliable. It helps us to relax when we believe there is a safety net.

About His Wall of Reserve

When a man's masculinity is attacked, it makes him feel invalidated. It can cause him to build up a thick wall of reserve. Men hide behind these walls and, to outsiders, they seem to become distant and defensive. Men can even distract others from this defensive position with preemptive aggression. Anger is a great shield and is not a primary emotion—it's a cover-up for a deeper emotion such as fear, hurt, or guilt. You may recognize this survival state from chapter nine, Brain Matters.

In order to reach him when he is behind his wall of reserve, you're going to have to satisfy his guard dog. In other words, you'll have to learn how all this happened in the first place, and then address it with him so he can take his wall down. You can't take it down for him — it's an inside job.

Men are often not in touch with their feelings and usually aren't at ease talking about them. Besides, a lot of men aren't that good at expressing themselves verbally. So addressing the issue may not be as simple as trying to discuss it with him. How you behave and treat him is going to make the biggest difference, until he is ready to put things into words and trust you enough to talk about it.

This can be an interesting learning experience for men because they get to practice something that is more intuitive for women. Remember that you are probably quite good at talking about your feelings by nature. He most often has to approach this as a skill to be learned, or a foreign language to be spoken. It may be kind of mysterious to him until he gets better at it.

If men perceive a deficit in themselves, they will likely hide it to the best of their ability. They may seem grouchy or short-fused, leaving us at a loss and wondering, "What's wrong?" The answer is often related to his sensitive pride.

Tips for Melting Walls

How do you go about convincing him he can trust you again and feel safe letting his wall of reserve begin to melt?

Be non-judgmental. If he likes what to you is a weird TV show, and you make a snarky comment, he might not feel comfortable talking about his preferences around you again. Because he doesn't feel accepted by you, he can't emotionally trust you when you are being judgmental about his personal interests, passions, and hobbies. So avoid unnecessary criticisms of such things, but also avoid thinking about him in critical terms. It's not enough to pretend to be non-judgmental: you have to learn to not judge him.

Show sincere interest in him. This is where a man really begins to feel like a woman is on his side or has his back. It won't work if you just pretend to like what interests him. You need to spend some time and energy trying to share his interests. If he loves studying cryptocurrency or politics and you just aren't interested in them personally, learn to appreciate and understand why he enjoys these subjects. If you discover what someone finds interesting in a hobby or activity, the chances are that you will see value from your own perspective as well. As you show sincere interest in him on a regular basis, he will gradually begin to trust you more and his wall of reserve will begin to melt.

Find and appreciate his manly qualities. Admiration is so important that it has its own chapter in this book. To summarize: look for specific qualities to admire about him on a daily basis.

Admiration must be sincere and tailored to the individual, but there are general areas of admiration that all men will appreciate. As you "treasure hunt" for his positive assets, it will begin to develop into a wonderful habit.

Emphasize your own femininity. As you emphasize the differences between you, your own feminine qualities and his masculine ones, gaining and maintaining his trust will come easier and more naturally for you. He will recognize that his relationship with you is one of mutual care, and this will help to convince him of your intentions and loyalty.

Show sympathetic understanding to him as well as others. As you do this, over time he will gradually begin to confide in you and trust you more each day. Treating others around you with the same consideration will show consistency and reliability to him and will deepen his trust for you.

Keep confidences. Knowing that his deepest secrets and desires are safe with you is paramount in developing trust. He will know deep in his soul that nothing he tells you will ever be shared with someone who does not have his permission to know. This is a truly wonderful gift to give to anyone, but it is an essential part of intimacy with your man. If you've made a mistake, apologize, and then start all over again and be vigilant.

Be patient. When we first meet someone, we want to extend a limited amount of trust to them simply because we have no reason not to trust them. But, this type of casual trust isn't the deep sort he needs to feel for you as a wife. This kind of deep confidence takes time and consistency to develop and so patience will be essential.

Are Vulnerable Men Wimps?

So men have vulnerable pride. Does this mean they are inherently weak? The answer is: not necessarily. Everyone has a vulnerable side. He's only a wimp if he doesn't also have a strong side. Bullies and man-children are often like this. Bullies are actually some of the biggest cowards you will ever meet. They must work overtime to cover up their weaknesses, and underneath the posturing and bravado, they are downright fragile and not manly at all. Man-children are just overgrown boys with "Peter Pan Syndrome" who refuse to leave Neverland and want a mother to take care of them. They will tend to choose pleasure over responsibility, and so they never grow up. But real men, even the strongest you will ever meet, have a vulnerable side — and thank goodness. Otherwise they would be nothing but stone, with little to no capacity for intimacy or compassion.

When a man feels safe enough to show some of his vulnerable side to the woman he loves, it can also provide an attractive boyish compliment to his masculinity — this hearkens back to a time when he was more innocent and purer, and it can be endearing.

Vulnerabilities are often what connect people. They can also help a person be more genuine with themselves and others. Rather than preferring the perfect characters in movies and books, we tend to more often admire the flawed hero — the one we can relate to, because we know we're all a mix of virtue and vice.

The people we really admire persevere and succeed despite their weaknesses. And if they can do it, maybe we can too. We all have an upstairs and downstairs side to ourselves, so we appreciate when we can see these aspects in other people.

Insecure women sometimes pounce on men when they show vulnerability because it threatens the woman's sense of safety. To her, the man is there to insulate her from fear and to make life comfortable, and when he seems to show cracks in his armor, she can become terrified and resentful. When she attacks him for having vulnerability, she is attempting to train him to never show it again so she can maintain an illusion of perfect safety and stability. But when a woman also wants her man to be sensitive to her feelings and needs, she's really giving a mixed message: she's asking him to be vulnerable and invulnerable at the same time. She puts great emotional distance in the relationship when she does this, and she undermines trust in favor of a father-daughter dynamic. Relationships like this can last, but only rarely and with very little true intimacy. These women spend a lot of time downstairs and often grow up with phony men who never learned to show much vulnerability in their relationships either.

His Emotional Needs

Masculine men have a need and desire to protect and provide for their loved ones. It makes them feel manly and is part of their personal fulfillment. A man needs to feel he significantly contributes towards the care of his family's primary needs, even if his wife works and makes more money than he does. They key phrase here should be 'significantly contributes,' because some women are very financially successful. A mature man will not be threatened by this as long as he plays an important role as a protector and provider and is validated for it

Women are very capable of meeting life's demands. It's not that women constantly need men in order to stay alive in this world, but we need them to reach higher levels of fulfillment, and the same is true for men regarding us. Being a single man can be a joyous thing, but he is arrested in his development without the opportunity to serve and protect; he is kept from the learning experience of belonging to something bigger than he is as an individual.

A man develops and benefits greatly with a family he helps to build. For a him, establishing a family includes maintenance and ongoing progress. It's not enough for his wife and children to merely survive, they must thrive for him to feel like he is doing well. His responsibility in this regard may occupy him productively and selflessly for a lifetime.

When my husband Bob watches out for me, I appreciate the sense of safety it brings. I know many women can relate to this. It's not that we can't do it alone, but we can go so much further with masculine help. And men can do a lot on their own as well, but they accomplish so much more with the support of good women. Masculine men instinctively know they need femininity to be complete.

Matt and Amy

Matt loved his wife Amy very much. Whenever she was sick, he tried to think of things he might do to make her life more comfortable. Sometimes, in the middle of the night when she couldn't sleep because of an illness, he would offer to run to a store and get her pain medication, cough drops, or whatever she might need. Amy struggled with her feelings of wanting to protect Matt from having to go out in the middle of the night. He often had to get up early for work. Early on in their marriage, she would sometimes say, "Are you nuts? It's snowing outside." When she learned that he loved taking care of her and wanted to feel like he was helping, she realized where the hurt look on his face came from. It was good for her to let him provide this kindness because it made him feel like a good protector and provider.

His Need to be Your Hero

A man bonds with a woman when he feels like he is successfully taking care of her. He wants to be the best man in her life. When he does well in his role as protector and provider, he sees himself as important — essential to her well-being and that of the family's, but also as a competent man in a competitive world. This is where he gets enduring self-esteem and confidence, especially if he feels like he's earned it. He doesn't want to have it given to him. For men, competence is incredibly rewarding: both in the workplace and in his personal life. A man who excels in the roles that his masculinity naturally assigns to him will feel like a hero. If you can help him feel this way, he will feel like he cannot live without you, or even stand to be deprived of your presence for too long.

Your job will be to communicate to him that he is competent, or even masterful, at being your hero. This display of confidence will inspire him to reach new levels of accomplishment and bring out his true potential. Criticism can have the opposite effect. Even if he does not currently fulfill either his or your vision for his potential, what you believe about him will have a powerful influence on what he becomes.

Here are some quick tips to help him become your hero:

- Focus on his strengths and try to imagine his positive potential. Look for evidence that he is your hero and you will find it.
- Constantly look for proof of his manliness in what he says and does.
- Allow him to protect you and show physical, mental, emotional, and moral strength for your benefit. Compliment him and appreciate him when he does this.
- Show trust and faith in his ability to provide for you.
- Allow yourself to be a "beauty in distress" sometimes and give him trust as he tries to calm your fears.

Sexual Fulfillment

While both men and women have sex drives, men often have a different motivation and experience. Both men and women seek release and euphoria from sex. They both strive for an answer to loneliness and can sometimes use it as a quick and easy proxy for

179

intimacy. But there is much more that differentiates sexuality for both genders, especially when they seek a truly meaningful and lasting relationship.

Men are less susceptible to the natural bonding chemistry that takes place in the body during affectionate interactions. So for women, sex adds more to the emotional experience of intimacy than it does for a man. The higher-minded man realizes that building a foundation for a sexual encounter has a goal to it which is greater than his experience of pleasure. His often-greater sex drive, which is more a physical impulse for him, must be addressed. Experiencing it in the context of something meaningful and lasting will be much more fulfilling to him.

When a woman marries a man, she claims exclusive access to his sexuality. If she then withdraws her physical attentions, he is left with a powerful need that may be too much for even a good man to suppress. Both men and women can have a strong sex drive, but for men it involves less complication with bonding. It may be more difficult for some men to see the risks of having multiple partners, and it is certainly easier for them to end a physical relationship and begin another.

Good men are principle-driven in this regard. They care about their partner's feelings and the consequences of having the bonding experience severed. They derive pleasure from not only her sexual enjoyment, but also her happiness. They would not intentionally abuse that arrangement. But it is often a challenge for men to focus their sexuality without some assistance from a good woman. This is another reason why women are the gatekeepers of civilization.

When a man commits to being faithful to one woman, he is trusting that she will help him stay faithful. She can support his healthy sexual needs and, in doing this, influence his desire to reciprocate. This doesn't mean a man has the right to expect you to do things that you feel are demeaning or that you aren't comfortable with. It also doesn't mean he can expect sex on demand. But a woman should invest in and cultivate her ability to satisfy her man sexually. A man's sexual need is as important to him as a woman's security is to her.

He Needs You to be Attractive

Men are biologically programmed to be extremely visual, especially where it concerns female beauty. Their visual orientation is important in dealing with conflict and acquiring mastery of physical and mental tasks. It is vital to his role as the person most often put forward in a relationship as protector and provider. But it carries over to many aspects of his life and it makes him very attuned to a woman's physical beauty.

Young boys can be almost paralyzed when they see their first strong presentation of feminine beauty. They may not even know the girl personally, but the image before them can be like a visit from a heavenly angel and it will sear an impression in their minds forever. A boy may experience something like it several more times in the future—perhaps even when he first meets you, though the initial event is much more about coming to the realization that femininity exists and that it is extremely powerful to him; it's less of a romantic concept and more an introduction to the idea of a reward tied to his visual experience of female beauty.

Males are born this way and it is helpful to them, but there is a price. Men may not realize that an emphasis on all things visual adds a lot of pressure on women to constantly look good.

We already want to be beautiful for ourselves and for each other, but we must also pay attention to it to attract the man of our dreams, especially if he is in high demand with other females before we win him over.

Your being perceived as beautiful also feeds in to his sense of social status and accomplishment. It may sound objectifying, but to be with a beautiful woman feels like a great reward for a man. He can feel this way in your presence while also appreciating you on a very personal level. This is something about men that you need to understand and accept. They really can't help it. But they can work on their depth of character, and this can be their gift to you. Don't judge your man too harshly for this, especially if he is mature and tries to balance his visual and social needs with other higher perspectives.

The good news is, not all men find the same kind of woman attractive. So there is more than likely a good man out there who will be attracted to you if you try to make the best of what you have been given. It's amazing how charm and femininity makes you more physically attractive. You don't have to be a classic beauty for your man to find you fascinating. And more happy news: if you have a timeless romantic marriage, as you age he will continue to see you as beautiful. You can't lose!

Don't give up on your physical appearance and count character as a substitution for presentation. Self-care maximizes feminine power. Don't sell yourself short. Some of us have used childbirth as an excuse to give up and dress down: no makeup or hair preparation, and a preference for comfort over appearance. When you take care of yourself, the first beneficiary is *you* because it feels great and boosts your self-confidence and esteem. It then helps those around you, but most especially your man. When you are feeling your best, you will *be* your best and he will adore you for it. Men like to be proud of the woman they're with.

He Needs to Have Fun

Everyone likes to have fun, but most men have a powerful need to spend time unwinding. Men can get very stressed from their lifestyles of aggression, ambition, and competition, so they have a particular need to blow off steam and relax. He will sometimes have buddies he associates with who share in similar activities and the need to diffuse tension, and he probably had an arrangement like this before marriage. These friendships can be quite important to him. But you can also help him in this area by providing relaxing companionship. Bonding and trust are promoted when a couple engages in activities which they both enjoy, and it is relieving for a man to know that he has a reliable way to release stress with his partner.

Efforts to decompress like this can be more effective in a social context. So, when you join him in stress relieving activities, you meet many of his needs simultaneously and you relieve him of the need to spend time without you in order to unwind.

You probably have some tension that you would like to release as well. Women tend to have different ways of decompressing, which are often more verbal and relationship-oriented. We tend to like talking things out, especially with our girlfriends. Men don't mind our verbal processing so much when it is metered-out, and when it can be combined with activities he enjoys.

You may not share all interests, but you should have an open mind and be willing to try new things for the sake of sharing recreation. Don't worry, you will find something you both enjoy if you are willing to find it together.

If you aren't already in the habit of doing fun things with each other, it can take time to get into a rhythm. You may find that your first few attempts aren't as enjoyable as you want, and it may take a while to find the right activity to do together. Some people need to learn how to relax and have fun. It seems counter-intuitive to say that you need to *try* to relax, but this can be a matter of focus — or rather defocus if you tend to have a hard time getting your mind off stressful things.

Some couples like to have a regular date night, for example. You can make it romantic and recreational by having a nice dinner and then maybe seeing a movie or going for a walk. Let him pick the movie as often as you do.

Dates don't have to cost a lot to be effective, as long as you're together and taking your minds off life's stressors. And if there are financial options, some find taking dance lessons or having gym memberships rewarding. There are many ways to have fun on a date. My husband Bob and I count anything as a date that we do together and alone. We've even gone to the garbage dump for a date when we had trash to get rid of and no money for luxuries. It was one of the most fun dates ever. We laughed and talked about how this was the poorest excuse for a date so far and now it's one of our favorite memories.

Look for His Manly Qualities

Men have a need to feel successful, that they are doing something of worth in the world and are good at it. They need their masculine pride to be validated, believed in and understood, especially by the one they love. You may never hurt him on purpose, unless you're trying to change him (which is almost always a big mistake). But if you understand what wounds him, you will avoid appearing like you're attacking his masculinity. You must never attack his manhood. Pay attention to and appreciate his displays of true manliness and always validate him.

Some areas of vulnerability where you can validate him are:

His Masculine Body

Tina was a newlywed. She and Jack hadn't been home long from their honeymoon before she started complaining he needed a total body makeover. She moaned about his hairy back and chest and insisted he get professional hair removal. This he did willingly. But that wasn't the end of it. Next, she told him he needed to lose weight even though he ran marathons and was athletic.

The tragic thing about Tina's story is, from the sound of it, Jack was a good husband with many good physical attributes — and he was interested in making her happy. It was her narrow focus which kept her from seeing these qualities and ultimately cost her his love.

Men are usually sensitive about their bodies and they like to be admired for their physiques. For some men, this means their impressive height. For others, it's their manly beards. It could be their performance on the basketball court. If your man doesn't seem to take pride in any aspect of his physique, you can start doing it for him. He'll feel amazing and love you for it!

Masculine skills

Jim was a very intelligent and successful man. He worked hard and provided well for his family. Carla felt that if she complimented him on being smart he would get a big head and become arrogant. Once when a friend remarked how smart Jim was, Carla retorted: "He's not that smart. He just reads a lot." She was trying to keep him humble, to change something she perceived was a weakness in him. She didn't notice his wounded pride. Carla's indifference resulted in her husband withdrawing emotionally. He just focused his attention on his career instead of her. Both were sad in the relationship.

Men take pride in their abilities in sports, tasks that require physical strength, courage, or anything they excel at. They may enjoy mechanics, building, mathematics, solving problems, writing, or other creative or analytical activities. It could be one of any number of talents they have developed or want to develop. When you validate and specifically compliment these skills and endeavors, his feelings will deepen for you. You have to be careful to avoid suggesting or implying he is incompetent or incapable of doing things well. If he isn't good at something, you can appreciate his efforts.

Dreams, Goals and Achievements

Gloria was a good woman who prided herself in being practical and realistic. Her husband Scott was a dreamer. He was bright and had dreams beyond being a school teacher, such as wanting to run for the school board or do something that made him feel important. Gloria often complained that he just wanted attention. It embarrassed her when he would get "too ambitious." She constantly undermined his next big idea, and it seemed Gloria's goal of holding him back actually motivated Scott to aim higher. Instead of resigning himself to a routine life, his attempts at success got more grandiose as the years passed. He sometimes invested in projects that weren't wise, trying to somehow gain her approval and the attention he couldn't get at home. She was constantly frustrated and so was he. She could have become his

187

biggest fan. He would have adored her for it and probably not acted in such a frantic manner to prove himself.

Men will often talk about an achievement or goal in order to be appreciated or admired. If you see this as purely bragging or boring and try to either change the subject or worse, belittle him, or if you yawn, or roll your eyes, he can be wounded. He will likely withdraw and not trust you, though he may not admit it. Men need to be believed in. If a man comes home from work and tells you of an accomplishment and you are too busy to listen, or you act disinterested, he might stop telling you. He may even find someone else who will appreciate him.

This is very powerful for any children you have as well. They will watch the way you treat him and will tend to copy your style, or perhaps internalize the mistrust he feels for you, or that you feel for him. On the other hand, you can encourage your kids to great accomplishments and a more open view of intimacy by the way you behave towards your husband.

His Masculine Role as Protector, Builder, and Task Leader

My maternal grandmother, May Berry, was a naturally optimistic person. She totally believed in her husband Herbert (my grandfather). They lived through the Great Depression of the 1930s. At one point, they even lost their beautiful home and had to move to an old rundown storage building due to financial reversals. Grandma's sister, Martha, came by one day and saw her on her hands and knees scrubbing the old wooden floor.

Martha felt so sorry for her dear sister and asked how she was handling the loss. Grandma surprised her by saying, "I feel like a brand new bride again! Like we're just starting out!"

She knew her husband would always find a way to take care of her and their children in spite of economic conditions. She didn't mind living minimally and understood that he couldn't control the economy. But mostly, her belief in him made their love deep and lasting.

She could have taken this situation as an opportunity to wound his masculine pride. If she mocked their poverty and his ability to provide, she would have had a lot of support from her friends though she would have made life miserable for everyone.

Anything to do with his work or career: money, success, achievement and skill all involve his masculine pride. His concern that his family is cared for and has the comforts and advantages of life help a masculine man feel competent. Complaining that you can't afford things and admiring others who make more money than he does are terribly wounding. Constant commenting on how you have to save and do without doesn't help. This is often hard for us because it conflicts directly with our need for security. Reminding him of how much your parents do for you or how hard you work is counterproductive as well. If you try to live within your means you'll have a greater chance of him wanting to take better care of you than if you always point out how much he falls short. When you appreciate what you have and take good care of it, the value of your relationship will become more important than what is in your bank account.

His Courage

Men have a need to feel that they are courageous. They often face great challenges in life that take a lot of valor. Appreciating his efforts will deepen his feelings for you. Attacking his bold nature will cause him to retreat emotionally from you. Look for ways he is courageous in the risks he is willing to take or to improve. You can help him feel like a lion instead of a kitten. Like your hero.

What Else Wounds Him?

You can be sensitive to his masculine pride if you understand what wounds he might have experienced growing up or in his career on a daily basis. Men are sometimes humiliated by bosses, co-workers or clients. They may also be hiding behind a wall of reserve that has been up since childhood because of an invalidating mother or father.

He may be his own worst enemy, feeling like he's a loser. A man desperately hopes that even when being self-critical, someone will believe in him and encourage him to regain belief in himself once again.

This is a great opportunity for you. Women are talented at being sensitive. If you accept and admire him, realize his potential, and look to the best in him, this will bring you much closer together. The trick is to not be the one who wounds him.

We are great at helping to heal wounds, especially with the ones we love.

In Summary:

- Whether we have ever had our own babies or not, women are biologically compelled to the soul-refining experience of motherhood, or we are nurturing with others in our lives. Men lack such compulsion and must therefore rely on women to inspire them to a more evolved state—to become truly masculine men.
- Men build, organize, and protect civilization, but women are its gatekeepers.
- Masculinity in its purest form is a man's source of power and reflects the best he can offer.
- Brutal and crass men are not masculine, but rather subjects of ridicule and pity who neither build, repair, nor protect.
- All men are biologically predisposed to seek competence in a world of conflict. This perspective gives them masculine pride and a corresponding weakness to emotional injury.
- Anything that invalidates a man's physicality, his social role, or his role in a relationship, can injure his sense of masculine pride.
    - When a man's pride is injured, he will build a "wall of reserve" to protect himself. You will need to win back his trust in order to inspire him to tear it down himself—it's an inside job.
    - Men long to trust the woman they love. As he learns to trust you, he will let down his wall of reserve.

- The masculine man needs to achieve competence, and ultimately mastery, regarding his need to protect and provide for himself and his loved ones.
- He needs you to see him as your hero.
- He has a powerful need for sexual fulfillment and for you to be attractive.
- He needs to have fun in order to release the tension he gets from being a person who is attracted to conflict.
- Masculine qualities where you can help to validate him are:
  - His masculine body
  - Masculine Skills
  - His dreams, goals and achievements
  - His masculine role as protector, provider and guide
  - His courage.

Chapter 13
Making Him Number One

For a deeply romantic union, both men and women need to feel like they are top priority in each other's hearts. When a partner is made number one, it calms their guard dog and makes them feel safe in the relationship. It should be the priority of a woman to make her man first in her mind and heart.

If you talk to a young woman in love, there is no need to instruct her to make the man in her life number one. She already does it. In fact, it's hard to get her to think of anything else. She will seem like she's always on the phone with him, going out with him, texting, or talking to others about him.

Why does that special feeling so often fade after marriage? When does it start to dwindle? Some say romantic love is not meant to last. That it can "run its course." I hear women complaining about their husbands and how they let them down. Are these women even still in love?

In a marriage, there is a tendency over time to take each other for granted. New relationships are always going to be exciting because they contain more elements of the unknown. There is constant newness and excitement. But novelty must lose out over time to familiarity if the relationship is to last, and we really want both.

Even though familiarity erodes novelty, we need a certain amount of it because we constantly gravitate towards safety and comfort, and we want to build a comfort zone around ourselves. But we also hate boredom. We often grow to miss the excitement of a new relationship. Many choose to see the loss of excitement in favor of familiarity as proof that romance can't last, or that the relationship wasn't meant to be.

You are the magic in your relationship. Those who let romance die often wait for their partner to do all the work, or simply don't understand that romance is something we create and maintain, not something which spontaneously charms the relationship while it's "meant to be" or while the magic is still there. The excitement of your new romance was only a preview of what the relationship could grow to be with the distilling effect of time and a commitment to renewing the romance on a daily basis. You can create a sense of novelty and romance in the safety zone of a relationship with Fascinating Womanhood.

It's important to start by making and then keeping him number one in your life. Do you want your romantic marriage to flourish? Of course you do, or you wouldn't be reading this book. So just remember this: If you want to be everything to your man, he must be everything to you first. If he isn't, he may look for someone else who sees him that way because he craves feeling important just as much as you do.

Quality Over Quantity

Some women think that when they have outside careers, or when children come along or are small, a husband can no longer be made number one because of the lack of time they are able to spend alone with each other. The act of making someone number one doesn't necessarily mean spending the majority of time with him or dropping everything the moment he needs you. These things might be impossible when you have a hectic schedule. A man can think of his wife as being his number one priority even if he works 80 hours a week—it's all about his intent. And so it is with us. When your husband comes first, you will think of him, his comfort, and care about his worries and dreams. And you will make time for him. You can do that in a life that requires you getting up constantly in the night with a newborn nursing infant or scrubbing a bathroom on your hands and knees, or working at an outside job that takes a great deal of your time. It's not totally a matter of time spent—though you spend as much as you are able at all stages of your life. What's important, what's vital, is how you honestly think of him. And he will know.

Putting our men first in our hearts and lives isn't hard. We can consciously appreciate and find specific qualities we admire and love about him. We can show him in the things we say and do every day. Make a habit of putting him first as the initial step in understanding men and inspiring masculinity, and you will find it gets easier every time you do it.

In Summary:

- The most romantic and lasting unions are those in which the couple make each other number one.
- Whether you have other commitments such as small children or even outside work, making your husband number one isn't only a matter of time spent with each other; it's a matter of the priority you give him in your heart and intent.
- *You* are the magic in your relationship. Make and keep your man number one in your life, practicing the principles of Fascinating Womanhood, and you will revive the excitement that can exist in a safe and reliable relationship.

Chapter 14
Acceptance

"When you accept a man, you see him as a total man, and are content with what you see and prove your contentment by not trying to change him."

~ Helen B. Andelin, Fascinating Womanhood Vintage Edition

have found over the years that if a woman is going to succeed with the timeless principles of Fascinating Womanhood, it will be because she understands the principle of accepting a man at face value and makes use of it. Those who have tried to apply Fascinating Womanhood principles without success have most often failed to understand what acceptance means.

Acceptance cannot be faked. You will get no good results from pretending to accept him for a finite period of time because it will have no power to change you, and this is what is needed to influence the change he should embrace in himself. Acceptance begins with you, in the way you think and feel about him. You love him and should be grateful to be with him. If you focus on what is wrong with him, it will dominate how you feel about the relationship. You can be aware of his faults while choosing to focus on his better qualities.

Additionally, you must understand that none of us can change anyone but ourselves.

Women tend to understand on a certain level the effect they have on men and how much they need our civilizing influence. This is not to say that we have the power to change them as we see fit, or that this should even be our goal. The only change that can be meaningful and lasting for him is change he makes himself. If we were to succeed in changing him, for however brief a time, we would mostly just rob him of masculine pride, and he would eventually rebel. A man can be made into a slave, but he will then no longer be much of a man in his own eyes or yours. He will always know on some level that he has the potential to be someone greater and he will long for it.

When we influence a man for the better, we invite him to access and develop the great potential that is already there in him. Rather than control or manage a man, we inspire him to be the masculine ideal we both hope he will become. We can inspire him to play to his own strengths — his surest path to greatness.

Even before a woman has children, she usually has a model for raising people in the form of a mother figure. Women get used to the idea, from watching their mothers from an early age, that their role in society is to manage people, and they most often excel at it. We females come by mothering naturally, but we sometimes find it hard to transition from our motherly identity to an adult in an equal relationship with a masculine man.

And so many of us attach ourselves in marriage to men we suppose will suffice with a bit of tweaking. Women sometimes choose this type of relationship dynamic because it puts us in a position to control the relationship. We may have a vision of what he could become so long as he complies with our rehabilitation program, and we forget that he hasn't necessarily signed up for it. Though we have very good intentions and suppose we're doing this for his happiness, we're really doing it for our own; our focus is not on his development or personal fulfillment. Marrying a man you plan to manage bears more resemblance to single-mother adoption than to romance.

So we are often tempted to think we can change our men — that it is our decision and for his own good — and that their change will be the result of our hard labor. But this approach is doomed to failure. There is a vast difference between influence and control; we can't have control over another person in a relationship, but we may exert powerful influence when we have the right perspective and motivation.

Presuming to change someone is different than inspiring them to make changes in themselves. One is manipulative, the other is supportive and based on a real belief in their great worth and value as a person. We don't realize it is actually damaging to the relationship to presume changing another person. Don't you hate it when someone sets out to transform you, to tell you what is wrong with you and how you should follow their good advice and example? If you knew your man was never going to change, would you be able to accept him and be content? The trick is in accepting what is even if he never changes. If you simply find you can't live with that, you will need to decide what you are willing to do or not do and make some important decisions. The only lasting change comes from what we choose as individuals.

The core of our identities is the choices we make and what they mean about us. Attempt to take choice away from anyone, and they feel like they have lost the essence of themselves. They feel a kind of death has occurred and they will do almost anything they can to break free, to find themselves and return to an autonomous state where they can make their own decisions.

We all want to feel accepted and loved for who we are *now*. No one is perfect, and so acceptance must involve an understanding of weakness. When we unite with a partner we bring both strengths and weaknesses to the relationship with the understanding that we're going to work towards growth together.

When you work on yourself, not your husband, boyfriend or others in your life, it takes a tremendous burden off you. The expectation that you must change anyone is daunting, and you won't be appreciated for it anyway. People never enjoy criticism in any context, but especially as an involuntary training regimen. Since the attempt to fix another person doesn't work, this approach is a lifetime pursuit of disappointment. Acceptance of anyone, especially the one you love, will bring you happiness and freedom from the need to try to change them.

Socks

When I was first married, I expected and wanted to keep a tidy, orderly house just like my mother had. I adored my husband Bob, but I discovered early that he had a habit that really bothered me. He has always been very careful about his clothing, even folding pants before he puts them in the laundry. He regularly hangs up his clothes—he is a professional and wears suits and ties daily. But he would take off his socks, fold them together, and chuck them across the room. I knew it would not be a good idea to complain or scold him, but I wanted those dirty sock balls gone, so I didn't know what to do. I began to think he looked at me as somewhat of a servant—that my job was to just pick up stuff and put it in the laundry basket. I read about a woman who got so desperate she nailed her husband's socks and clothes to the floor. I knew that was a lousy idea.

Then I heard about someone else who kicked each item of clothing on the floor under the bed. When her husband asked where all his clothes were, she would say: "Maybe they are under the bed?" and let him get the hint. Men hardly ever get hints. I'm ashamed to say, I tried this. A mistake. It hurt his feelings and then I felt bad.

Finally, I decided I would accept him just the way he was, whether he ever changed or not. I also decided to go one step further: I picked up his socks and took care of anything else he left around as an act of service and a gift of love to him—one I didn't expect any thanks or praise for. I thought about how much I loved him and how much he always did for me. The resentment disappeared.

The amazing thing was, about 6 months later, I noticed there were no more socks on the floor. Without me saying a single word or even expecting anything, he had changed. To this day, he never leaves those things around. In fact, he claims to have no memory of changing—or even of throwing his socks around. I forgot the issue too, and only remembered it recently while I was working on this book. Putting his laundry on the floor is so unlike Bob now, it's hard to imagine life another way.

You can see from this example that acceptance is a matter of focus. It comes down to being aware of the good and the bad in a man, and then choosing to focus more on the good with the idea that he is wonderful the way he is. It is also deciding to not try to change him, but rather to accept and love him in thoughts, words, and actions. The magic in the example above was that I changed myself and then he changed himself. Though I understood the influence this could have upon a man for the better, I didn't focus on that part. Perhaps this is why we both forgot the issue until recently.

The Gerbil Cage

Jennifer's husband Tom was a kind, intelligent, optimistic and friendly man. He was hard-working and fun.

Unlike Jennifer, who was a "neat freak," he tended toward some clutter and didn't notice if things were not always put away. Jennifer once remarked that his car looked like a gerbil cage: old paper, soft drink cups, and fast food bags here and there.

When they were first married, she talked to her sister Ann about a time when he left one shoe and a newspaper on the floor in the living room. Jennifer cried and accused Tom of not caring how much she had to work to keep the house tidy. He was baffled at her reaction. To her, this was a major issue.

One day, when Jennifer was feeling particularly annoyed, she found herself thinking: "Why can't Tom be tidier like my father?" Jennifer's father was an extremely clean, careful person: his shoes were always lined up perfectly in the closet. He hated to come into the kitchen and step on bread crumbs or worse, something sticky. He was a very good man but a prolific worrier and developed ulcers as a young husband and father. He was high-strung, a perfectionist, sometimes grumpy and very hard on himself and others.

Jennifer realized if her husband became obsessed with tidiness (like her father), he might also not be as carefree and optimistic. She loved her husband's cheerful, naturally positive disposition, and could count on him to say everything would work out; a positivity she realized she needed desperately. Jennifer was more like her father: prone to worry and perfectionism. The last thing their relationship needed was two obsessive types.

This knowledge has helped her ever since. Jennifer is now able to overlook the small inconveniences of her husband's somewhat untidy habits in favor of the greater parts of his personality — the ones she loves so much. She sees this as a good tradeoff and wouldn't have it any other way. This is acceptance.

Sometimes when we wish another person was different, we don't realize we can't change fundamental personality types. But we can influence each other to become much more civilized and charming. We can encourage good habits and relationship-affirming choices. But Jennifer could not change Tom's basic fun-loving nature, and she realized that she didn't want to. It was a natural weakness for Tom to be insensitive to household orderliness, but this is because his real nature was to have a bigger perspective on life, not letting minor clutter disrupt his cheerfulness.

It is natural for everyone to have a corresponding weakness with strength. The tidy person often struggles with letting go and having fun. The fun-loving person sometimes miss the details. But we really need all kinds in this world, and relationships are usually the stronger for our differences. Acceptance is acknowledgment of the good with the bad, and choosing to focus on what is good, even if it isn't your own style. When you can accept a man the way he is, he will feel it and love you for it.

Stand Up Straight

Carl was a new husband and in love with his wife, Eva. She thought Carl was a good catch but quickly realized some of his imperfections. Soon after the honeymoon, she began to put her hand on his back and say "stand up straight." After several reminders to do so, he told her it embarrassed him. He hadn't wanted to marry a mother figure. She then softly said she wouldn't say it out loud anymore — she would just put her hand in the middle of his back and "this will be your signal." It didn't help.

Eva's intentions were good. She wanted the best for her new husband, or so she thought. In reality though, she was undermining his masculinity. Even sons rarely like their mothers to tell them to stand up straight. But a husband? Much worse. Comments like that are demeaning and can make him feel like a child. And Eva's motivation was more for herself than for him. The unintended side effect for her was Carl's wall of reserve thickening.

Always remember, the only person you can change is yourself. The good news is, you can.

Have you ever wanted to go on a diet or exercise program? It's hard to even start one or stay on it long enough to affect a lifestyle change. But when you do, the euphoria you experience is amazing. It boosts energy and self-esteem. There is almost always a tendency to resist when a person tells you to lose weight, even if it's your doctor or someone else who doesn't have a personal relationship with you. Being told to change your body can feel humiliating and even invalidating. You would never want this sort of response in your husband. Everyone wants to be accepted as they are, your husband included.

We use our energy most effectively where it has the most power: in changing ourselves. Your self-esteem will increase, your attitude will be much more positive, and your relationship with the man you love will improve dramatically.

In Summary:

- Acceptance can be one the hardest principles for some women to master in Fascinating Womanhood.
- Women have a tendency to default to the role of mother or people-manager in relationships. But masculine men don't sign up for a rehabilitation program when they get married. They want a wife, not a mother.
- We do not have the power to change another person, but we can change ourselves in powerful ways which inspire masculinity and lifelong love affairs.
- You must accept your man at face value, contemplating the good with the bad, with a focus on what is good and with no intention of changing him.
- Acceptance cannot be faked. It must be real to be effective.

Chapter 15
Admiration

All people long to be admired, but men tend to be even more responsive to it. Men are wired to receive an emotional reward in recognition of their competence, and so they long for it. You may even notice they sometimes give compliments based on your performance rather than a more direct expression of how they feel about you. When they do this, they are giving what they like to receive and perhaps don't appreciate that women would more often prefer an expression of emotion, such as 'I love you.'

As women we like to be told often that we are loved, and it is more effective when it is spoken in a passionately sincere way. We thrive on a regular diet of it. It's not that men don't appreciate this, but saying "I love you" may be too vague for them at times, and what they really like to hear is how specifically they have done well at a task they are trying to master. Most men are starving for this recognition. They would rather be told they are admired than loved, though they appreciate being told they are loved as well.

We are all programmed to first notice negative things. Before we learn better and practice a different way, we tend to point out what is wrong in any given situation without thinking. If you have a job, you may find that you do one hundred things right, and your boss might compliment you, but more likely is going to focus on what you do wrong. We do this often in our relationships, thinking we're just managing and improving things, but we discourage each other when we don't promote positive behavior as much as we could if we practiced admiration.

This principle should govern most of our communication. But we must practice and overcome our nature in order to accomplish this. In time and with repetition, you will find that it comes more naturally because you will learn how effective it is and you'll love the results.

There were probably many things you admired about him when you first met the special man in your life. Maybe it was the way he dressed or how ambitious he was. But how about now? Do you struggle to find things you admire about him? Maybe you're not sure what he longs to be admired for.

When love is new, the excitement demands focus and we tend to pay attention to what is amazing about our man because it is novel. But in time, we grow familiar and we tend to exchange excitement for comfort — we lose touch of what was exciting about him as we grow complacent. Practicing expressing admiration is an additional way you can be the magic in your relationship. The effects of sincere admiration will seem like a miracle. They will renew the electricity in your love affair as long as this skill is practiced correctly.

Finding and Targeting His Greatest Ambitions

To be most effective with showing admiration, you must understand the deepest ambitions of your man. You must learn his personal aspirations and target his efforts to master them by giving him sincere compliments. You will find the most success in convincing him to share his deepest dreams with you when you cultivate trust with him. You can do this in many ways, including with general statements of acceptance and admiration. But you may need to do a bit of detective work as well, and you may also find that he needs assistance to discover his dreams himself. Here are some tips for learning more about the deeper side of your man's ambitions so you can more specifically target them in your expressions of admiration:

Listen to him: When he wants to tell you something, pay attention to what he says and let him do most of the talking. Look into his eyes. It's amazing what you can find out about any person if you are truly interested in them and what they have to say. Learn how his mind works specifically — what he loves and is interested in. This will also make him feel accepted. Be sure to ask questions that indicate to him you are listening, that you are interested to learn more. Ask him to clarify if you don't understand by saying something like: "Do you mean…?"

If he is expressing his feelings, listen carefully and be understanding. Everyone needs to feel they are heard and understood, that how they feel matters. If you don't agree with a particular point of view, you don't have to get into an argument. Just listen and try to learn why he feels the way he does. We don't always have to express our opinions. This is good practice whether the relationship regards romance or not. It doesn't mean you can't ever disagree with him. But if you want to understand and get to know someone, listen.

Think about him: You face a lot of distractions in a given day and you may not easily notice clues he occasionally drops that could indicate his deeper side. You may need to set aside some time to just think about the evidence he gives in the things he has said and in his reactions to certain situations. Does he get excited when you go to the theater or a museum together, for example? This may indicate an artsy side to him. A lot of men may instinctively suppress artistic interest for fear of judgment. But this could be wonderfully liberating for him to embrace and receive admiration. Perhaps he gets really cheerful when the subject of fixing things comes up, or maybe he lights up when he engages in physical activities. You may have a sporty husband or a closet tinker with anything mechanical or electronic. He will give you many indications over time of his true nature, and he will be amazed if you can identify it without much help. It will feel like true love and acceptance to him.

When he is expressing himself in a personal way, give him your full attention. Set anything else you are doing aside. We do great damage when we ignore a man who is pouring his heart out, and we make amazing gains in trust and intimacy when we show sincere interest in these vulnerable moments.

Notice his body language. Men will often show how they feel with physical expressions rather than words. Notice the way he is sitting, moving his hands, and the expressions on his face in a given situation. These observations can tell you a lot about how he feels. If he sits forward during a show, it might concern a subject in which he has a particular interest. If he smiles to himself during a speech, it might indicate something he likes to do or think about. If he hums or taps his feet to a song, you may discover his taste in music or even an interest in music in general. What he laughs at may show what he thinks is clever.

Any of his physical communication can display his sense of values and priorities, and these can lead you to a deeper understanding of him.

General Admiration

Even once you have discovered his deeper desires and ambitions, you will not always have the best opportunity to express admiration for them. And you will want to show sincere admiration as often as possible. I have addressed some these qualities in a prior chapter but from a different perspective. You will find the following is a reliable list of areas in which almost all men crave admiration, and where you can complement them on most occasions:

Physical Features: This includes his physical strength: lifting heavy things, opening jars, greater physical endurance, masculine features such as build, larger hands, muscles, and other things.

Presentation: If he makes any effort to present himself well, compliment it. Be specific. If he is handsome, even if only to you, tell him often. Admire him for the way he walks and moves, even the aroma of his cologne if he wears it. If he has great hair, tell him. If he has beautiful eyes, let him know.

Chivalry: Good men want to be thought of as gentlemen. They want to be heroes to women. Chivalry includes bravery, respect for and courtesy to women, generosity and patience, protection and providing, and their usefulness in a tough situation. Recognize your man's work in providing for and protecting his family and loved ones. Even if he loses his job or has difficulty at work; if he is trying, he needs to be admired for his persistent desire to take care of you. Admiration of his chivalrous behavior will inspire his masculinity and will encourage it in future.

Courage: Men are expected to face physical challenges, specifically ones where they stand in the way of danger and discomfort for the ones they love. Some of them choose a career in the military, police, or as firefighters, for example, and they literally fight bad guys or dangerous situations as first responders. Women also pursue careers in these areas, but they are still dominated by men—partly because of the physical demands, but also because men are naturally drawn to action and even danger.

They can sometimes get quite high on the experience of facing peril and overcoming it.

Even though he might not have chosen an occupation with physical danger, he may still face a lot of awful situations in order to provide and protect. The workplace can be emotionally brutal and wounding, and he may think of it like a battlefield.

We can make a habit of admiring and verbalizing appreciation for these qualities. We need men to be courageous. Life demands bravery from all of us at times, and men feel a particular need to be admired for their bravery.

Success in his field: Men crave being recognized and appreciated for their efforts in their occupation, especially if they have chosen a career that doesn't exactly align with their personal ambitions, but which they pursue regardless in order to take care of their woman. Most men aren't fortunate enough to be paid for what they'd really love to do, though they may get there some day with a supportive woman at their side. Recognize his loyalty and willingness to sacrifice to make sure his loved ones are taken care of. It's a selfless and noble thing he's accomplishing.

Character: Character is principle-centered living, and its essence comes down to the way we speak and behave when we do not expect punishment or reward. It is what we do when we think we are completely free to do as we please. Men need to be admired for choosing good over bad, especially when they could get away with bad behavior. Men and women are obviously both capable of great character, but men will be more inspired if they are intentionally recognized for it.

My father used to say a deal was only a good deal if it benefited both parties. I always appreciated him for this and found it made him more masculine. It's easy to be a villain and we already have enough of them. A great man stands up for what he believes in and behaves in an honorable way, no matter the perceived consequences. Look for signs of character in him and offer specific and sincere admiration for them. Consider listing them in a notebook as a reminder.

Sense of Humor: A man perceives instinctively that his sense of humor is his ability to diffuse or manage tension. You could think of it as an approach to conflict resolution. It is generally known by men that humor is an attractive quality to us, and they often seek to exhibit great cleverness in this area. It is endearing to them when we laugh at their jokes or attempts at wit. Using humor is also a way of showing bravery in the face of dangerous or tense situations.

I love the way my husband uses humor to help me relax, and it often shows me how masterful he is when things get tough. I express this to him by allowing myself to laugh as he finds humor in these types of conditions. His ability to do this shows confidence and makes him strong in my eyes, and I can't help but admire that.

Intelligence: Intelligence is a type of mastery and display of strength, and it's something that should be easy for a woman to appreciate in her man. Not all men are or want to be intellectuals, but every man has to use intelligence to understand the world he's in and solve problems he faces on a daily basis. He will be at his best when he is upstairs using his rational and intuitive minds, and he will have more confidence in relying upon this if you encourage him. He may not be academic, or he may make his living with his particular gift for intelligence, but all men want to be thought of as smart.

Sympathetic Understanding

Sympathetic understanding is active listening with expressions of admiration. It doesn't mean mere agreement of opinion. Two friends who understand and appreciate each other often hold opposite points of view on politics, religion, and many other subjects. But the trusted friend understands the motive that underlies the friend's contrary opinion and appreciates the sincerity of that motive. So, despite differences of opinion, each can understand and appreciate the intent of the other.

Active listening is a communication technique that focuses on what an individual is saying, both verbally and non-verbally. It requires listening carefully to what a person is saying, but also involves something called mirroring, which is to adopt the mirror image of a person's body language as they are communicating to you. Body language includes the sound of the voice: tone, volume, and speed. If they are talking in a near whisper, you should talk softly too. If they are talking fast, try to keep up.

If they are leaning towards you, do the same. If their hand is holding up their chin, copy it.

This is not a manipulation technique if it is done sincerely because mirroring doesn't just win their trust or make them feel calmer, it puts you in a position to understand. It's a little like putting on another person's shoes, in the figurative sense. People naturally copy the body language of another when they have a great desire to understand. When you mirror another person, you are more likely to feel the same feelings. It helps your imagination to almost become the person you are trying to connect with. Being good at this requires that you care a great deal and expend mental energy to imagine what it must be like to be the other person. Some people are naturally good at this and others can learn with practice.

Mirroring also helps someone to accept and trust you. People tend to feel closer to, or identify with, those who seem like them. As you seek to imagine their point of view and become more familiar with it, you will naturally become more like the person you're trying to connect with. That person will notice, and if it is done with good intentions, it will come across as a natural thing.

Another part of active listening is restatement. It helps to show that you understand his feelings if you reflect them by asking clarifying questions. That means to state in your own words what you think the other person just said in order to assure that you are hearing correctly. You will have many opportunities to ask for clarification because understanding someone, especially if they are upset or passionate, can be challenging. And it is important to be sincere because it can be annoying for someone to hear what he is saying repeated many times, especially simple statements. So, keep the clarifying questions essential.

For example, suppose he says: "I am so mad. I didn't get that promotion at work." You could respond by reflecting a sympathetic question and statement of admiration: "They didn't give you the promotion? How terrible! I can't imagine anyone more qualified than you."

Or suppose he is venting about politics. That's often a hot topic. He might say: "I'm so angry about the election. We're really in a mess now!" He may even rant for a bit. In his voice you might hear frustration, anger, even some hopelessness, perhaps that his vote has so little power. You can invest in your relationship in a circumstance like this and earn more trust by saying something like: "I love the way you feel so strongly about things you believe in," or, "I understand how you feel. It makes me feel safer knowing you are keeping up with these things." This will help to diffuse his tension and distract him from his wounds in favor of something uplifting and relationship-affirming. He will love you for helping him in tense moments like this and it will inspire his masculinity.

You can also ask leading questions like: "So what did you say next?" or, "And then what happened?" This encourages him to explain himself fully and reinforces that you are listening and trying to understand—that you care and are on his side.

Many marriages are compromised or strengthened by the hundreds of small things we say and do every day. Even if you have differing political opinions, you can still find much to appreciate about your husband in everything he does. You can find common ground and show sincere admiration for him.

Sometimes, as a man who has deep wounds begins to trust, a phenomenon we call "Pandora's Box" results.

Pandora's Box

You may be familiar with the Pandora's Box from Greek mythology, and this is similar. In Fascinating Womanhood for the Timeless Woman, we use it to describe how powerful emotions, pent up over time, can sometimes spill out seemingly all at once.

Men tend to hold their feelings inside, often for many years and for various reasons. He may feel rejected or invalidated but not express it in words. In fact, he might not even be in touch with these feelings on a conscious level.

As you begin to express admiration for him and he begins to trust you just a little, part of the process of repairing trust might involve releasing some of this previously controlled hurt in the form of verbal anger.

He will need to find a way to put his feelings into words, and this is often difficult for men. You might think if you are saying sincere and complimentary things about him, his response will be immediate tenderness. He may have to get some repressed pain out first before this can happen.

You will need to listen and let him empty himself. It might take more than one day and it will certainly involve some patience on your part. Once he has expressed himself, the release of this emotional pressure will make room for intense romantic feelings that may surprise you.

Not all men do this, but you need to be prepared. If he doesn't have any pent up negative emotions, he won't ever feel the need for this release, so it doesn't always happen.

Below is a real example of a couple who experienced a Pandora's Box reaction.

The Darkest Time of My Life
~ By Anonymous

My husband and I had been married for 20 years. I always thought we had a good marriage. Still, I was plagued with depression, worry, and moodiness. My husband would come home from work, eat, and then watch TV for the rest of the night. I began to gripe and nag that I had too many responsibilities as a teacher and at home, and I needed his help. If I kept on him, he helped reluctantly. We started criticizing each other severely. I became more sensitive and demanding. I felt marriage was a fifty-fifty proposition and I wanted him to help more. We went to a counselor and the word "divorce" would creep into the conversation, though I felt sure we were just threatening and nothing else.

I began to feel fear. For the first time I was thinking he didn't love me anymore. I was depressed and worried. The only thing I wanted to do after work was fix supper, eat, and go to sleep. I had frequent crying spells, feeling sorry for myself. Sometimes I would go to bed weeping, hoping my husband would comfort me, which he did by patting my head and talking to me. This was not at all what I wanted. I wanted to be close and it just wasn't there. I told him we were growing apart and I didn't like the feeling. The next day he said: "You rejected me and now I'm not sure I love you." I was scared out of my wits. I am Catholic and had been on an ovulation method of birth control which requires a lot of abstinence. He never liked this method.

I decided to get my tubes tied despite my religious convictions. I was not going to lose my husband because of too little sex (about twice a month). He tried to discourage me and said it was too late anyway, that he felt impotent and had no desire for me. I went ahead with the operation hoping against hope he would one day love me again.

On the dreadful day of the surgery I had a visit in the hospital from a strange woman. I was woozy from the medication when she started talking to me and told me she had been my husband's mistress for the past nine years. I got hysterical, my world came tumbling down. That was the darkest moment ever. A priest came and told me to forgive my husband. My husband came in and was shaken but admitted he had found her after he felt rejected by me. He has not seen her since that day. I said I would forgive him, though I found it hard, and I didn't want to leave him. He said he didn't want to leave me and our three children either.

I found Fascinating Womanhood at about this time. I knew God had a hand in leading me to it. As I started reading, I cried at all the mistakes I'd made. I couldn't believe I had actually smeared a dirty diaper in his face when he wouldn't help me change the baby.

I applied the principles I was reading. I listened to him, praised and admired him without sounding too gushy.

One night, Pandora's box opened for the first time. He reminded me of some of the most humiliating things I had done. He said after the diaper incident, he had felt like killing me and decided he would never forgive me. He mentioned several other serious infractions and I listened. I told him I was sorry. Then we went to bed. He put his arm around me several times during the night. When he got up, he put his hands on my face, kissed me and told me he loved me. All this happened the first time Pandora's box opened. The Box opened once or twice a week for three months. He had stored up hurt and anger for twenty-one years and was finally releasing it. I listened and humbly apologized.

Today, my husband and I are happy and content. He can talk to me about his innermost feelings. His confidence in himself has gone up one hundred percent and he has been promoted at work.

Every time I'm around women and they talk about marital problems, I tell them the things I've learned from Fascinating Womanhood. Some of the younger women don't agree because they like the idea of a fifty-fifty relationship. I ache for them because I know what will happen. I can never go back to my old ways.

I appreciate this story so much. It illustrates how relationship healing can occur even in the darkest of times when everything seems hopeless. Fascinating Womanhood principles are truly timeless.

In Summary:

- Men are particularly responsive to admiration, seeing it as a reward in recognition of their competence. Most would rather be admired than told they are loved.

- Admiration can renew a tired romance like magic.

- Effective admiration is always sincere and is most powerful when it is specific to the man.

- You may need to do some detective work to figure out his deepest ambitions in order to target them for admiration. He will probably not just tell you and he may need help discovering them.

- All men will respond well to certain categories of general admiration, and they welcome admiration of their physical features and appearance, their acts of chivalry and courage, success in their fields of employment, displays of good character, humor, and intelligence.

- Practice showing sympathetic understanding by active listening with expressions of admiration.

- When you can convince a man to take down his wall of reserve with acceptance and admiration, a phenomenon called Pandora's Box sometimes occurs: a powerful verbal display of pent-up emotions. This may require some patience on your part to endure, but it will create intense romantic feelings towards you when it subsides.

Section 3

Creating a Lifelong Love Affair

Relationships necessarily start out with little information: we present ourselves in a certain light and we make first impressions, which lead to ideas of who we are to each other. We marry these ideas, full of hope and good intention, and our good will carries us through difficult times and to greater intimacy with each other. This leads to familiarity, and romance is sometimes lost in the complacency of this comfortable state. Femininity and understanding men has the enormous power to reawaken masculinity and rejuvenate the spark that started the romance. Now let's discuss how to take it further and make it last.

This section will teach you the importance of relationship levels and how they are built, how the division of labor in a relationship can take it further, the gravity of having clear boundaries and character, how girlishness can diffuse ordinary thoughtless behavior by your man and deepen your relationship, and more.

There is nothing that surpasses timeless love. It's scarce in today's world of selfishness, greed, and ambition. It can't be bought or sold, but you can earn it. There isn't anything else in life that offers greater dividends.

Living Fascinating Womanhood timeless principles has brought boundless joy and romance to my marriage and those of countless others around the world. It goes against my basic nature to share such private things, but I want you to know what these teachings have done for me and my husband. He tells me things like: "You are the best thing that ever came into my life," and, "Some people say you only fall in love once. I disagree. I fall in love with you again every day." I could fill a book with his statements of love and devotion. My marriage is my greatest treasure, but it didn't come from luck. It came from many years of practicing Fascinating Womanhood's timeless principles. If I have it, you can too. Let's work on this together.

Chapter 16
Four Levels of Relationships

"A healthy relationship is with someone who accepts your past, supports your present, and loves and encourages your future."
~ Anonymous

Whether you are married or single, there are important principles that underlie any long-term successful relationship. When you hear about couples who are married for decades and are still in love, you may wonder what their secret is. One secret is building and nourishing a solid foundation that includes four levels of intimacy. You will have your best chance at success if you develop these levels in this order:

1. Intellectual

2. Emotional

3. Spiritual

4. Physical

When a couple first meets, they don't have much to go on besides presentation and imagination. It takes time and mutual investment to even begin to know another person. When we make too many assumptions about each other and rush in to deep commitments, we set ourselves up for trouble. Sometimes we start the physical and chemical bonding process before we know who we're bonding with. Then we get married, buy houses and cars together, and even start families, without much knowledge of who we've united with. It's vital to spend time together to build a foundation for lasting and rewarding intimacy and to avoid potential catastrophe. Understanding the four relationship levels will help you to develop and repair relationships in a more efficient way, and you will probably save yourself a ton of grief.

Intellectual Connection

When you first get to know someone, you share thoughts and ideas often related to who you are, where you come from, interests and work, possibly even politics, sports, or current events. Most relationships never go beyond this point. We all do this with our casual friends or acquaintances. This affiliation level may never go beyond the weather, as with a neighbor or a stranger you talk to while in line at a store.

Your rational mind dominates here because the process is so verbal. This intellectual level is a pleasant way to relate to someone—it's polite and friendly. It's also a way to learn about people and gain experience with them for future reference. These experiences become an important part of your memory bank. But you won't tend to progress to the emotional relationship stage unless you get to know each other a little more.

What does intellectual closeness look like when you're married? It's important to have conversations with each other.

They don't always have to be profound, but it's important to share ideas and discuss common interests as well as differing opinions to help you stay bonded. Often couples start out with this connection but lose it over time after marriage because they take it for granted. This intellectual level is kept high when you consult each other and negotiate as you work things out.

Intellectual closeness is especially linked to the beginnings of developing an emotional connection with a man. It is a little difficult to know where the one ends and the other begins with men, so don't discount it.

Bob and I regularly share thoughts on something new we've learned from the news, things he's learned in his practice, or from reading. I often can't wait to tell him about something I've learned. It might be as simple as a new recipe or as complicated as something troubling going on in the world. Sharing this information with each other builds friendship and a sense of having things in common.

When it comes to dating, this sort of sharing forms a basis for moving to the next level. If you neglect this first step or jump too soon into emotional dialogue, you will miss important facts and it will come across as a bit pushy and weird to people.

Too Friendly, Too Soon

Luke got a new job at a sports equipment store. He had recently moved and didn't know many people. He was anxious to form new friends. One of his tasks was to be gracious and help customers relax. Sometimes he went a bit too far.

One time he met some very nice people and struck up a superficial but sociable conversation. Suddenly he said "I like you. Let's exchange phone numbers and get together and hang out sometime!" The customers were comfortable with the intellectual development of their conversation, but Luke's enthusiasm for friendship came across as too fast, too personal, and too soon, especially since they were customers and he was supposed to be helping them. They excused themselves without buying anything and left quickly.

Luke meant well, but the context of his forwardness was as critical as his haste. It's true that relationship chemistry is personal and can be felt powerfully in very little time, but it absolutely must be mutual to work, and Luke made assumptions without finding out. He pressed the point and practically dared the recipients of his affection to reject him—which they did. He probably seemed a little looney to them.

If Luke had met these people at a social gathering, they might have been more receptive. Perhaps if they had been regulars at the store for some time and were on a first-name basis, Luke could have proceeded to the suggestion of hanging out sometime with more success. If he had only proposed trading phone numbers without the pledge of immediate friendship and social activity together, they might have also been less intimidated.

Have you ever engaged in a conversation with someone you thought might be interesting but after a little while you thought, "He's kind of strange." Maybe all he obsessively talks about is himself or some subject. You may totally disagree with his political or religious views. He may have odd habits. Suddenly he doesn't seem as attractive as you thought. He might not even be a potential friend. You might begin to sense a vibe that says, "He's not my type."

Rather than taking the time to find these things out, imagine that you get some drinks together, spend the night at his place, and then wake up to find out he just got out of prison for a violent offense, that he's married, or that he looking to borrow money from you. These are things you could have found out with a little time and conversation.

You will always be grateful if you first take the time to get to know a person before advancing to emotional intimacy.

Emotional Intimacy

As your relationship develops, you will begin to express feelings. You won't just talk about your views on something, you'll add how you feel about them. This will increase your level of vulnerability with each other, which is why this level should come after intellectual bonding.

When you begin to form emotional intimacy, you will share how current events impact you personally. You will show the passion you have for certain subjects in words, tone, and physical reactions. And if things go well, you will advance to sharing past experiences, hopes and dreams, doubts and fears. Shared knowledge and experience of these things is intimacy, and this is a healthy thing when there is acceptance, respect, and love. At this point, you feel comfortable enough to risk invalidation because you have faith in the recipient—that sharing will create bonding rather than injury. When a person returns validation for your risk, your confidence in them begins to grow. Your history of love and acceptance becomes your story and your identity. You feel closer to each other. This increasing trust can feel liberating because it signals you are not alone. It's easy to love people with whom we can be accepted as our real selves: this is the core of emotional intimacy.

The difference between intellectual closeness and emotional intimacy is similar to that between thought and feeling. Thoughts tend to be based in reason and attempts to describe things, especially in language. Feelings are not naturally expressed with words, especially for men; and people are often not entirely aware of them, or able at least to put them into words. They're often expressed in non-verbal ways like body language, facial expressions, or tone of voice. Intellectual bonding is safer by itself but limited in terms of the sense of closeness it may achieve. Emotional intimacy is far more dangerous because it is shared vulnerability, and this requires trust because it can be abused terribly. But emotional intimacy permits greater bonding and the intensely fulfilling sense of safety and comfort this provides.

If you feel this reward is worth the risk, you'll need to let your guard down with him.

When you're married, it's important that you feel comfortable around each other. Your husband may not feel as relaxed talking about feelings as directly as you do. Does he let out his emotions by venting? If so, be a good listener. If you cry a lot when you're emotional, explain to your husband he doesn't need to worry; that this is a more natural, physical, even chemical reaction for you — that there is no problem to solve, nothing to fix, and that you're just sharing. Men are action oriented and he may need to hear from you that all you need is for him to listen.

When dating, some are tempted to jump into an emotional relationship a bit too quickly. They might be starving for validation from a man, especially after a breakup, a rebound, or a divorce.

So Eager

Caroline went through a painful divorce two years ago. She tried to move on but was lonely and starving for validation from a man. That's when she met Henry at a conference. They hit it off right away, finding that intellectual closeness was easy and comfortable. They talked about the meetings they were both attending, and Henry asked her to have dinner with him.

It began well. They talked about the conference and their respective jobs. But soon, things got awkward. She launched right into her divorce, how painful it was, and how it had cost her both financially and emotionally. She even began to weep.

Though Henry was attracted to her and had asked her to dinner, he began to think she was emotionally unstable and maybe a bit crazy — certainly not safe to share his own vulnerability with. As the evening wore on, he felt increasingly uncomfortable and couldn't wait until it ended.

Caroline rushed into heavy emotional issues without building a foundation of trust and the basics of intimacy with Henry. This is why he became uncomfortable.

If you aren't aware of relationship levels, you might get married before you realize you don't even know your husband. For example:

The Accountant and the Beauty Queen

John was a very successful accountant. He married Margot, a former beauty queen, and they had several children. Other than physical attraction, they had nothing in common. Emotionally, there was no sharing whatsoever and others couldn't understand how they had ever gotten together in the first place. It was like they were from two different worlds. They never connected on any level except the physical one — and that part didn't last. Though they were financially successful and had a family, this wasn't enough to keep them together. If Margot had understood the need to develop intellectual closeness, and then bond with her husband emotionally, she could have made a difference, or may not have married him in the first place.

You Have an Advantage

To be successful, close relationships require you to balance your rational and intuitive minds and involve a process of learning to put feelings into words. This is usually easier for women to do, partly because we start life with more connection between the left and right hemispheres of our brains, and this may be why we are more persistent at it.

Talking about feelings is more difficult for men because they must think about it more than we do. They frequently consider it either draining or something to be avoided because it makes them feel more vulnerable. Women don't like feeling vulnerable either but are perhaps more used to it than men who may work harder to protect themselves emotionally. Men feel much safer in a logical state of mind and struggle to put emotions into words. They do have very strong feelings, and they express them a great deal, but less so in words and more in action.

The female advantage is our greater tendency towards rational and intuitive mind balance. We can help men if we are patient and realize they need support and safety in learning to identify and share their emotions. Whether you're dating or married, it's important to create a secure emotional atmosphere where he can process and express his feelings with you.

Have you ever heard men say women are the emotional ones? This may seem to be true because women are more verbal about their emotions, and we may be more willing to show them in the form of tears or dramatic expressions, but men are no less passionate and emotional than women. We may observe intense male passion by watching men play or watch sports. Note the intensity of their emotion-driven behavior. They can become downright feverish! Men who are merely watching sports on TV, yelling and slapping each other on the back, show very intense emotions. For the men playing these sports, in their minds they are engaged in a life and death struggle. After a win, they let out their passions, sometimes by shouting or cheering, and may even hug each other.

Other than these acceptable displays of emotion, men tend to find it easier and safer to hide out and not let anyone see how strong their feelings really are. Women often misunderstand men when they retreat. We take their aloofness for disinterest or even rejection. But if you bear in mind that he is just hiding his vulnerability because he lacks awareness of it and how to deal with it, you can be more sensitive to him in these moments. You can let him have his alone time to sort things out. You can forgive him a pause in the conversation to take extra time to process everything—something which takes you little to no time at all. You can react more appropriately and judge him less, and this will bring you closer.

When we started out, Bob protected himself by hiding out emotionally quite often, despite being in training as a psychologist. It took time for him to acquire his present-day skills, and it took patience on my part for us to build the trust we have in our relationship today. Though he has helped me a great deal in understanding men, he still had to work on expressing his emotions with words — it's one thing to study it in graduate school, and quite another to do it on a personal level. Bob is now wonderfully fluent at expressing his emotions with words and, in fact, he often helps me. We have faced great emotional challenges together; we have overcome them and grown, developing a feeling of safety with each other that only deepens as the years pass.

Appearing to be Emotionally Connected

There are some people who are good at appearing to be emotionally connected for the sole purpose of using others. Because men and women don't always have good motives, you need to be careful who you trust. This is another reason why it is wise to spend some time getting to know the person you are dating, exploring intellectual and emotional depths, before going to the higher level of spiritual intimacy.

Spiritual Intimacy

If you have progressed through the first two levels of a relationship, you will naturally begin to seek connection on a deeper level. If you're already in a committed relationship and you haven't developed this level, it's probably not too late to start.

Spirituality at its most basic level is your sense of purpose and how you fit into the grand scheme of things — your connection to the human race and the earth you live on. It includes your values, your perspective of beauty and worth, your sense of right and wrong, your beliefs in the nature of life and death, and your reasons for waking up, working hard, and enduring the "slings and arrows of outrageous fortune," rather than simply ending it all, as Hamlet mused. For many, religion provides a framework for a lot of these questions; for others, meditation and simple awareness or care for the world around them constitutes spirituality. Whatever its source, spirituality can be powerful, and when it's shared between two people who love each other, it can become a beautiful and living thing which transcends time and death.

When forming healthy relationships, people don't usually trust these deep and personal feelings to another until they believe there is a foundation of safety based on successful intellectual and emotional bonding. Men usually share spiritual feelings when they are in touch with them and feel safe enough to do so. If you have built a foundation for emotional intimacy, you will naturally want to share this deeper level because it will bring you closer together. You can help him get in touch with these feelings, and support him in identifying and talking about them, by recognizing and validating him on the first two levels.

A relationship built on intellectual, emotional, and spiritual intimacy provides a foundation that will last, and establishes context for the next and final level of bonding: physical intimacy. This approach to building intimacy is a timeless principle and an imperative part of romantic relationships that last a lifetime.

239

Having a spiritual level of intimacy will lead to the most comprehensive relationship you can have. It enhances the meaning and potential of intellectual and emotional bonding. People who have developed to this level have a union that can last even if one partner's health deteriorates, even if they die. It can create a timeless romantic love — the one dreams are made of.

If you do not have this three-part foundation in place, physical intimacy can be deadly to your relationship.

Physical Intimacy — Affection

The early levels of physical intimacy may include non-sexual touch such as holding hands, hugging, and cheek kissing or just sitting close to each other. These things are common and not necessarily even romantic in nature. We can all have physical contact on this level with family and friends. It's bonding and healthy. Somehow, perhaps only in North America, holding hands implies sexual intimacy, but this is not the case for most of the world. Physical contact can be a part of your relationship that can endure no matter your age, and it produces a lot of pleasurable body chemistry.

Sex Before Marriage

When it comes to romantic or sexual contact, another level is added. This includes kissing, foreplay, and the most intimate of physical expressions: sex. This can deepen and enrich your relationship, but it can also destroy it if done prematurely, without the other levels being developed, or without a long-term commitment. You might get away with it, but you might not. If you don't, the price can be devastating. It's high-risk because there really is no such thing as *casual* sex.

This is because sex involves a lot of potential complications: health, economic, psychological, legal, and even social. Without knowing a person well, you potentially share fluids with everyone they ever shared fluids with, and the risk of disease becomes a factor. In addition, pregnancy can result and can have an enormous impact on health and everything else in your life. Having a child is a big economic commitment, and one or more partners may not be ready financially or even psychologically. Raising a child requires a minimum level of maturity and responsibility, not to mention a lot of sacrifice.

Sex also releases bonding chemicals, and you may end up emotionally connected to someone who doesn't respect you or treat you well, and who may be willing to sever the bond casually. This can cause enormous psychological damage and decrease your ability to trust and bond with future partners. There is no prophylactic, or prevention, for psychological vulnerability. Are you ready for this? Is he? And if you're not, you may also have consequential legal issues to deal with such as custody or child support, especially if you don't agree about issues with this person you didn't take time to get to know.

And finally, sex before commitment can have a deep impact on friendships, family, and even society in general. Again, I'm not saying you can't navigate these tricky waters, I'm just saying it's very hard to do without figuratively getting kicked in the teeth. Life is already overwhelming enough. There's a safer and smarter way.

The decision to offer your body to someone is a big deal. This should be an important choice and should not be considered simply a reward for a nice date, or be made by default, under the influence of body chemistry, alcohol, or drugs. Rash downstairs choices sooner or later must face rational and spiritual realities and consequences.

Why rush in to it? Ask yourself: who is in control? You, or your sexual impulse? What directs your future? Who is watching out for you, if not you?

Let's consider a real example of a dating couple who didn't bother to pay much attention to any of the levels except for one — sex.

Mixed Up Intimacy

Natalie was very young, only 20 when she met Peter. Both had prior relationships that had failed. There was instant chemistry between them and soon they were having sex. After a few steamy months, they moved in together. They decided not to marry because, to them, their commitment was the most important thing — they didn't need a piece of paper to feel bonded. Besides, all their friends who had gotten married had also eventually divorced. They felt they were safer just living together.

But after two children, they finally decided to make it official and put on a large wedding. A few years passed, and it seemed to their friends everything was working. But things weren't. Natalie discovered that Peter had been unfaithful, and more than once. And on top of everything, he began to drink heavily and became verbally abusive. She was devastated. She regretted getting married. If only she had taken more time and invested more effort to get to know him she might have seen the selfishness and duplicity he often displayed. She missed early cues because she was physically and emotionally committed.

The exuberance of their early and intense physical relationship pushed Natalie and Peter into a false sense of intimacy. Sex became a shortcut to what initially felt like a deeper emotional bond, and this made her complacent about building a more genuine foundation to the relationship. They thought they knew each other. Natalie thought she could trust Peter, and both invested minimally in the other levels of their relationship, only to later find they didn't share much other than two children together. They were practically strangers on emotional and spiritual levels, and eventually divorced. Both felt bitter, each blaming the other for their failure.

If Natalie and Peter had taken the time to get to know each other on deeper levels, they would have avoided the false sense of intimacy that passionate sex can bring. They would have either worked out their differences and married on a better footing, or they would have avoided marriage altogether, and thus escaped the heartache and cynicism that resulted.

243

Sex in Marriage

Physical intimacy is a significant and worthy part of a romantic marriage. An honest and safe sexual relationship with your husband is a powerful way to express love for one another and it strengthens all levels of intimacy. However, your lifelong love affair can still survive if sex is interrupted or cut short for reasons such as health, age, or disability. Intellectual, emotional, and spiritual bonding are more lasting than your sexual relationship.

People sometimes have different sexual expectations of each other in marriage. If he is more interested in sex than you are, you need to remember that you took him off the market as far as physical intimacy is concerned when you married him. When you marry a moral person, you put each other in a potentially vulnerable situation. If you either close the door to your marriage bed, or even if you only accept it every once in a great while—only when you feel like it—you can potentially place a great burden on your partner.

People who are dating have a greater chance of marrying the right person if they follow the levels of intimacy in order. Once married, couples have the greatest chance of an enduring love affair when they balance and invest in all four levels of bonding.

Fixing It

It's a lot more difficult to build a foundation under a house after the structure is already built, but with a marriage, repair is still possible.

The study and application of the timeless Fascinating Womanhood principles is an important key to your success. It includes developing all levels of intimacy as well as your own femininity, charm, and character. Understanding men is also vital. If a marriage lacks intellectual, emotional, and spiritual intimacy, it can't thrive, no matter how great the sex is. When marriages lack intimacy, of whatever sort, both husband and wife will tend to seek it elsewhere. Finding a proxy for intellectual bonding with one's spouse is perhaps the most forgivable, but most marriages will be in danger if there is a substitute for emotional, spiritual, or physical intimacy. Relationships have different needs and pressure points, but we should never be complacent in letting an area of potential intimacy with our spouse be neglected, if we can help it.

If your relationship has gotten off to a bad start, your challenge will be to inspire real romantic love beyond that which is merely physical. Doing this may feel like starting from the beginning — because it basically is. You will need to get to know each other on a deep level, and this may feel scary because you might uncover some surprises, maybe even deal-breakers. But you're going to have to find some courage, humility, and perhaps above all, patience in this endeavor.

Deep trust, especially if it has been undermined in the past, cannot be built quickly or easily. Humility is the great leveler of humankind. Seek it. If you can just refrain from running your mouth at him and making rash decisions, you'll probably find some courage and humility along the way.

245

You may have to exercise forgiveness. This is where humility will be essential. Remember that neither one of you is perfect, and it is a lot easier to be forgiven if you are willing to reciprocate. Also, if you have anything spiritual in common, you may look to a higher power together for perspective on imperfections, forgiveness, and becoming a better person.

I realize that this discussion may seem judgmental or critical but that is not my intent. So many women experience great stress and pain because they had no idea they weren't building a solid foundation under their relationship prior to getting involved physically. Most of us lack psychological and relationship education. Many women who engage in premarital sex have been taught erroneously that there is no real emotional or mental risk.

The risk is real because sex so often substitutes for other levels of intimacy and is therefore an unstable foundation. It takes time and investment to develop intellectual, emotional, and spiritual bonds—increasingly so, and in that order. Beware the deep and lasting hurt from severed bonds that can cause enduring cynicism and difficulty with trust. Such emotional damage could hold you back from the greatest relationship of your life. You might think of yourself as having only so many heartbreaks in you before it really begins to harm your ability to be close to anyone ever again.

People who make appetite their priority are eventually governed by it. They come to live for novelty for its own sake and increasingly objectify their desires. Where it concerns sex, these people develop something akin to an aversion to commitment and for the sort of sacrifice that relationships require. You need to be much more to him than a nightly meal. You will have much greater success, more fulfillment and meaning, and a lifelong love affair, if you build the relationship on more lasting terms.

Sexual Satisfaction and Being Sure

Some people think they will have the best luck finding "the one" if they experiment and have multiple sexual partners. They believe part of finding the right person requires having sex to see if you fit or work together. They rationalize that they will be ready to settle down and be faithful to one person after a period of adventure and exploration. Sleeping with multiple partners won't help you find the right person. Finding out if he is a good lover doesn't determine if your relationship will last. The other pillars of intimacy need to be established and will give you much more information to decide whether the relationship has a great chance of becoming a lasting one.

The greatest physical intimacy and even sexual pleasure comes from a complete intimate connection on all levels. Nothing else compares.

How Long Does It Take to Move to Each Level?

The speed with which people move through the four relationship levels depends on the couple, their maturity and readiness to fall in love and build a lifelong romance.

Some relationships take years while others may take only weeks. Some couples begin to develop each of the levels on the first date. Here's an example my sister, Merilee, gave me of how she and her husband Craig's relationship evolved.

Merilee and Craig

"I met Craig on a blind date that I did not want to go on. In fact, I would say I dreaded it. The only reason I agreed was that my good friend Marcy set me up and was adamant I go. She worked with Craig and insisted I would have a good time. I had never had a good time on a first date and had been on plenty by the ripe old age of 22. To me, first dates meant I had to be an actress. I had to entertain and be polite no matter how bored I was or nervous the guy might try to kiss me before I knew how I felt.

"Craig was attractive, but I was still uncomfortable during the first 30 minutes or so while we made small talk. By the time our dinner arrived I decided there was nothing worse in life than engaging in frivolous conversation, so I asked him, 'Tell me what you are like?' To this day Craig insists that asking that question is a poor way to find out about a person. Perhaps he's right, but he took me at my word and we transitioned from discussing music and movies to philosophy, politics, religion, and our personal values. It was a riveting conversation which I did not want to end. Unfortunately, I made plans for later that evening and had to leave sooner than I would have liked. He never complimented me on my appearance or hinted that he found me attractive. Still, he asked for my phone number and I was glad.

"It was two weeks before Craig called me. Enough time had passed that I assumed he wasn't interested in me. We made plans to meet again and when we did, we had a great conversation. Despite having had two previous boyfriends, I had never experienced a deep connection like I did with Craig. Maybe I didn't know it was possible. All I knew was that it felt really good and I was very attracted to him. He seemed to like me but he never told me or held my hand. We dated for six weeks before he kissed me. When he finally told me he thought I was beautiful I asked him why he never mentioned it before. He said, "I could tell you were used to hearing it.

The truth is that if Craig had tried to kiss me on the first date, I would have let him. If he had told me I was beautiful, I would have liked it. I'm glad he didn't. We might have gotten caught up in a physical relationship and never developed the layers of intimacy that are the foundation of our deeply satisfying marriage."

For some, six weeks might be either fast or slow. The issue isn't so much time, or what you think should be a rate of progression, but the quality of your time together and the communication you share. Couples can acquire a fast and genuine intellectual connection, and they can even find emotional intimacy rather easy if they discover they are in sync with each other. Spiritual intimacy may take a bit more time, but quality of communication and the degree to which two people feel a sense of safety and reciprocity with one another is what will determine their story together.

We most often find that it takes time, courage, and effort to develop a bond that will truly last, but each couple is different. We will all be tempted to believe we are the special ones who didn't need much time to fall in love. But beware of chemistry alone being the basis of your romance. Knowing when you have a relationship you can build a reliable future on is a matter of good judgment. You should carefully consider the strength of your intellectual, emotional, and spiritual levels to gauge your ability to judge and move to new and deeper levels.

In Summary:

- Whether you are married or still dating, understanding and learning to grow all levels of your romantic relationship are important in developing your lifelong love affair. It is safest and most effective to develop the levels of intimacy in order, from intellectual to emotional, and then to spiritual as a foundation, before physical.
- When you develop these levels in order, you have a greatly improved chance of finding a man you can love your whole life.
- If you are already married, you can still develop the other areas of your relationship and deepen your marriage even more.
- Building a foundation for a lasting romance is not so much about the time you commit, but the quality of your time and communication together.

Addendum

William Tucker, author of "Marriage and Civilization: How Monogamy Made Us Human, stated that, "Western European, American and East Asian societies live in relative peace and prosperity because they honor and enforce monogamous marriage, as did the earliest human societies.

Joseph Henrich of the University of British Columbia, Robert Boyd of UCLA and Peter Richerson of UC Davis summarize the civilizing benefits of monogamy:

- The pool of unattached men is reduced so that they do not form a potentially disruptive residue of society.
- Crime is reduced since most crimes are committed by unmarried males. In addition, longitudinal studies show that fewer crimes are committed by the same men when they marry.
- Political coups and factional fighting become less common because there are fewer single men willing to enlist in rebel armies.
- Society becomes more productive because men work more when they are married.
- Children do better because men invest in them instead of using their resources to obtain more wives.
- Spousal relations improve because men and women are more dedicated to each other instead of merely entering an economic/reproductive relationship.

- Child marriages disappear and the age gap between husbands and wives narrows. There is reduced inequality between men and women and spousal abuse declines.
- Young women are no longer hoarded and sequestered by their families in order to protect the value of the bride price. Marriages become elective and more stable.

These conclusions, though referring to monogamous relationships over polygamous ones, apply to uncommitted and casual relationships vs. committed ones, and support the institute of marriage.

Consider the following:

- According to statistics by US Attorney Legal Services, living together before getting married doesn't accomplish the goal that couples think it will; *i.e.* testing the relationship to see if it will last.
- A couple who do not live together prior to getting married has only a 20% chance of being divorced within five years. Contrast that with a couple that has lived together beforehand, in which case the number jumps to 49%.
- For couples who decide to move in together, just over half marry within five years. Within that same time period, 40% of couples split up. Roughly 10% will continue living together without being married.
- People who decide to live with a partner may also be more likely to divorce if they are unhappy with the relationship

after taking vows, since they may have less conservative views on marriage.

- During the time couples live together, they know the situation may not be permanent. They often divide bills and property in terms of yours and mine, but don't necessarily have the notion that assets belong to both of them. Living together may be more stressful than being married, due to lack of stability.

Here are some more statistics on living together before marriage by Michael McManus, author of the book "Marriage Savers." He says, "Statistically speaking, living together is not a trial of marriage but rather training for divorce."

- More than eight out of ten couples who live together will break up either before the wedding or afterwards in divorce.
- Couples who do marry after living together are 50% more likely to divorce than those who did not.
- Only 12% of couples who have begun their relationship with cohabitation end up with a marriage lasting 10 years or more.
- McManus reports a Penn State study that even a month's cohabitation decreases the quality of the couple's relationship.
- Children of cohabiting parents are ten times more likely to be sexually abused by a stepparent than by a parent.

- Children of cohabiting parents are three times as likely to be expelled from school or to get pregnant as teenagers than children from an "intact home" with married parents.
- Children of cohabiting parents are five times more apt to live in poverty and 22 times more likely to be incarcerated.

Family is the fundamental building block of civilization. A man and a woman falling in love and getting married are the beginning of every strong family. We are driven to create families because of a powerful biological imperative, but also because we observe and experience how rewarding it can be. Family is one of the few things we can possess in life that can really last the test of time and tragedy. It addresses the universal problem of loneliness and provides a safety net in disastrous times. A lot of couples these days are choosing to not have kids, or they can't have them due to physical reasons. Marriage can be a beautiful thing, even without children. But in the grand scheme of things, getting married and having kids is a supremely meaningful experience. It is one of the greatest opportunities for learning and personal growth that a person can have.

However, it can be as challenging as it is meaningful without structure and routine. Without these things, we tend towards chaos and inefficiency. What keeps us from effective unions is a lack of intimacy and trust. What threatens our families when we have children is a lack of understanding of the benefits of organizing and dividing labor. When families lack trust and organization, conflict and disorder tend to dominate. We constantly fight each other for validation, domination, and the pursuit of individual agendas—the concept of togetherness is under continual strain. We can doubt why we are even together because we are stressed and unhappy, when the original goal was to support and lift each other up. United and with a plan, we can bring order and happiness to our families, overcome great difficulties, and build amazing things.

Relationship roles are somewhat cultural, though we can see throughout the world a modern tendency for women to want greater equality and enhanced options to pursue their dreams. Though we may embrace our excellence in relationships and the home, women don't appreciate having their lives pre-programmed for them. In pursuit of this, many progressive relationships attempt to carefully negotiate roles in such a way that everyone, but no one in particular, is equally responsible for everything. In our attempt to protect sensitive feelings, we can create role confusion and this leads to conflict that undermines the whole concept of marriage and family.

The promise of marriage, or indeed any union, is the notion that we can accomplish more together than we can alone. But families require cohesion. In business, division of tasks is a major issue. In many organizations, confusion about leadership can lead to waste and collapse. Few can survive a sense of not knowing who is in charge or how we can help each other. Families may seem like they can absorb more chaos than a business, but they often fail for similar reasons: a failure to pay the bills, a lack of morale, and internal conflict. Much or all of this can be ascribed to failure in identifying and observing roles.

But how do we reconcile specific roles with equality? Equality can be very affirming to the individual but it is also limiting, especially where you have more than one person trying to accomplish something in partnership with another. Equality is really a sort of social fiction we adopt in order to affect better outcomes, and it's valuable in some contexts because life can be unfairly competitive. But some kinds of relationships, especially intimate ones, are best when they're not adversarial, but cooperative. In families with deep trust, role specialization creates progress rather than imbalance.

Much of what we have focused on prior to this chapter is foundational to relationship roles because it builds a basis for trust. Without trust, we will tend to look for more equality in a relationship—and when we do that, it is tempting to erase role distinctions. If we have low confidence in anyone else taking responsibility, we will find it difficult to delegate roles.

In relationships, especially in a home with children, life can get overwhelming fast. To have a reliable partner who excels at specific roles can make all the difference in the world. It frees you to do the same. If you can coordinate your efforts towards similar goals, your union will accomplish far more and will be able to overcome any difficulty.

Understanding relationship roles and our expectations of how they are carried out is crucial to marriage. In order to avoid unnecessary conflict that can damage relationships, these roles need to be clarified and agreed to. When we embrace the idea that we can each excel at a specific and complementary role, we can greatly add to the tranquility and progress of our family.

There are solid, basic rules for relationship building and productivity that can be used in any group or family unit no matter what size. A marriage or family is a small organization, in some ways like a business. As with most organizations, a home will be more efficient and produce better outcomes when each participant knows how they can best contribute.

Task and Relationship Leaders

One vital role in any association is that of a leader. Because it has the most potential for abuse, the subject of leadership often prompts discussions on equality and power abuse. Leaders are unfortunately needed sometimes for subjugation, but their greatest contributions are for coordination. Good leaders are productive and talented at meeting the challenges before them while maintaining group unity and morale. To be most effective, situations sometimes call for different skill sets. Men and women are generally inclined to certain sets of leadership skills, both of which can be critical in different ways, in different contexts of life.

Let's revisit some of the predispositions of gender and how they can relate to leadership.

259

Men naturally seek their identities and meaning in competence and responsibility — what else do they have?

A flood of testosterone is introduced in the first few weeks of the development of a male fetus. It changes everything physically for a boy, transforming the potential of genitalia from female to male, changing the way their brain develops, predisposing them to specialization rather than generalization, and a focus on survival. It also sets the body on a path for physical development that emphasizes physical aggression and competition. Young males instinctively seek conflict and hierarchy in their play styles, which usually center around intense physical action. This instinct carries through to adulthood. Men develop 75% more upper body strength than women do. Their brains and bodies are developed to maximize coordination in order to excel at physical action, and therefore they are predisposed to it and the roles it implies.

All the above implies that men excel at protection, physical labor, and mental tasks which require focus and objectivity, often at the expense of emotional sensitivity and verbal expression. In other words, men tend to be really good at focusing on a task and getting it done. Women are more interested in relationships while men are more interested in things. This is why we describe men ideally as the builders, protectors, and organizers of civilization. A man's tendency towards task objectivity helps to explain why men are drawn to STEM (science, technology, engineering, and math) occupations. Women are smart enough for STEM jobs, but statistically they are just not as interested in those fields. When men live up to their potential, they take care of the next generation and help to ensure that the human race continues.

Without the requisite testosterone, human fetuses all start out and will ultimately become female. At its basic level, everything in female fetal development is geared towards future reproduction. The female body is prepared for menstrual cycles, and the eventual ability to give birth and lactate (or breastfeed). Our female brain is wired for a greater sensitivity to sound and emotional reaction to sensory information. We're going to hear a baby cry better then men, and we're physically and mentally designed for the job of nurturing it. Because of their emotional interest, infant females will attend to faces longer than boy infants will. Young females are prone to simulate motherhood and homemaking with dolls and toys. They tend to seek group cooperation activities from an early age and through to adulthood. Women find themselves at their best in motherhood and relationship development occupations.

These rather simple summaries of gender development and predisposition are not meant to emphasize limitations so much as core competencies — areas in which we particularly excel. The cult of equality will seek to minimize our physical and mental differences in order to make the point that males and females can compete with each other and accomplish many of the same things — that there is no real meaningful difference. It is true that men and women can excel at the same skills. But men have evolved to be particularly good at a certain style that some may refer to as "task leadership." On the other hand, women tend to be best at "relationship leadership."

Task Leaders

Task leaders are more concerned with getting the job done, sometimes at the expense of feelings if necessary. They're not all rude or even insensitive, but their priority is task first and feelings …later, if they can be afforded. Task leadership generates great productivity in the right contexts and can weather even extreme stress and chaos. Good task leaders can bring order to a disastrous situation, and it is in these times that feelings are often least convenient. Again, men tend to focus on one hemisphere at a time in problem-solving.

Task leaders are great for powering through a quagmire or conquering in an adversarial and dangerous situation. When an organization has low skill levels, we need task leaders. Their impact is decreased in times of great prosperity, when people are doing their jobs well or assuming responsibility appropriately, or where delicate feelings are critical to outcomes.

The primary objectives of a task leader are:

Career: Someone has to take primary responsibility to provide adequate income for the family. Women can be task leaders, and are often forced into the role of bread-winner. But it's hard when a woman has to do everything — give birth, recover, bond with the kids and take first responsibility for raising them, and hold down a job that provides the main source of income. In divorce, we are most often the ones who take on both roles, even if we can afford services to help us. This is a staggering amount of responsibility, and it's not an effective or efficient approach.

Men are the more obvious primary breadwinners and they are the more natural task leaders, and ideally they take care of these burdensome outside tasks so women can focus more easily on relationship leadership.

One of our primary needs as women is to feel financially secure. We appreciate it when we can count on a man to provide necessities of life, especially when we are vulnerable either while being pregnant or raising children. But even if we aren't, it is comforting to be taken care of physically, emotionally, and financially. It's not a sign of weakness but interdependence. Men need us too.

Efficiency: Task leaders appreciate the need for efficiency, for getting tasks done in a timely, accurate manner. No matter how privileged we may or may not be, there is always only so much money, time, and resources to focus on our wants and needs. Efficiency is about organization and making the best of whatever we may have.

Teaching Responsibility: When there are children to be raised, the task leader usually takes responsibility for orienting children towards the eventual realities and responsibilities of adulthood. Most parents don't want their children to be dependent on them forever. Teaching responsibility requires self-discipline, structure and routine, as well as setting a good example.

Teaching Principles: This includes learning to become a productive, law-abiding citizen as well as understanding the basics of values: the meaning of life and how you relate to others, learning right from wrong, kindness, honor, and integrity. This is mainly a task leader's job because it involves setting limits and boundaries — saying no, and even applying constructive disciplinary action. Relationship leaders add to this tremendously by supporting the task leader in this role. We also add by gently reinforcing our husband's teaching and discipline and by further explaining to the kids about values and principles.

Motivation: Energy to accomplish tasks requires mental focus. It's easier to avoid personal responsibility by focusing on one's rights and sense of fairness, and this attitude tends to decrease motivation. Task leaders must redirect a lack of motivation that comes from focusing on entitlements to concentration on the exciting and limitless possibilities of self-improvement and personal initiative. They must teach self-reliance and a sense of responsibility by showing children how making good choices leads to a better life. This includes modeling a strong work ethic and high self-expectations, as well as the need for education, both formal and informal.

Leadership in Major Decisions: This one is often grossly misunderstood and misused. It is frequently thought to mean some sort of tyrannical master/slave arrangement. It sometimes does, but this sort of relationship is seldom happy. There is another, healthier definition:

When there is a decision leader in the home, he keeps the family focused on primary objectives and redirecting, when needed, discussions and priorities to what matters most. It's a matter of objective focus, and so it is a natural job for the task leader. Taking the lead in major family decisions means to organize, guide discussions, emphasize valid points, offer opinions, and actively seek the advice and thoughts of the relationship leader before coming to a final conclusion. For efficiency purposes, someone needs to have a final say in major decisions. Small matters can be delegated, but life often punishes the indecisive.

A wise task leader knows the importance of input from the relationship leader. Such managers often work the hardest and they're often harder on themselves than others. Good leaders ultimately see themselves as good servants who are not superior to others. They just accept their responsibilities and embrace the opportunities presented.

Discipline: Discipline really should be a shared responsibility but someone should have the final word, especially if there is any disagreement. Consequences should be consistent. Teaching is the most effective when children can see cause and effect clearly. Most mothers love it when they can rely on the child's father to back up the discipline she has started. In other words, to be able to say, "Do you want me to tell your father?" is nice when needed. Men have lower, deeper voices that sound more authoritative, which inspires respect, and they're usually bigger and more intimidating.

Pipe Down

When I was a child, my sisters and I shared a bedroom and would often talk and giggle late into the night. I remember how scared we were when we would hear the sound of our father's footsteps walking heavily and deliberately toward our room. We could feel his frustration at us for failing to obey him. He would open the door and sternly say something like, "You girls need to pipe down!" I can still hear it in my head after all these years. I don't know why we were so scared. He was never abusive, but I guess our imaginations provided what reality didn't. We hated to hear his deep voice telling us to be quiet. We weren't as impressed when mother told us to be quiet, for some reason.

The Importance of Task Leaders:

- Task leaders are important to others' self-esteem: they set limits and boundaries which lead increased productivity. They help you feel like you've earned something.
- They work towards building security and stability.
- They get the job done.
- They are instrumental in skill training in the family. They emphasize the importance of knowing how to do a job and do it well.
- Task leaders believe it is important to build a successful reputation. They appreciate the good name they can pass on to their descendants.
- They provide expectations and goals and like to outline steps to reach those goals.
- They help everyone else's guard dogs feel safe!

Relationship Leaders

Relationship leaders place feelings as a top priority, especially where feelings concern important relationships, but they sometimes do this at the cost of productivity and order. These leaders are very capable of getting the job done, but they tend to excel in leadership positions when members of the group have high skill levels and are self-directing. They can be the best leaders available in times of prosperity and relative calm, being particularly good at maintaining a strong group, and they can be vital where feelings and relationships are the most critical element in a task.

The relationship leader is essential to the happiness not only of a family but also to a romantic marriage. Two dominant task leaders seldom attract each other and when they do, their union is often turbulent. It's been said the only person who can live happily with a strong task leader is a relationship leader. They seek to understand and are tolerant of the more insensitive side of others. Women excel at this more often than men. We are better suited to the extensive interpersonal requirements which raising children and running a home demand.

The division of labor which has been described as typical between men and women is not a fixed rule. The roles are reversed in some cases. Even with these exceptions, men more often lack the higher level of physical bonding we form with our young. I do know of some successful unions where the husband is a stay-at-home parent and mother is the bread-winner; there

267

may very well be romantic arrangements like. But these are the exceptions more than the rule.

The list of a relationship leader's responsibilities is longer than the task leader's and is also much deeper, though some are supportive of the task leaders' primary jobs.

Primary Objectives of a Relationship Leader:

Career: When you are a wife as well as a mother, being a homemaker and/or stay-at-home mom is a career in spite of what some might say. Just because you aren't paid directly doesn't mean you don't have a serious job. Your work in your home may exceed the amount and intensity, and almost certainly the long-term value of any work you could find in the more formal workplace. Anyone who would argue against this point probably lacks the credentials to do so, because if they ever had occasion to be a mother and homemaker, the truth of the matter would shame them to silence. Don't let amateurs lecture pros!

If you have a job outside your home as well, you will work even harder. Many women with external careers work to bring in extra money. Often it's out of necessity for survival or for self-expression. We usually get little praise and sometimes even derision for all of this.

Homemaker: This role is extensive and includes not only the day to day tasks of maintaining the home but also the creation of atmosphere, preparation of meals, shopping, and many other things. This area is important whether you have children, or both of you are working, or your children are grown. The creating and maintaining of a home provides the safe and comfortable atmosphere in which we all need to relax at the end of each day. This role could also include gardening, home decorating, minor home repair, and cleaning.

Lover: We all have a great need for physical affection, but relationship leaders tend to excel at the giving of physical comfort. This could be considered part of creating a sense of the home as a sanctuary from stress. It is a great service to your partner and spouse to focus on their needs in this area, to make their fulfillment your priority. Investment in physical comfort is particularly satisfying to the relationship leader because it strengthens bonding and romance. It strengthens a sense of well-being and that the home is a place you both want to be.

Friend. Acceptance and admiration are described in earlier chapters. But in this context, we can say generally that relationship leaders are good at being a companion because they're tuned to feelings and needs. Being a friend to a partner and spouse means also embracing their idea of fun and recreation, being a sympathetic and active listener, and keeping confidences.

Amateur Nurse. Though you may lack formal training, if you are the relationship leader, you're going to find yourself in this position often. Many relationship leaders become highly accomplished in this area, though you should always consult a professional in more serious cases. An experienced mother learns to tend to everyday issues such as scrapes, bug bites, fevers, colds, and upset stomachs. This isn't a mere hobby for relationship leaders: development of in-home health care improves and even saves lives. No one can get to someone in medical need faster than the relationship leader who's already there. And no one cultivates more trust and bonding in the home than the amateur nurse.

Chauffeur. This does not apply to a lot of countries where public transportation is extensive and readily available. But in much of North America, it is a critical role that someone has to fulfill in the home. When my children were growing up, I had to balance numerous responsibilities with driving them to appointments, lessons, activities, and social events on a daily basis. Some may think this amounts to a recreational pursuit, but it can be stressful and require a lot of planning and sacrifice, especially if you live in a big metro area where driving is challenging. The relationship leader is almost always the default chauffeur. I used to think I needed a special cap to wear because I drove my kids around so much.

Amateur Counselor. Getting tired just reading this? There's a lot more. As a relationship leader, even if you don't have kids you're going to fill a vital role in being your spouse's confidant and shoulder to cry on when needed. Life is hard and relationship leaders are the best counselors. They're also the most accessible and readily available, despite their enormous workload. If you have kids, it's going to be a central role for you. Counseling is part of raising children and helping them cope with the stress of growing up and facing life's challenges. It's part of helping them find healthy and productive identities and becoming responsible adults. The task leader is going to be a key partner in this as an example and teacher of principles. But the relationship leader has particular skill in the emotional nuances this job requires. And if you had to hire someone to take care of all the emotional crises that members of your family were to encounter, you'd be looking at a hefty bill. Serious psychological issues should be addressed by professionals, but like with amateur nursing, the day-to-day stuff is critical and not only improves life immensely, but saves your husband and children and adds tremendous meaning to relationships and family. A relationship leader can invest in this area through self-education and consultation with professionals.

Cook/Baker/Entertainer. If you're not going to eat out or hire professionals for three meals per day, someone is going to have to step up to this challenge. People don't want to eat gruel everyday, so the home cook is going to have to invest in some skills. And you're going to have guests occasionally if you have a balanced home. You may bring the boss over, and it will eventually be your turn to have the friends by for a visit. The person who excels most at preparing food is going to end up directing these activities. Even where entertainment is concerned, it has to be coordinated with the preparation, serving, and clean-up of food and drinks. Cooking can add so much to a home that it comes to define it. The smells of a wonderful kitchen can be the thing you remember most when away from home—can be the most comforting thing about it. Some say the kitchen is the very center of the home. A lot of the nursing and counseling will be done while food preparation is in process because relationship leaders have to be

271

multi-taskers. No wonder women are so good at this. If you ever encounter someone who says homemaking isn't a real job, ask them if they ever worked in food service. It's a complicated and important job that can take countless years to perfect. What is the value of someone who is highly skilled in this area? I dare you to tell me the generous cook doesn't have enormous influence in the family, the home, and the world.

Teacher/Tutor. This is most applicable to homes with children and is heavily related to the task leader's skill set—a close partnership between the two can make a huge difference. Whether your children are in public or private school, or if they are home-schooled, experts agree: parental involvement is critical to a child's education and future success. Even if you can hire a tutor, you're going to end up supporting a child's educational development in a personal way. Most of us can't afford the best life has to offer, so this is going to be a serious job if you want your kids to do well. It implies being educated yourself to some extent, though informal efforts will go far. It's also part of counseling, because education can be quite stressful for children and requires emotional and psychological growth, along with skills acquisition. It cannot be overstated that the most effective approach to educating children will be with a close relationship leader and task leader partnership.

Tailor and Launderer. Tailors make and repair clothing, and sometimes even upholstery. This is another one of those cost issues where, if you can't afford lots of new stuff or to constantly have professionals repair it, the relationship leader will likely be called in to save the day—especially if you have kids, because they grow out of their clothing fast and they're hard on them. Kids have a lot of energy and like to run and jump around all the time, and they have frequent accidents where they rip and stain their clothing. It can take some skill and serious labor to save clothing from this abuse and keep it in good order. The relationship leader is often a homemaker, and therefore on the front lines of this constant battle to maintain and balance resources in the home.

Inventor/Problem Solver/Repairer. This is another limited resources issue and one that compounds with kids. Homemakers are often called upon to fix things and solve weird problems, and so often to make do. Modern life requires limited, and sometimes extensive reliance on machines and equipment as well as plumbing, and the task leader is sometimes really good at fixing stuff. But if he is the primary bread-winner, and the relationship leader is the homemaker, the latter will face most problem solving tasks in the home. Kids break toys and important things around the home like lighting and furniture, dishes and electronics. Repairing such things may require a pretty broad skillset, and a partnership with the task leader can be crucial to maintaining home repairs while solving day-to-day problems.

Home Manager. Much of the above is implied by this role, but more is involved. Homemakers usually have to work with a budget, and so are at the heart of planning and coordinating activities and expenditures. They have to know everything that is going on to balance wants and needs and to run an effective and happy home. With kids, this may involve organizing and managing further division of labor, and most effectively will be done in partnership with a task leader. You could think of the relationship leader as a foreman to the task leader, who is an executive, though homes are often more horizontal than a business in terms of communication and even ultimate authority.

Support System for the Task Leader. Backup and adviser for the task leader in areas of efficiency, motivation, teaching values, responsibility and discipline. The task leader needs the support of the relationship leader in carrying out family and personal objectives. They often explain in a kind way what the task leader is trying to accomplish.

Women tend to be more interested in and good at homemaking and mothering than men are, partly because of our continuing interest in relationships. Men are better suited to be protectors and providers. We are better at multi-tasking. We can talk on the phone, fold laundry, cook and keep an ear out for kids, even listen for whether there is a strange sound in the furnace or roof, all at the same time. Men aren't usually as good at this. We take this ability for granted most of the time and get frustrated with men for not being able to do what we do easily. This is usually because we don't really understand them. My husband Bob is a very intelligent and educated man but says things like: "When I'm grilling, I'm grilling." He can barely even talk to me while he's cooking meat on a barbecue grill. It's just how he is—he's not trying to ignore me. He prefers to do one thing at a time well, and he enjoys it, even getting a little annoyed if he has to change focus before the task is done. It's not that men can't multitask, they just tend to avoid it and to not be quite as effortless at it as women.

The relationship leader is a better index of how everyone in the family feels at any given time. We more quickly sense when someone, even the task leader, is down, stressed, or sick. It's also important to us that everyone feels good about themselves. We worry when someone is crying or even too quiet, and we're often willing to give someone the benefit of the doubt long after reasonable doubt has vanished. In these cases the task leader is needed to balance things out.

When a woman is doing it all alone, meaning the task and relationship roles, her job is even more difficult. It's possible for women to do well at it but it's tough and this hybrid type of leader is often taken for granted by those who should appreciate her the most.

Aunt Elva

Bob's aunt Elva lost her husband in a farming accident when the oldest of her seven children was only about twelve. Their marriage had been very close and she never wanted to remarry. She kept many pictures of Morgan around the house and would often refer to him, saying to the children, "What would your father think of...?", or "Your father wouldn't approve of you doing...", using him as an example and a role model. Morgan left Elva debt free with a large farm but she still had to work very hard. The older boys had to grow up fast to help her fill their father's shoes. It was very difficult for her and she was lonely. She successfully raised all seven children who grew up to be mature, productive members of society. She had to be both task and relationship leader, recognizing the need for both. Though the path she chose was very hard, it was a testament to the strength women have when they need to draw upon it.

The Importance of Relationship Leaders:

Fill many crucial roles in the home:

Build self-esteem in others. They believe in the potential of everyone, especially family members, not just in attending to tasks at hand.

Help to build emotional security in the home. Family members feel safer psychologically and more valuable for who they are now, not just for their potential.

Repair damage done by an insensitive task leader whenever possible.

Care about how family members feel while they are learning or fulfilling tasks.

The sensitivity of a relationship leader allows them to *sense when something is amiss* with a family member or in the marriage, usually before the task leader is even aware. This can prevent serious problems from being full-blown before they are noticed.

Support the task leader in teaching values, goals, honor, integrity, spiritual growth and other important qualities in a successful family.

Help everyone else's guard dogs feel safe!

The relationship leader is the heart of love at home.

Task and Relationship Leader Partnerships

In the home, as in many organizations, there can be no more dynamic and effective leadership than a task and relationship leader who work well together. But in order to coordinate well, you both need to understand and respect what each other brings to the partnership. This implies taking responsibility for your particular role and supporting your partner in theirs. It suggests enough trust to let the other do their job without supervision. And it often means that you must defer to each other when particular skill sets in you or your mate are most required.

Practically speaking for most of us, life is often more challenging than it is convenient. We rarely have enough money or resources to do or have everything we'd like, and we sometimes find ourselves on the edge of disaster for prolonged periods of time. Competition and scarcity create tense and unpredictable environments, and this can present challenges to the serenity of our unions. And though marriage is a partnership, practical life puts the task leader most often in the driver's seat.

Consider the chaos of a home full of immature (low-skill) children who run amok. If you have ever turned your back on a young child for 5 minutes, you might find flour all over the kitchen floor or the dog painted with honey. They're like little tornados wreaking total destruction and chaos if they're not constantly supervised.

Running a home can feel like a battlefield. Mom is usually the one who is there to comfort the child with a skinned knee, but in such cases Dad may also need to give a speech about foolish activities or disobeying rules — neither of which are going to feel convenient to the child's sensitive feelings at the time, but which may teach valuable skills and principles in order to avoid similar or worse instances in future.

In a relationship between a man and a woman, both should be leaders — both are directors of a home and family even when there are no children or the children are grown. They should be goal-oriented partners. But unless responsibilities for each are understood, agreed upon , and respected, problems crop up quickly.

Effective and happy marriages have both a task and a relationship leader. Sometimes these roles are reversed. Being able to be flexible at times is ideal. Men are more natural task leaders while women tend to prefer and be good at the relationship role. Bob sometimes says, "My dad was the law and my mother was the love."

In Summary:

- Families are the building blocks of civilization. A man and a woman falling in love and getting married is the cornerstone of that foundation.
- Marriages and families are challenging when there is little structure and routine. Without these things, we tend towards chaos and inefficiency.
- The most effective marriages have two leaders: a task leader and a relationship leader.
- Men tend to be more natural as task leaders while women tend to more often be the relationship leader.
- Task leaders are good at getting the job done and reaching desired goals.
- Relationship leaders are most concerned with how everyone feels while getting the job done. They are usually the ones who children go to for comfort and who care most about their emotional state at any given time.
- In a relationship between a man and a woman, both should be leaders—both are directors of a home and family even when there are no children or the children are grown. A husband and wife can be goal-oriented partners.

haracter is the foundation for mature, lasting romantic relationships because it helps you respect yourself and expect better treatment from others. The quality of your relationships will add the most meaning to your life of anything you do, and developing character is the surest pathway to the best relationships possible.

Corruption abounds in the world today, as it always has. Many are willing to complain about it but fail to adhere to the values which would prevent it. We can't continue to ignore basic principles as individuals and then be surprised when society and its leaders fail us by their immoral choices. C.S. Lewis warned that, "We laugh at honor and then are shocked to find traitors in our midst." If character is in short supply, we must look inward because we can only change ourselves.

Life is a constant struggle to balance immediate and delayed gratification—a daily choice between living a reactive or an intentional life. We often find ourselves overwhelmed by immediate sensory stimulation and needs or engaged in a search for greater principles to guide us. And so, life can be thought of as an internal battle between the demands of the downstairs versus the potential for fulfillment and joy available from the upstairs portions of our minds.

We make our greatest progress toward a wonderful life when we struggle against baser instincts and seek a degree of self-mastery. Progress produces happiness, and the greatest progress is made by living a life of worthy character. Such a person wants to be the best version of themselves they can be—not only for their own benefit, but also for that of others. And so, we should think of character as the extent to which we master ourselves toward *noble ends*.

Worthy character always commands admiration. The rewards are well worth the effort because lifelong love affairs depend on it. Without character, you and your man will never build something that lasts because selfishness will rule, and self-serving relationships are never happy for long.

It's Up to You

Character is something you must build yourself, though others may be of some assistance to you, and you to them. But only you can take responsibility for your self-improvement, and you will have to do all the hard work.

You can start today by believing that you have this potential. I assure you that your true capacity for greatness is much more than you or I could ever imagine. It is truly limitless. Contemplate this and try to believe. If you look, you will find plenty of supporting evidence from your life and the lives of others. In doing so, you will take an important step forward.

A Lonely Struggle

Much of your experience in life, and most of the people you meet, will do little for your sense of self-worth or confidence. That's because the important battles are fought and won from within. It is a lonely struggle that we must all face if we are to develop character. I have felt the fear that is common to everyone who dares to take the first step towards self-improvement. Beginning this process takes courage.

A person of worthy character will try hard to be brave and show humility, honor, charity, and self-restraint—they will constantly practice self-improvement. Achieving this goal is a lifelong pursuit, rather than a destination you arrive at. Building and exercising character is a way of life.

Courage

Courage is an attribute which is just as native to women as men. There are many types of courage, and life will test them all, but the timeless quality of *noble* courage is choosing correct action in the face of fear.

"Being brave does not mean you are not scared. Being brave means you are scared, really scared, badly scared and you do the right thing anyway."
~ Neil Gaiman, Coraline

Courage may include facing physical or psychological harm, and it may consist of active or passive choices. There is the courage of a first responder to a crisis like fire or violence; or in that of the outnumbered believer who stands up for something true and good. And there is perhaps as much courage in the person who stands down when they don't have to. It takes courage to confront and to forgive, to justly restrain another or to apologize when in the wrong, just as it requires courage to believe that taking a risk may result in a worthwhile reward.

It takes courage to be consistently kind in this cold world, and only the brave are up for the challenge of bearing and raising children. We must sometimes risk life and limb for the ones we love, and sometimes while at a physical disadvantage. Women often face even more scorn than men when we are outspoken in what we believe, and we are less often remembered for our sacrifices in history. Therefore, if it could be said that women excel at any particular type, it might be moral courage — perhaps the most difficult of them all.

Fear is natural, and often a sign that you are perceptive or wise. But few if any good decisions are based out of fear alone. Your guard dog will always demand reassurance of safety, but your upstairs capacity for reason and inspiration have more than enough power to manage fear. Remember that fear is a necessary downstairs function which helps to keep us alive, but your guard dog will always be primitive and lacking in the perspective needed to go beyond mere survival.

A lack of courage can be remedied with regular meditation on the order of personal values. As Goethe famously wrote, "Things which matter most should never be at the mercy of things which matter least." Consider whether being right in an argument is more important to you than the general and lasting tranquility of a relationship, for example. Sometimes you may find you have to let go of being right for the greater good. As you set and refine your priorities, reminding yourself constantly of what matters most, you will build a strong instinct to act or refrain appropriately.

Many also find personal prayer a helpful way to find strength and faith. Belief in God can inspire you to grow in character. Belief or commitment to anything that's greater than you can increase your courage and desire to live a principled life.

Each act of courage will build confidence for the next. Start small and you will find it easy to build upon past victories. The greatest opportunities for building courage may therefore be in the smallest contexts of life. Consider the relatively small courage required to admit and apologize when you've made a mistake. Or perhaps the bravery it takes to speak in front of a crowd or go back to school. Relish these opportunities to fine-tune your character and prove your mettle to yourself and others.

Humility

Traits of worthy character often have a great deal to do with one another—they are mutually supportive. As noble forms of courage depend upon a commitment to things which matter most over those which matter least, so humility is also a gauge of perspective. Courage requires us to prioritize and humility helps us to know how, and so the two values are related.

Many understand humility to mean lowliness, or submission—these words are listed as synonyms for humility in many dictionaries. While such qualities can be noble, they can also be cowardly and weak, and depend upon context. To be counted as a *virtue*, humility must ultimately empower the person who employs it. Therefore, a better definition of humility may be *courageous insight, or the willingness and ability to perceive, accept, and when required, act upon what is true but personally challenging.*

A person of worthy character understands her great potential, but is simultaneously capable of knowing her present limitations, however temporary they may be. The Christian Bible states: "And you will know the truth, and the truth will set you free." An arrogant person is more in love with fantasy than reality. Such people are ultimately delusional and self-defeating because of their selfish desires and motives. There is a great freedom to humility because, at its core, it embraces truth wherever it is found, however frustrating it might feel in the moment.

Humility is an often-underrated virtue because it is so commonly associated with weakness. The secret you can carry away from this chapter is that humility is one of the few real cores of strength a person can possess, and it is integral to character. Humility is also one of the most powerful talents we can have for keeping ourselves and others safe. It banishes self-defeating influences like ego and bias, helping us to think and feel clearly. It also comforts because it confirms a commonality to all living things rather than drawing contrast. And it is open to self-improvement without engaging in a personal sense of competition with others.

A humble person values truth for its own sake before selfish agenda, and resists being offended by truth in any form. As my husband likes to say, "Truth is always user-friendly." While it is often a heavy thing, carrying it regularly will build strength of character.

Honor

Honor takes courage and humility. It will be next to impossible to find an honorable person who is not also humble and courageous. Simply stated: honor is consistency in correct action and includes virtues like honesty and an individual sense of personal responsibility. Sooner or later, honor eventually becomes reputation.

We value honor because it promises dependability and a measure of safety. These things generate trust and encourage you to be close to other honorable people. You can allow them to see your vulnerability and you can let them help you. If you can find a person you can trust, you will acquire a potential solution to loneliness. And if you can find many, you will be rich in a way money can't buy.

Honesty is a necessary part of honor and is essential for relationships. This makes it a central part of an enduring marriage. Whether they are professional, platonic, familial, or romantic, relationships need trust, and so they require honesty.

But we cannot simply communicate everything that crosses our minds or divulge everything that happens to us to everyone we're close to. There wouldn't be time for much else in life if we had to share everything, and some things are best kept private. Honesty is not necessarily *candor*, which is simply speaking one's mind without thought or consideration of impact. Candor is overrated.

Virtuous honesty should be centered on actions which are uplifting. So many people say, "I'm just being honest," like speaking thoughtlessly is being true to yourself and should never require apology. This behavior is often just an excuse for rudeness.

Knowing when to speak, and what and how much to say, are marks of high wisdom. It takes a shrewd eye to understand the needs and sensitivities of relationships, especially in the delicate context of romance. But honesty compels us to say certain things, at times even though they may hurt or cause disorientation. You may be attached to someone who is acting in a self-destructive way, or you may have an opportunity to make a significant difference in the lives of people in great need simply by speaking up. Honesty is tied to courage and humility when life thrusts us on to the center stage of important events, and honor compels us at times to be bold in action and in word.

We must practice courage and humility when making such judgments of ourselves and others, but we will tend to do well if love permeates our thoughts and actions. Exercising humility will help us repair damage when we say too little or too much.

Charity

Charity is love in action, which can require courage at times, especially when a cause seems hopeless. It walks hand-in-hand with humility, and a person who practices it regularly will develop great honor.

Charity flows from the love we cultivate for friends, family, community, and all humankind. Its twin enemies are selfishness and apathy. Without charity, there could be no lasting unions. Charity mends and uplifts broken relationships and broken people. When it is channeled, it is a means of distribution with almost limitless potential to alleviate human suffering. Many courageous men and women who have devoted their lives to charity have changed the world, like Mother Teresa, Albert Schweitzer, Princess Diana, and Mahatma Gandhi.

Charity may be an expression of generosity, but it can also include mercy in the form of forgiveness or forbearance. When we forgive someone of their wrongs, we potentially repair and uplift. We give encouragement to another that, despite their weakness, there is hope. When we advocate mercy on behalf of another, we encourage others to see value in all life. We promote caution in judgment and the perspective that though we cannot change others, we can always change ourselves. And when we are merciful, we refine our souls.

Charity can be shown through ambitious endeavors, but it can also have a powerful effect in the form of small acts of kindness. A charitable organization called Random Acts was founded in response to the 2010 earthquake in Haiti. They started an initiative to encourage *random acts of kindness* throughout the world, and it has become a global viral phenomenon.

See randomactsofkindness.org for lists of little acts you can engage in to make the world a better place. This website has lists of things you can do for strangers, friends and family, and things you can do in public places and even for special groups like the elderly or animals. The ideas range in degrees of simplicity and creativity, and most of them will cost you little to nothing. The idea behind random acts of kindness is that the world is changed one person at a time, one act at a time. It's about uniting people in a perspective that each person's choices matter.

Everyone is empowered to make a difference, and small acts make a big difference in the world when many people engage in them. You will be amazed at how energizing and upstairs such acts can be, how they can change your day and even your whole life, as well as those of others.

Good men notice acts of kindness. It has an influence in their lives and the way they feel about us. Women tend to excel at this virtue and men are drawn to those of us who are feminine and caring.

Self-Restraint

A person of worthy character also seeks to control her less than noble impulses. Life and the downstairs portions of our minds relentlessly urge a potentially all-consuming sense of danger and corresponding need for both *immediate* and *equivalent* comfort and reassurance. To become a person of great character, we must escape the pull of our downstairs minds and find a way to live in a more balanced and uplifted state. We must make our upstairs minds our focus and manage our downstairs tendencies.

Pleasures and ease make for a comfortable life, but they severely limit us when they constitute our greatest desires and actions. Too much of even a very good thing can often lead to a pleasure-obsessed life. And the same applies to excess comfort. We do not make much progress, and mental balance cannot easily be achieved or maintained, in the prolonged absence of at least a little stress. Sometimes losing some comforts can reset our gratitude. And as we know, gratitude gets you back upstairs. Seeking pleasure unceasingly is a very downstairs mentality.

People who live impulsively tend to wait for things to happen to them rather than take responsibility and make big plans. They would perhaps like to improve but either don't believe they can or find it hard to conceive of working hard to earn it. They will also tend to believe that life is unfair because things don't come easy, and they live their lives with a sense of victimhood, helplessness, and hopelessness. Self-control teaches you to live a deliberate life with the long-term in mind and tends to maximize your potential, rather than minimize it.

The challenge we all face is to evolve beyond a sense of merely surviving and to live an intentional life. This includes creating and fostering loving relationships with our husbands, our children, and all those we know.

Self-Improvement

Change begins with you, but it radiates outward from you and has the potential to uplift and inspire those around you.

People of great character are constantly engaged in efforts of self-improvement because they believe in their limitless potential and understand the effect it has on others. They do so because they have love and hope, and a vision for the future. They are guided by the faith that one person can have a meaningful impact, and that this is worthwhile, even if their impact is never officially recognized or celebrated.

With courage, humility, honor, charity and self-discipline, you will constantly seek progress for yourself and others because you are connected to each other. You will have respect for life and relationships and you guard them carefully, in every way that you can. You see opportunities to beautify and repair constantly, and so you maintain a consistent sense of progress and satisfaction in life. This gives your life a steady and happy rhythm which others will be inspired to follow.

Character in Romantic Relationships

Good men find a feminine woman of character irresistible. She inspires him to be better. Knowing this, you can be the great catalyst for change in your life and those with whom you come in contact. Your man will respond to your character if he has any intention of living a meaningful life.

If you are beautiful, charming, and feminine, but lack moral fiber, you won't find and keep what you are truly looking for. With character, you will have self-confidence and esteem. This won't guarantee success on preconceived terms, but your risk will be minimized, and you will tend to attract — and be attracted to — a man who has the potential for a lifelong love affair.

Tia, Jane, and Jerome

Tia was a beautiful girl from a wealthy family and could afford the best life had to offer. Jane was also beautiful in her own way but was from a poor family and was raised by her grandmother.

Tia and Jane worked for the same employer, the mother of a young, rich and handsome doctor, Jerome. He had occasion to visit the place of employment and meet both girls. Tia fell in love with Jerome and the two dated for a time.

Jerome also got to know Jane and was initially impressed with her kindness to everyone, including strangers. As time passed, he witnessed further evidence of her worthy character.

The two became friends, but at first Jane was not romantically interested in Jerome because she witnessed some shallowness in his behavior.

As Jerome and Tia got to know each other, he began to see that Tia was shallow and even mean to people. Though she was very beautiful and sophisticated, she was also highly self-centered. Tia's lack of character highlighted Jane's abundance of it. Jerome eventually fell in love with Jane, who inspired him to develop his own character to be worthy of her affections. Happily, she also fell in love with Jerome when she got to see what a great man he could be.

This story is meant to illustrate the importance of character in winning a man who also possesses at least the potential for it. It also shows how a woman of worthy character inspires the same in good men who aspire to be with her.

Some men go for the woman with greater presentation. In terms of character, like tends to attract like. When a fascinating woman has character, she will attract men of high quality and become irresistible to them.

Happiness vs Pleasure

Are you consistently happy?

It is important to contemplate what motivates you, what you spend your time searching for. Is it short-term pleasure or long-term happiness? How disciplined is your ability to delay gratification for larger goals? Do you find yourself constantly compelled to seek little highs in order to get through the day? Through the hour? Or do you find yourself relatively calm and steady?

Happiness and pleasure often get confused for one another. The body chemistry can feel similar, but happiness is much more enduring.

For me, pleasure is eating a warm apple fritter doughnut when I am extremely hungry. But it doesn't bring me happiness, especially the next morning when I wake up and weigh myself. Then I experience regret.

In contrast, happiness is the by-product of living a life of character. It springs from one's personal sense of growth and accomplishment, but also from the ever-expanding connection we feel to all life. As our self-definition expands, so does our joy, while our fear and loneliness recede to a half-forgotten memory.

The Importance of Learning to be Happy

Happiness can make anyone more attractive. It's basically a skill which you can practice and master. Marilyn Monroe, the late Hollywood film star said, "A smile is the best makeup any girl can wear."

Though we must all deal with hardship and grief in life, living a life of character will help you to keep your chin up. It will instill hope for the future and teach you to smile again. And when the going really gets tough, remember there are people to help, tears to dry, and service to give all around you. Getting involved with helping others will have a positive side effect of making you happy as well. And people will love being around you.

Kristine

My sister Kristine has always been a great example of someone who prefers to stay upstairs and is there most of the time. She gave birth to and raised 9 children and has a wonderful husband. With that much going on in her life, she's been through a lot. But she has an ability to put things in perspective quickly. She can change her mental state by what she chooses to focus on. I've seen her go through a particularly stressful event, only to bounce back, telling me something she's grateful for or what she has learned from her experience. All her siblings know and appreciate this about her, and I know her husband Steve does too. He gets to live with a loving upstairs lady every day.

How Character Affects Appearance

A person's character, or lack of it, can have a profound effect on appearance. The chemistry that your body produces has a very real effect on the body, just like the impact of what you consume. Negative thinking produces negative chemistry.

Too much time spent with an excess of the stress chemical cortisol, for instance, diminishes the immune system and promotes premature aging. Consider negativity as something akin to having a bad smoking or drinking habit. I know many people who are very careful about their diet and exercise but spend most of their lives fretting and anxious. Your health regimen is not complete if it does not include character.

On the other hand, positive emotions that come from developing character promote copious amounts of positive body chemistry such as natural dopamine, endorphins, serotonin, and oxytocin. These can do wonders for your health. If you are cautious in what you consume, you should also think about mental and emotional self-management. Consider building a life of character as a very natural complement to going to the gym regularly.

Developing good character will lead to happiness not only for you but will promote the marriage and relationships of your dreams. Your self-confidence will grow, and you will be lovelier to others than you ever thought possible.

In Summary:

- Being a person of good character will attract and inspire the love of a good man.
- Character is something you can and must build yourself.
- Though women can be courageous in many areas, we particularly excel in moral courage.
- Humility is one of the real cores of strength a woman can possess and is integral to our character.
- Self-restraint and self-improvement are hallmarks of a woman of good character.
- Good men find women of good character irresistible.

- Happiness and pleasure often get confused for one another. The body chemistry can feel similar, but happiness is much more enduring.

- Happiness makes anyone look more attractive. It is a skill you can practice and master.

- Character can affect your appearance. Developing your own good character will lead to happiness and will promote a marriage you always dreamed of. As you become a better person, you will be lovelier than you thought possible — in spite of age or natural beauty.

Chapter 19
Boundaries

Everyone has a sense of personal boundaries, or the guidelines and rules by which we determine what is safe and reasonable behavior for ourselves and others. Our boundaries are an important basis for our identities because they form the core of our own values and the example of what we present to the world. They also help us determine what is normal behavior in *others*, and this is how we sort people out quickly in social situations and how we safely navigate relationships. When the temptation to do something self-serving at another person's expense arises, our sense of boundaries — or our sense of acceptable behavior in ourselves — becomes relevant.

We will likely have a different set of boundaries with strangers, family, and romantic partners. And sometimes boundaries evolve over time. Our boundaries with ourselves also evolve, and this can relate to character, or how much we actually live by the guidelines and rules we place on others.

You may know people who pride themselves on always speaking their mind. They're just "being real", and when they have a big opinion about politics or clothes you're wearing, they can't help themselves and they see it as a sort of virtue. But what if you have an opinion that contradicts theirs or is not perfectly flattering? Suddenly 'being real' isn't a virtue, it's rude. This is a person with different boundaries for others than they have for themselves, and people like this are often viewed as having a problem with character.

Our sense of boundaries can come from diverse influences such as culture, community, family, education, and various social exposures, and is often at least partly formed by the sense of boundaries others place on us. But ultimately, we decide what our boundaries are for ourselves and others. They are an important key to personal happiness and self-esteem, and they are vital to achieving and maintaining successful relationships.

Boundary issues can be one of the most challenging areas of relationships because when you assault a boundary, you assault the person. And it's difficult when different expectations and perspectives collide. In marriage, there will be a period where husband and wife learn about and make adjustments for the differences in each other's boundaries. For example:

Oh Hello

A newly married couple was just learning how to live together. One day, the wife, Joy, ran into an old friend from college and they decided to go to lunch. She was surprised by how much he had matured, and he was surprisingly handsome. Joy's husband Bart called her and wanted to take her out for something to eat.

Joy said she was already having lunch with a "friend," preferring to remain vague.

A male co-worker then called Bart and asked him to celebrate his new promotion by joining him at a restaurant. No problem. Joy was busy anyway.

As luck would have it, both Joy and Bart ended up at the same restaurant at the same time. When Bart saw her from a distance with a handsome man, he was shocked and felt betrayed. He went over to their table and greeted them. Joy seemed a little embarrassed and introduced Bart as her husband. The friend responded, "You are married?" She hadn't told him. This bothered Bart too.

Later, Bart confronted Joy, who minimized the incident saying he was just an old friend and there was nothing to worry about. Bart was still hurt.

Joy was not clear with her husband or the friend from college because she wanted to pretend she was single for a while. She enjoyed the attention and thought she could get away with it. If the tables were turned, Joy would not have appreciated the situation any more than her husband. Deep down, she knew this, but she did not behave in a way that was consistent with her own boundaries or her husband's. She was embarrassed because she knew what the situation looked like. Adding up, first, her presence with the handsome stranger, second, his surprise at hearing she was married, and third, her omission to her husband, made it look like she was not faithful to either of them. All three ended up embarrassed and trust was undermined for all.

If Joy had stayed true to the mutual boundaries of her marriage and invited her husband to join her with the handsome school friend, Bart probably wouldn't have thought anything of the encounter, and nobody would have felt compromised. The relationship would have been defended from a potentially hurtful event and doing so would have reaffirmed trust.

People earn trust by actively and consistently protecting the feelings of others while maintaining their own basic boundaries. If they are not maintained, boundaries will constantly be pushed, and the relationship could be seriously undermined.

Doilies

Viktor just bought Anna her first new car. She'd had vehicles before, but they were always older and had a lot of miles on them. Victor had his own car, but soon after buying Anna's, he started to ask if he could borrow hers for various reasons. She adored Viktor, but he kept his car rather neglected. He threw stuff over his shoulder all the time while he was driving: old papers, cups, and water bottles.

Anna did not want her brand-new car cluttered, but she didn't want to hurt Viktor's feelings. She also wanted to add feminine touches to her new car. So, she pinned doilies on the head rests of each seat and found pretty mats for the floor. She enjoyed driving around in her new feminine car.

One day, Viktor asked Anna if he could borrow her car to run to the bank. His car needed a few minor repairs and he had put off getting them done. She said: "Of course," but worried how it might look when she got it back. When Viktor came back, he looked very frustrated and announced: "I'll never drive your car again!" She asked why, having no idea what happened. He said with a grin: "You should have seen the way the tellers looked at me when I drove up to the bank with those doilies. I'll never do that again." The next day he took his car in, got it fixed, and never again borrowed Anna's car.

Some may critique the above example as passive-aggressive. Anna avoided a potentially hurtful encounter with Viktor through her already established feminine nature and girly touches to her car. She also accepted her husband at face value. She sincerely wanted to let him borrow her car if it made his life easier, even though it caused some small anxiety for her—which ended up being quickly and smoothly resolved.

Special Issues: Venting

Women love to think out-loud. My husband and I refer to this as "verbal processing." Women often have a need to talk things out more than men do. As women, talking about what happened and how we feel about it is a way for us to organize complex thoughts. However, we sometimes find ourselves speed-talking in a way that is insensitive to our husband's needs.

Sometimes when you're venting, if a man doesn't know what you are doing, he might think he's being personally attacked, even when that's not your intent. Or he might think you want him to take action and solve a problem, while you just want to process. But you need to feel heard and understood, right? Making sure your husband or boyfriend understands beforehand why you need to vent can make a difference in whether or not he realizes you are just processing and not upset with him. Next time you have a lot of pent-up emotion you need to express, try saying something like: "Can I vent about something? Is this a good time? I just need you to listen, I don't need you to do anything else."

Getting the Right Balance

Your ability to perceive others' boundaries will be important to acquiring and keeping good relations with them. You will also need boundaries for yourself, and it takes time and experience to learn what boundaries provide the right combination of protection and vulnerability in a relationship. This is true of friendships, dating, and marriage. Relationships need trust, but they take time to perfect, and you will need to guard some of your feelings during that time of discovery and adjustment. Don't be frustrated with missteps, just choose to learn from them.

The most effective sorts of boundaries require a degree of self-awareness, a desire for the happiness of others, and some courage. Relationship repair is a sort of ritual all healthy associations engage in, because minor damage along the journey is to be expected. If these incidences are not dealt with as they come, pressure mounts until it explodes. The daily practice validates and strengthens the relationship.

Women are often the most powerful influence for men in learning self-consciousness. Men tend to be objective, task-oriented, and therefore oblivious — to some extent — to the impact of their words and behavior and the effects of their insensitivity. When a man marries, in order to maintain the relationship he must respond and adjust to frequent cues from his wife. She will need to respond to his feedback regarding his boundaries as well. Look for little cues such as a smile or eye contact when something is pleasing, or a frown or avoidance when something is not. We might sigh, hunch our shoulders, shudder, jump up and pace, gesture energetically with hands, laugh, or initiate physical contact. We are often not aware of how much reward and punishment we provide in the context of even daily communication.

You can learn to tell if your man is either displeased or distracted. If he is engaged, his eye contact will be good. He might even learn forward as you talk and ask for more clarification.

If he is bored or maybe isn't comfortable with the conversation, he might just be ill-at-ease because he isn't in touch with his own feelings. He might change the subject, start looking at his phone, get visibly angry, or even leave the room. Men sometimes become a bit weary with our need to explain things in more detail than they would, which can make us feel like they aren't interested in what we are saying. Micro-expressions such as a very brief frown, smile, raised eyebrow can give valuable cues to his emotional state. So can the warmth of his voice or the amount of words he uses, if he looks away from you while talking, or twists his body away from you. When you make it a priority, you will observe many such simple feedback prompts and they will provide a roadmap for you to make adjustments and work together towards building intimacy.

In Summary:

- Everyone has a sense of personal boundaries, or the guidelines and rules by which we determine what is safe and reasonable behavior for ourselves and others.

- Our boundaries are an important basis for our identities because they form the core of our own values and the example of what we present to the world.

- They also help us determine what is normal behavior in others, and this is how we sort people out quickly in social situations and how we safely navigate relationships.

- When the temptation to do something self-serving at another person's expense arises, our sense of boundaries — or our sense of acceptable behavior in ourselves — becomes relevant.

- The most effective sorts of boundaries require a degree of self-awareness, a desire for the happiness of others, and some courage.

- Relationship repair is a sort of ritual all healthy associations engage in, because minor damage along the journey is to be expected.

- If these incidences are not dealt with as they come, pressure mounts until it explodes. The daily practice validates and strengthens the relationship.

- Relationships require constant and mutual training through feedback and adjustment, and we only learn through this process if we have some humility in accepting corrective cues.

Chapter 20

Girlishness

The original Fascinating Womanhood taught the principle of *childlikeness*. It is described as "extreme girlishness" and "the charming qualities of a little girl." The idea is a powerful one and it has helped a lot of relationships, as gauged by the many success stories we have received and by the testimonials of women we've witnessed over the years. But there has also been a fair amount of confusion surrounding the topic.

The trouble with this term is that it contains the word *child* and it sounds a lot like *childishness*. Some use the two words interchangeably, and it has been supposed by critics of Fascinating Womanhood that we teach women to be weak, ignorant, or to feign helplessness to affect a certain set of behaviors from the men in our lives—that the principle is either invalidating, immature, or corrupting of women. The truth is that childlikeness is not an exclusively feminine trait and it can be good or bad, depending on how it is employed.

Like with charm or admiration, intent determines the value and overall effect of behavior. To give a gift without strings attached is generous. To grant favor in *order to obligate* is manipulation. The difference is in the motivation: selflessness versus selfishness. Childlikeness, more than any other principle in Fascinating Womanhood, has great potential to become manipulation if its intent is not clear with the practitioner. As a branch of charm, it can be used to uplift but also to demean, to strengthen or weaken a relationship.

At its core, the Fascinating Womanhood principle of childlikeness is *a willingness to show sincere innocence and vulnerability with a twist of humor for an unselfishly beneficial purpose.* That purpose is usually to diffuse tension in a relationship and it requires a careful touch to be effective. It is a playful way of behaving that can be attractive, and it has the potential to renew and also strengthen romantic feelings in your marriage. Childlikeness includes not only ways of expressing anger and hurt, but also endearing ways to ask for things, playfully expressing vulnerability and trust, showing a continual sense of newness, and a joyful delight in life.

With women, the principle of childlikeness takes the form of *girlishness* and its particular flavor is endearing to *good* men, encouraging their natural masculinity. This is a term I prefer over childlikeness because it applies specifically to women. It includes distracting a man from tension through the expression of childlike trust, appreciation, or displeasure. It is a wonderful expression of feminine power because it is uplifting and subtly assertive, but not aggressive.

Men can sometimes practice a male version we might call *boyishness*. When it is done in an immature or selfish way, it looks just as childish as it is for women. If the focus is not relationship-building, but rather the pursuit of private agenda or control, it's just a type of manipulation and won't work for long. But when the purpose is to build trust and intimacy, and when the timing and situation is right, it can be remarkably effective for either gender to awaken the best in a romantic partner.

There are those who are naturally gifted with girlishness, and others who need to learn and practice it as a new skill. This can take time and some trial and error. There are different ways to practice this timeless art, and I like to think of them in girlish terms of: (1) Exaggeration, (2) Distraction, (3) Appreciation, (4) Trust, and (5) Asking for Things.

It should be stated before we go much further, and it will be repeated later by necessity, that girlishness in any form is not right for truly hurtful situations where abuse, serious betrayal, or deeply destructive behavior is involved. It is a playful art grounded in humor and trust and cannot therefore have anything but a negative effect where such critical elements are absent. Professional help should be sought in these cases.

Girlish Displeasure and Exaggeration

Girlish exaggeration is a mild form of confrontation. Women sometimes need to confront men in a relationship because we occasionally get hurt, annoyed, or angry in the natural course of things due to his grouchiness, thoughtlessness, and his taking us for granted. Such situations can breed tension and conflict which, if it escalates further, can seriously damage the relationship. These are critical relationship moments where dark clouds have gathered, but there is still time to avoid a storm and strengthen the relationship.

Whose Fault?

When such situations arise, always take a moment to look inward and consider whether you or he, or both, are at fault in a tense situation. Start with yourself. Were you downstairs: tired, scared, or not feeling well? If so, the issue may have started with you, and further expressions of your source of stress may only escalate the issue. You may hold the keys to unraveling the whole problem with a simple apology, or an acknowledgement of his feelings and your mistakes.

If it really is him who has acted poorly, it may also be that he is unaware of his feelings or the impact of his behavior around you in that moment, and if he is a fair man he probably did not mean to hurt you. He may be in a temporary downstairs frame of mind and simply need help to get back upstairs. This is the golden opportunity in which you may be able to help the higher, more genuine man within wake up with an artful display of girlishness.

Here are some examples of girlish exaggeration:

Approach #1: Exaggeration of *Words* or *Manner*

To diffuse a mild or moderately tense situation, display your emotions in a girlish and exaggerated way. Direct words at him which emphasize his masculinity such as *big, tough, brute, hairy, bully, beast,* or *stubborn.* If these don't suit your personality, you can think of others that fit for you. It will help if the terms are gently accusative, but ultimately should be more magnifying than diminishing. The idea is to refer to him in such a way that highlights his masculinity, suggesting strength in his behavior even if that strength is being used in a negative way. Avoid using adjectives that are in any way belittling, and therefore a challenge to his masculinity, such as stupid, dumb, weak, lazy, little, pipsqueak, or anything else that might decrease his manly stature in his or your eyes.

A Giant Example

In the 1956 movie Giant (starring Rock Hudson, Elizabeth Taylor, and James Dean), there is a scene where Elizabeth Taylor's character Leslie is told by her husband that she and other women present are not welcome to participate in a political discussion, explaining in a somewhat condescending way that it was "men's talk" and "boring." Leslie is surprised and mildly offended because she was raised on the East Coast of the United States, near the capital, and was used to being included in political discussions.

After a gentle attempt to insert herself in to the conversation, her husband tells her curtly that she is "tired" and that she should say goodnight. She responds with a speech that accuses all the men present of "dating back at least 100,000 years" in their treatment of women. She then marches off to bed with her head held high.

Much later that night, her husband comes in the room to find Leslie asleep. He is still very upset and loudly takes off his boots, throws them on the floor, and stomps around the bedroom. Leslie wakes up and immediately apologizes for her "caveman speech" from earlier. Her husband responds with a tirade of how terrible her behavior has been.

Now, here is where we have that golden opportunity we just talked about, when the use of girlishness is a perfect way to save the situation. Notice how Leslie chooses to react to being bawled out.

She responds with a girlish pout: "Honestly, you make me sound just awful! You knew what a dreadful girl I was when you married me. I did not deceive you sir!" Then she adds gently and with a touch of humor: "Besides, you love me very much." At this, she delicately picks off a bit of fuzz from the blanket and flicks it carelessly.

Her exaggerated but sincere girlish vulnerability, along with trust in his good nature—and with a touch of playful levity— disarms her husband completely and in an instant. They end up spending the rest of the night in a loving embrace.

What Might Have Happened Without the Use of Girlish Exaggeration?

Let's look at what might have happened if Leslie had done what many women do.

We often react to a perceived offense with defensiveness. Her husband insulted her intelligence and social relevance in front of his male friends, and then in turn, disregarded her apology. If she had justifiably renewed her defense of a woman's right to discuss politics, the whole thing would have escalated further, possibly into a name-calling shouting match. Both would have gotten even angrier than they already were, and this could have led to long-lasting bitterness, resentfulness, and even a loss of trust in the relationship. Instead of spending the night in each other's arms, her husband would have probably slept in another room.

Instead of defending her position intellectually, Leslie expressed playful and slightly humorous defiance and self-deprecation with love. It's doubtful she really sees herself as an awful person, but this was not the response her husband expected. The quick addition of her confidence in his love for her melted him. The lint flicking showed a playful and innocent mood and gave him a little time to respond. Because this was not yet a serious situation, and because she knew him well, it worked like magic.

Another successful example of girlish exaggeration was submitted by a fan of Fascinating Womanhood:

Burnt Spaghetti

One evening, during a discussion between a married couple, the husband referred casually to a woman his wife's same age as "an older woman." His wife took offense and shot back with: "She's my age! You think I'm old! You meanie!"

She then walked away in an exaggerated huff, though honestly a little ruffled at the comment, and pretended to clean a neighboring room. The husband was getting ready for work during the conversation and needed to go, so he followed her to the next room to kiss her goodbye, hoping to apologize for hurting her feelings.

As he was leaning in, she responded with: "You don't want to kiss an 'older woman!' I should have burnt your breakfast burrito, you brute!" She added a stomp of her foot.

He smiled and tried to pinch her. That's when she knew it was working. She tossed her hair, stepped back playfully from his pinches, and said: "I think I'll just burn your spaghetti tonight, you hairy beast!" He was giggling at this point and reached playfully for her in a way that made her feel anything but old. Spanking him as he turned to go, she told him he'd better get to work. He gave her a look of parting that said he was looking forward to coming home as soon as he could.

Benefits of Her Childlike Response

The wife took a thoughtless comment and turned it in to a playful lesson that diffused tension and increased chemistry in the relationship. The husband got the point and learned from the exchange but was amused and aroused rather than belittled. She was rewarded with a confirmation that he still found her attractive. Together, they turned a potential fight in to a romantic and positive memory.

Out of the Mouth of Babes

You can also learn how charming girlishness can be by observing it in small children. It's easy to see their lack of sarcasm and bitterness when they are offended, and you can also note how they don't tend to carry grudges.

We Wear Bows in Our Hair!

My niece Sarah has identical twin daughters, Daisy and Violet, age 4 at the time of this story. They are very girly and constant adorable stories about them circulate through the family.

One day, a boy their age confronted one of the twins, Daisy. He informed her she didn't look like she was 4 years old—the girls were small for their age. She insisted she was indeed that age and the boy's mother confirmed the fact and told him to leave her alone. The boy then said to her: "I bet I could beat you up!" Daisy replied with unimpressed disdain: "We don't do things like that! We wear BOWS in our hair!" She then raised her head high and stalked off with the dignity of a queen.

This girlish response left the little boy speechless and disarmed.

To Daisy, it was an attack on her femininity to assume she would want to engage in a physical fight. This charming story delighted everyone who heard it, especially the men in the family.

Approach #2: *Reflect His Treatment of You* in an Exaggerated Way

This technique is similar to the first, but its focus is for you to turn yourself in to a sort of mirror of his behavior in an effort to awaken his self-awareness. Rather than copying his behavior, you should indicate in an exaggerated manner what it is like to receive his ill-considered or callous treatment. Try using phrases like: "How could a great big man like you pick on a helpless girl like me?" or, "So this is the way you treat a little, defenseless woman!" or, "Oh, what a dreadful thing to do!" Remember here that we target the behavior and not the man in a personal way, suggesting that he simply had a lapse in judgment.

You might also make exaggerated and feeble threats such as, "I'll never be nice to you again," or "I'll tell your mother on you." It is often helpful to add a playful smile or wink, so he knows you're not deeply offended or childish. The manner with which you employ such a tactic should fit your personality and come across as natural. Responses will come to you when you tune in to your innocent nature and practice a bit.

Girlish Distraction

Sometimes confrontation does not fit a situation. In these cases, it may be helpful to redirect the energy of a situation by drawing attention away to something innocuous or even humorous. Girlish distraction invites him to be more self-aware and to change his focus to decrease tension.

Backseat Driving

Jill's husband Greg often fell into the habit of giving unwanted advice while she was driving and he was a passenger. He was a classic backseat driver and Jill grew tired of it. She decided to use girlishness to diffuse the situation and introduce more charm into their relationship.

As Jill was trying to merge into highway traffic, Greg told her: "You can make it now if you hurry up. GO!" She replied: "It scares me to go fast like that right now. Can I help it if my feet are smaller than yours?" Then she just looked at him with head lowered from under her lashes.

Her statement was purposefully ridiculous: size of feet has nothing to do with merging quickly into traffic or pressing on the gas pedal. But he got the message that she didn't feel comfortable driving exactly the way he did, and that she found him very masculine with his implied "big feet." He was distracted and charmed at the same time.

Tough as Shoe Leather

Natalia hadn't been married very long to Sam. His mother was a good cook, but as he was growing up, she encouraged her children to tell her when a dish wasn't tasty, insisting she appreciated the honest feedback. Natalia came from a totally

317

different home where complaining about the cooking was considered disrespectful to the chef. When Natalia made pork chops for the first time for Sam, she accidentally over-cooked them and Sam remarked: "These are so tough they taste like shoe leather!"

Natalia didn't appreciate this insensitive comment but rather than confront Sam, she decided to redirect the conversation, saying with a wink and an ironic smile, "Yeah, I cooked it that way as a subtle message that you shouldn't leave your big dirty shoes laying around the house all the time. Clever, huh?" As she suspected, he got the double meaning that his comment was also quite invalidating to her efforts to please him. He was delighted at her soft touch and sense of humor, and the respect she maintained for him despite his insensitivity — something Sam was able to perceive because, after all, he was a good man. She invited the conversation to go in a lighter direction, but also encouraged him to consider his own behavior, and she did it in a way that preserved trust and affection in the relationship. He even ate his shoe-leather dinner with apologetic gusto.

She might have responded with resentment and hurt feelings, perhaps even with the intention of teaching him a lesson and laying some boundaries, and this might have even worked but it would not have deepened the relationship. It might also have escalated a mildly tense situation into a full-blown argument with hurt feelings. Natalia made a fast and insightful choice that Sam really didn't mean to hurt her and that she could use girlishness to gently inspire his better nature.

Approach #3: Girlish Appreciation

It is in the basic nature of all good men to enjoy giving gifts and doing thoughtful things for the women in their lives. And women reciprocate such expressions of love through charm. Responding with exaggerated grace, charm, and gratitude is another way to practice girlishness. It can fortify and renew romantic feelings. The key is to express sincere thankfulness with femininity and exaggerated excitement. This is a huge motivation and reward for men, and it will encourage intense love and devotion.

Easily Overjoyed

Ginger's husband surprised her with tickets for a romantic vacation in Hawaii. She responded with wide eyes, throwing her arms around him, and exclaimed: "Oh, William, are we really going? I can hardly believe it! You are so generous and thoughtful!"

Some women may forget to show gratitude, remarking that she needs to get a new bathing suit or that she should have been consulted first, because of her busy schedule. This is always a missed opportunity in any relationship, because gratitude is vital for maintaining romance.

Another time William noticed Ginger was not feeling well. It was midnight and he was already dressed for bed. When she admitted she had a sore throat he immediately offered: "Would you like me to go to the drugstore and get you some medicine? I don't mind at all." She protested saying it was late and she didn't want to think of him going out in the cold. He insisted saying he would happily make the trip. She responded by saying: "You are so kind to do that for me, especially at this hour. What would I do without you?" She was concerned about his well-being and health but also recognized his need to take care of her. She understood the art of receiving too.

Ginger's style works because it builds from sincere appreciation, and this stems from her humble and loving perspective of William. Pretending to be overjoyed is more likely to come off as cynical or back-handed. She plays up real emotions for William's benefit, somewhat like turning up the volume on good music. As you get to know the love of your life, you will acquire a greater sense of what makes him feel appreciated. If you keep his joy at the center of your motivations, you will make him feel like the luckiest man alive.

Approach #4: Girlish Trust

Girlish trust means believing in his intentions toward you—faith he will keep his word and be honest with you.

In a healthy relationship, expressing girlish trust is important to your romantic relationship. This trust means you are unwilling to easily believe he would do anything to betray it. It means you believe in him as a man, in his intelligence and ability to solve problems. Of course, he is human and will make mistakes. But when these infractions are not serious and can be repaired, basic trust is preserved.

It's a mistake to try to instruct your husband on things he is supposed to know more about than you. For example: if he is a welder, you shouldn't give him advice on his work unless he specifically asks for your thoughts. Just trust him. We don't appreciate unsolicited advice and neither does he.

If your husband or boyfriend gets lost while driving, let him figure it out, even if backtracking is necessary, rather than giving him unwanted advice. He will ask if he wants help.

When you trust him, don't expect perfection; you won't find it. Your main trust is in the *intent of his heart*, not his day to day decisions or actions. Men need respect from the world and they work hard for it, but they especially need it at home where they go to recuperate. This kind of feminine respect is a huge motivator for a man. He will work twice his normal capacity to avoid disappointing a good woman who believes in him. And he'll be almost physically incapable of denying her anything she asks, if he can grant it.

On the other hand, he'll drag his feet and act resentful if she criticizes a lot or puts him down. He may even try to get even or find comfort and respect elsewhere.

The Dreamer

There was a man who loved to invest in various businesses and ideas. He was a dreamer and longed to be financially successful and do more than teach school, which was his profession. He sometimes invested in projects that, to his practical wife, were foolish. Perhaps they were at times. Once he invested in a 3-wheeled car franchise that didn't succeed. To most of his family, the whole idea looked ridiculous.

Another time he tried to run for local public office and was not elected. His wife was embarrassed by his sometimes-unprofitable attempts that failed. Over time, she realized she needed to learn to appreciate his heart, which was to never stop trying to provide for and impress her. She began to trust him in a girlish way. He never became wealthy, but they lived comfortably and in their later years were very close because there was so much trust and affection.

If you are in a committed relationship and make a mistake by expressing lack of trust in him, don't be hard on yourself. Minor everyday infractions can be repaired and trust renewed. Developing girlishness is a learnable skill.

Approach #5: How to Ask for Things with Girlishness

Learning how to appropriately and successfully ask for things you need is a crucial life skill. When you are in any kind of relationship, whether at work, with friends, or most importantly with your husband, you will sometimes need to make requests. It doesn't matter if you are both employed, make great incomes and consider each other equal partners. What you want might cost money, it might not. You may need a favor or just some time to pour your heart out to him.

The best way to ask for anything is to speak up in a feminine way. Be upfront, sincere and specific, but also be girlish. Say something like: "I'd love to...." Or, "Could we...?" You might also try: "Know what I really need? It's..." or, "Do you think we could...?"

When I was growing up and on road trips with the family, we sometimes got hungry on long stretches and were nervous to ask our father if we could stop and get something to eat. We were taught not to be cheeky. Our answer was to get our little sister, who was much younger, to ask for us. Dad would almost always say yes. Looking back, I realize it was the way she asked, not her age that made him want to accommodate. She would just say "Dad, I'm hungry. Can we get a hamburger?" She not only asked him sweetly, but she was specific about what she wanted. She didn't make him figure it out. He would usually smile because he was charmed.

The Problem with Hinting

Why do we hint for things? In our own minds, it seems to soften the blow of what we want—it is meant to feel less aggressive and assuming. Hinting makes us feel less selfish, and we feel more protected from vulnerability if what we desire is met with rejection.

Stop hoping for men to be mind-readers. No one really is, but men tend to be particularly tone deaf to hinting. They usually don't even know we've hinted for something, or they misunderstand it. They would much rather we spare them the intrigue and just ask. Be a little outspoken in a feminine way and drop the hinting in favor of a better relationship.

If a man rejects a request, and if he's a good man who tries hard to provide, listen to his reasons and trust his intentions enough to accept a *no*, especially a kind one. Don't argue or push, nag, or manipulate to get your way. This makes him feel disrespected. And if it's a matter of not being able to afford something, then a man will feel even more put down by his inability to provide in the moment. It is one thing to ask correctly, and it is another thing to accept a no with grace and continuing support. Protect his feelings and he will always protect yours.

Let's say you've asked in your girlish way and he's ignoring it because he wants to avoid it. Hit him over the head with some girlish exaggeration. The following is an example where hinting and even asking didn't work, but girlish exaggeration did the trick.

The Light Fixture

Once, when we were in college, I acquired a large clunky light fixture that needed to be hung. It was heavy and hard to manage, so I hinted through some off-hand comments to Bob that I would like him to hang it for me. At least, that was the message I meant to convey. I wasn't sure at first if he understood what I was asking, and further attempts yielded no results. He was going to graduate school and was very busy, so his distraction at the time probably played a big role. So, days went by and the light fixture sat in the corner of our bedroom, unhung. I decided to give him a stronger hint and put it on his side of the bed hoping he would notice. I later noticed it back on the floor in the corner.

I realized at that point it might be years before he ever felt like doing it, so I tried another approach. I remembered Mom teaching me about girlishness, so I dressed up extra girly in a pretty skirt and felt very feminine. When Bob walked in, I carried the huge light fixture with great effort along with some tools to him and asked in a shy but direct way if he would be willing to use his strong muscles to help with something I couldn't do on my own. He happily installed the light fixture on the spot, visibly feeling great in helping and protecting me. And I felt great being helped and rescued from a heavy task that was really too much for me. From that moment on, I knew that asking in a girlish way was much better for both of us.

Another approach might be to attempt to do the job yourself while your husband is watching. Do it in a feminine way while demonstrating your girlish need for him—either because what you are trying to do is too awkward, too heavy, or you aren't sure how to do it but know he does. A lot of men love to swoop in and save us from a difficult task, especially when it's something they're good at.

Present your Case with Charm

Sometimes we try the attorney approach, logically convincing him that what we need or want is a good idea. You present your case with more pros than cons, of course. This sometimes works, depending on the personality of your husband, but it isn't charming and doesn't tend to deepen your relationship.

Why not try something that is charming and could also amp up the romance in your lives? It is much more rewarding than simply getting permission and can even be fun. You could try saying something like: "Do you know what I would really love? I'd adore a trip together. Just you and me. Do you think we might be able to do that soon?"

Another idea is to verbally give him a picture of what you want. Help him see himself and you in it. For example: "I was just thinking of you and me in Santa Barbara at that great beach where we got engaged. Remember the restaurant where we had that amazing sea food? I know it's probably too much to ask for, but doesn't it just delight your imagination? Do you think we could go there again sometime? Maybe even this year?"

Is it Childish?

Motivations do not come in neat categories of selfish or unselfish. Part of happiness and successful relationships is thorough and consistent self-care. It is not always a selfish thing to ask for something that you want or need. Your motivation can become a problem and can undermine the relationship when your desires ignore the wants and needs of others too much, especially when this becomes hurtful to them. You must balance your need for self-care with his need for the same. To do this, you will need to engage in some courageous soul-searching and might need to sacrifice what you want occasionally for the greater good. You will tend to be girlish if you care more about his needs than your own, but if you fail to take care of yourself and if he is sometimes oblivious, you might become resentful. Girlishness relies on love and good will to remain pure, otherwise its practice becomes childishness.

In Summary:

- Girlishness is a willingness to show sincere innocence and vulnerability with a twist of humor for an unselfishly beneficial purpose.
- When done properly, without manipulation, girlishness has the power to not only diffuse many situations where your husband has been thoughtless, grumpy, or in other ways unfair with you, but it can have a power to deepen your relationship even more.
- Some areas where girlishness is especially helpful are: in expressing your displeasure through exaggeration, reflecting his treatment of you in an exaggerated way, implementing girlish distraction, appreciation, trust and the way you ask for things.
- When you learn to present your case with charm, you will find these common occurrences can become ones that are fun, even humorous. You might even look forward to them.
- Girlishness relies on love and good will to remain pure; otherwise its practice becomes childishness.

*"The homemaker has the ultimate career... What do
shipping, railways, mines, cars, governments, etc. exist
for except that people may be fed, warmed, and safe
in their own homes? ... We wage war in order to have
peace, we work in order to have leisure, we produce
food in order to eat it. So your job is the one for
which all others exist."*

~ C.S. Lewis

This chapter is all about creating atmosphere. Everyone
wants to live in a space where they feel safe and
comfortable, and where they can rest. This is the definition of
a home. What we usually think of as home is something very
personal and having to do with the word sanctuary. It's something
we all know when we feel it. Even with great relationships, the
environment you live in impacts you and anyone who lives or
visits there.

Whether your home is a tent, an apartment, middle class
bungalow, or a palace, the ambiance you create is important. The

sense of any environment you enter or experience instantly either comforts or alerts your guard dog. You will either feel more at ease or more uncomfortable, though you may have no idea why unless you understand this part of you.

All your senses are involved in successful creation of atmosphere—not just sight. If you walk into a home that looks beautiful but smells like rotten bananas and mold, it won't feel as inviting as one that smells of freshly baking bread, potpourri, or just the smell we all know when everything is clean. As all sensory information must pass muster with your guard dog before anything else can be comfortably experienced, whatever you can do to put the guard dog at ease will allow your family and guests to feel comfortable.

You can use what you know about the guard dog to help people think of your home as a sanctuary where they can relax and permit the higher forms of their brain to operate freely. Within such a setting, relationships can flourish, tranquility abounds, children blossom, and welcome visitors are at their best. Everyone will remember how they felt, even if they don't know why, and will love being in your home.

Creating a comfortable environment is something women tend to excel at when we try. When we look for ways to make our homes more beautiful and inviting, we are creating this special feeling for ourselves and our loved ones. It's what my mother called being a "Domestic Goddess."

It's not difficult, or even necessarily expensive, to generate a pleasant atmosphere, but this does require focus and maintenance as well as some basic creativity — or the ability to copy what you see.

You can add womanly touches here and there, such as a table cloth, a potted plant, a rug or carefully arranged pictures on the walls. Make it obvious that a deliberate attempt is regularly made to keep the home pleasant and attractive. Show that you care about all who live there, as well as those who visit.

Consider all the senses — for your sense of smell, perhaps have something delicious cooking, fresh flowers, fresh air through an open window (or an open door on a nice day), or some sort of light air freshener. For sound you might add soft music playing in the background or a recording of the sound of birds. Make sure the temperature of your home is also as pleasant as you can manage. No one feels emotionally safe in a room that is either freezing or hot. A clean and tastefully arranged room is pleasing to the eyes, and for sense of touch, a soft throw or pillows helps to create a general sense of "sit down and make yourself comfortable" for all who enter, whether they live there or are a guest. Your atmosphere should say: "Welcome!"

There are so many free resources and ideas at our fingertips to draw from. We can even learn about and plan out these feminine touches while sitting in our homes, in comfort.

Creating Atmosphere

Providing a place where he loves to be, and to which he looks forward to coming home, involves a bit of interior decorating and homemaking. You don't have to be advanced to make your home warm and inviting. The main requirement is that you care about the comfort level of your loved ones.

Let's start with the sense that is usually activated first.

Visual Atmosphere

Visual atmosphere is simply the way your home looks. This includes not only furniture, wall coverings, and the color of paint used on walls, but also how these things are maintained, arranged, and kept clean. If a room is not tidy, it detracts from the other visuals you have carefully put in place. This doesn't mean you must have a lot of money. The important thing here is the effort you give in making your home look as good as you can.

Men are enchanted by a woman's touch, as long as she remembers his masculinity. A woman's touch can be balanced with the respect that a man lives there as well. A combination of masculine and feminine visuals is great and, like clothing, accentuates the differences. It can be any style of décor from modern to French Baroque, from Thai traditional to Finnish industrial, as well as repurposed garage sale "Shabby Chic" or hand-me-downs from grandma; the important thing is the thought and care that go into your surroundings.

When you are moving into a home that is new to you, carefully consider how to arrange the furniture, what to put on the walls, how to position beds, how decorating the bathroom will make it beautiful as well as convenient. This is creating visual atmosphere.

We all know it's not enough to create ambiance once and be done with it forever. If it is not maintained, it will deteriorate. You can buy beautiful furniture and even hire a decorator to create a fabulous looking place. But if you neglect it, your home could quickly turn into a dusty, terrible mess, especially if you have children, pets, or lots of guests. More men are taking responsibility for household chores these days, but the bulk of it still tends to be handled by women.

Aromas

The smell of cleanliness is the foundation for any other aroma you add to your home, car, or work space. How do you feel when you walk into a room that smells like mildew, old cheese, or any other unpleasant odor? We all want to come home to pleasant scents. What scents do you want in your home? You can display fresh flowers, but those can be expensive. There are also room fresheners, scented candles, and food cooking, frying, or baking. Essential oils can bring the aroma of nature indoors. When you realize how important smells are, you can decide what you like best. In my opinion, there is nothing better than the aroma of fresh baked bread. My husband feels that nothing tops the smell of bacon.

When you have dinner guests, do you consider how your home will smell as your guests arrive? Not all foods have the best aromas when they are cooking, even though they taste great. Watch out for cauliflower. I had some simmering away on the stove once when we had friends to dinner. I had soft background music playing, my table was set carefully, and I was very attentive to all my other visuals. When my friend Ami walked in, she wasn't sure what I was cooking but the smell worried her. I have never boiled cauliflower again. Fish is another one to be careful of; it might be delicious and even impressive to guests, but the aroma of fish bones in your trash can be awful and will mess up your evening's aromatic atmosphere fast.

I remember my mother saying if she'd had a particularly busy day and hadn't prepared dinner by the time Dad was due home, she would quickly start frying some onions. Onions frying is a delightful smell; they smell like dinner is being prepared. When Dad walked in, the wonderful aroma would hit him immediately and he was always reassured that something good was on the way. He seldom noticed that it took a while longer before we ate.

Sounds

Sounds could be the most ignored of the aspects of atmosphere, though they do have an important place. Show careful consideration for what others in your home would like to listen to, and be creative. There are so many sounds that can generate an appealing ambiance. I have a CD of the sound of birds in an English countryside. I love it. Some people like the sound of creaking wooden ships in a harbor or soft music in the background. Others love the resonance of water with either a real fountain or a recording of one. Still others prefer peace and quiet or the sound of children happily playing. Perhaps you have a lovely singing or speaking voice that can calm the people around you; don't underestimate your own power to create a mood wherever you go, especially in your own home.

Tastes

Who doesn't love good home-cooked food? Even if you could afford to eat out every meal, it isn't as healthy and there is a reason home cooking has such a good reputation. Cooking skills are easy to acquire with books, internet, and cable TV resources, and you can quickly gain a high degree of competency right in your own home. But it isn't necessary to be a Michelin-rated chef. Knowing how to master a few basic meals is not only rewarding, but it goes far in calming men's guard dogs. You can find almost any recipe you can think of online, many with instructional videos, or you might simply know a friend who can show you some special cooking techniques in person.

I'm sure you've heard the phrase: "The way to a man's heart is through his stomach." While this might be a little overstated, there is still a lot of truth to it. To most men, food is love and it can be like magic.

Good friends still share time-tested recipes, but we're lucky to have many of the advances in communication we have today. We don't even have to take big risks that the recipe will be good.

Many online sites have reviews. Some have hundreds of five-star ratings that practically ensure the dish will be great.

Women are often busy and, though you might love to spend all day cooking something amazing, you can still find many ways to calm his guard dog through delicious food that don't take all day to prepare. Sometimes cooking short-cuts like crock pots can be a wonderful solution to a hectic lifestyle.

Crock Pot Cooking Improved Her Marriage

Jada and Terrell started out their marriage with each having a successful but demanding career. The problem came about two years into their marriage. Terrell became increasingly grumpy and critical of Jada. Instead of coming home and enjoying their time together in the evening, he seemed dissatisfied and even a bit distant. Jada had no idea what was going on. They went out to dinner and she confided her concerns to Terrell. What he said totally surprised her.

He admitted that every day when he arrived home from work, hungry and tired, the house seemed empty and cold. Not only was Jada not there, but there was no dinner. He was struggling to get in touch with his own feelings but was able to provide at least this much information.

Jada felt bad that she arrived home even later than he did. What could she do? She went to her sisters for advice and they quickly came up with an answer. They told her she could have the inviting smell of home cooking by using a slow cooker or crock pot. Jada had little experience but soon had a handful of great tested recipes and a plan.

On the weekend, when she was home, she prepared a week's worth of crock pot meals and froze them. Each morning, she would dump the ingredients in her slow cooker and head off to work. When she and Terrell both came home, there was not only a wonderful aroma and no one frantically trying to pull something together, but they both enjoyed a delicious meal without all the stress. The amazing thing was, it had a big impact on their marriage. Terrell's grumpy attitude disappeared, and he was also much more affectionate and attentive.

Sometimes a relatively minor change can result in something fantastic. Don't underestimate the power of calming the guard dog. Paying attention to atmosphere can make a bigger difference than you might realize, as the above example illustrates.

Touch

The way things feel can make a difference too. Fabrics on your sofa, a warm or cold floor, rugs, towels and sheets can all contribute to your loved ones' feeling of comfort. You could consider plush pillows, velvety throws, silk rugs, soft towels, or even slippers and bath robes for guests.

You should reserve your deepest consideration for your husband. What kind of pillow helps him sleep best? Soft or crisp sheets? What about the fabrics you wear? When I dress in particularly soft or silky fabrics, Bob always notices and says how much he loves it when I wear these textures. He will sometimes just sit beside me and gently stroke my leg, feeling the texture. If I wore more rough fabrics, I would be less comfortable, and Bob might be less pleased. But wearing soft clothes results in him wanting to touch me even more!

In Summary:

- Whatever else you do in your life, realize that your role as a homemaker is the one for which all other careers exist. The importance of creating and maintaining atmosphere is not only exciting but challenging. It provides an endless source of potential for improvement and creativity.
- All the senses (including sight, sound, touch, aroma, and taste) need to be considered when calming your loved ones' guard dogs so that everyone can feel their best.
- Practicing and developing your skills in improving the atmosphere in your home will make you feel happier and more successful and can have a profound effect on your family in addition to all who visit your home.

"[Men] step into matrimony deliberately. They step into it under stress of prodigious emotion, when cold reason and calm judgment are not the question..."
~ Fascinating Womanhood 1922

The timeless principles of Fascinating Womanhood are not just for women who are already married and looking to improve their relationships. All the charm, skills, and practice of the powers of femininity can help single women too. In this section, we will discuss some principles that will benefit single girls who want to know how to find their hero.

Prince Charming

What we look for in a man will tend to have a profound effect on the nature of the relationship. If our focus is on looks, wealth, or status, and if our priorities do not mature beyond that at some early point, the romance will be short-lived. If you look for timeless qualities, such as character and charm, your relationship will last proportionately.

If a lifelong love affair is what you're looking for, you must ask yourself whether the things you value are the kind that stand the test of time.

The following is a story that illustrates some things I learned about myself before I was married:

When I was about fourteen, I asked my mom how I could find the perfect man for me. She gave me a blank sheet of paper and told me to write down all the qualities of the man I wanted. That was easy, and I made an extensive list. When I was done, she turned the paper over and told me to then write down the qualities that man would be looking for in a woman. One that he deserved. This was much harder and more painful since I didn't feel I possessed many of these qualities. When I finished the list, which took significantly longer to complete, mom told me to tape the list to my headboard — with the list of what he would want facing outward. She suggested I not look at the backside containing the qualities I wanted in him, telling me I would attract the type of man I desired when I resembled more closely the list of things he'd want. I took this to heart over the following years.

That list was taped to my headboard until I went to college and met Bob. I returned home after getting engaged to get ready for the wedding and was surprised to see that list still there, taped to my headboard. I turned it over to see the qualities I had hoped for and Bob fit all of them. I then turned to the part that applied to me. I had made some progress, in part because of the exercise my mother suggested. I imagine that taking self-improvement seriously helped me to win the love of such a great man.

If you are married, you can still do a version of this. List your husband's good qualities on one side and what he would deserve or want on the other. It can have powerful results if you refer to it daily and try to live it.

"We but mirror the world. All the tendencies present in the outer world are to be found in the world of our body. If we could change ourselves, the tendencies in the world would also change. As a [woman] changes [her] own nature, so does the attitude of the world change towards [her]. This is the divine mystery supreme. A wonderful thing it is and the source of our happiness. We need not wait to see what others do."
~ Mahatma Gandhi

It's important to work on yourself but it's also helpful to understand why some men are hesitant to get married.

Why Some Men Say They Don't Want to Get Married

1. *He can't afford it*

A responsible man is sensible to the financial obligations marriage implies, and he could be in legitimate debt from education or an investment that didn't work out well. Not being able to offer the woman he is in love with any sort of lifestyle or security could delay a proposal. He longs for a sense of competency in this world and he can sometimes fear invalidation from a wife for whom he does not care adequately. As he gets to know you and realizes your wonderful character, he can be assured that you love him for who he is, not how much money he makes. Your constant belief in him and understanding of Fascinating Womanhood principles can help him make even more of himself than he might alone.

2. *He's immature*

If you are living together or just sleeping together and using birth control, and he doesn't want to get married, he's probably grown complacent because he's immature. He may value your physical relationship to the point that he thinks he has everything he wants. This is a sad allegation because it will tend to mean he objectifies you to a large degree. Ask yourself what state your relationship would be in without sex. If there would likely be nothing left, his masculinity has not come into full bloom, and you may have rushed the physical side of your intimate relationship. He will need time to prove his masculinity to himself and to you, and during this period you can inspire him by developing your own feminine power. His masculine growth will prove his worthiness to you and his suitability as a mate if he has the right potential. You can protect yourself by focusing more on your intellectual, emotional, and spiritual connection with him. The relationship will mature according to its capacity and in its own time, and this process will teach you if and when he's "the one." A truly mature and masculine man will be interested in marriage and the commitment it brings in due course because he will see the greater meaning and opportunity for mutual growth.

3. *He's not done dating yet*

This means that he has his eyes on other girls, or he is not interested enough in you to commit. And it could mean he is planning to simply collect you, to keep you as a sort of pet or trophy and never really take things further. In other words, he is signaling his interest in using you, and he is not a masculine man.

It may also be the case that he's a great catch but there is something about you that is scaring him off, and he is looking at relationship exit signs.

Short Man Jokes

There was a pretty young woman who was dating a handsome but short young man in college. All seemed to be going well until she asked him one day, "Are you sensitive to short man jokes?" He responded that he wasn't, so she said, "Oh good. Now I can tell them!" Not long after, he decided he was not finished dating yet and needed more time. She had no idea why he suddenly stopped asking her out.

This young woman didn't recognize her boyfriend's sensitive pride. You may think, "Who would say something so rude to the person they're dating?" You might be surprised how few women understand male pride and how many make this mistake in different ways. We are often unaware of the impact of hurtful or insensitive words and actions, especially regarding masculinity—a subject in which we are frequently uninformed. So, if he is suddenly acting distant where he was previously interested, ask yourself if you've been insensitive or somehow injured his pride. This will help you avoid making unintended blunders that could hurt you and cause him to lose interest, and it may point you to an area of your relationship in which you can attempt repair.

4. *Fear of an uncertain future*

This is a legitimate anxiety, especially for a masculine man. It includes the first point above concerning finances, but may also involve a sick family member, legal trouble, his own health, or something complicated from his past that has a bearing on his present and future prospects. Or he might be uncertain of himself, having not yet obtained a level of competency in this world to satisfy his own pride. You can build him up faster than the world can with your feminine power. Through your example as a fascinating woman, and with the influence of acceptance and admiration, you can inspire his masculinity, which will improve his self-confidence.

5. *He is divorced, or his parents were*

Many get divorced and jump right back into marriage. However, it's not uncommon for a sensitive man to develop anxiety about potentially going through it all over again. Or, he might have seen parents or siblings go through painful, even ugly divorces and think to himself, "I don't ever want to go through that!" Patience here will go a long way with a man traumatized in any way by a painful breakup or loss of trust with someone else. Focusing on the appropriate order of intimacy levels and your influence as a feminine woman will help to heal his wounds and calm his fears.

6. *He has children*

If he has been married before, or has children from a previous relationship, he will have financial and emotional responsibilities. Perhaps he is concerned that you won't like his children, or they won't like you. How will you unite and become a successful family? Understanding and being sympathetic to these concerns will help him feel that being with you is a great advantage, rather than a risk.

7. *His family doesn't approve*

Sometimes a man might be put off by thinking of marrying a woman he knows his family won't likely accept. Does he fear he might be abandoned by them? What family obligations does he have? Being sensitive to these issues will help you understand him and avoid unnecessary conflict. It can also have a positive effect on him that can cause him to be more persuasive and creative in securing family approval. In addition, when you live the principles of Fascinating Womanhood, you might very well earn your way into his family's heart through your character, compassion, and charm.

8. *Inflexibility*

Some people create rules for themselves to help them feel more in control and safe. I knew a man who once said he could never marry a girl because she liked Miracle Whip®, a type of condiment in the US. Another man set his limit at the mispronunciation of a particular word. Others may feel strongly about differences in their political views or tastes in music or recreation. Whether significant or not, inflexible men make excuses to avoid responsibility and commitment, or because they're not really in love. A mature man will have a broader perspective and appreciate your feminine qualities. More importantly, he will desire commitment with you because of the potential he sees in you as an individual, and in your union.

9. *Emotional dependence on family*

Some men seem to be emotionally dependent on family even if they have a job and are financially independent. These are the men who must check in with their mother, father or guardian before making any decisions. If you find this to be true with the man you are considering marrying, this could be a real problem. You must assess if you actually want to marry a man whose parents' opinion of you overrules his. Remember, you must accept him at face value. If you can't, you might need to move on.

10. *He thinks you're high-maintenance*

If you are a high-maintenance woman, this might be a huge problem for a man you're interested in. He might feel like he will never be able to do enough, buy enough, or be enough for you. This most likely indicates an issue with your personal character, what you want or demand regularly of him and others around you. It may be that you are not as mature or perhaps not ready to build a lifelong romance yet.

When you have mature character, you will tend to put things which matter most ahead of those which matter least. You will have an ordered sense of priorities and values, and you will not seem high-maintenance to a masculine man because he will be in sync with you. High-maintenance women tend to be superficial and more concerned with material possessions, appearance, and status. These are transitory things that we can only barely say that we possess under the best circumstances; like saying we possess water in our cupped hands. It's only a matter of time before our circumstances change. Sooner or later, character becomes the only thing we really retain, if we have anything at all.

It's easy to say that you shouldn't be concerned about poverty, and that the quality of your relationships is what makes you wealthy. You can't eat friendship, and romance won't keep rain off your head or pay the electric bill. You do have a basic right to a certain expectation of lifestyle. Ask yourself if you could stay in love with a man even if only the necessities of life were available. Imagine that together, the two of you never really achieve much in terms of status, and that your access to adventure and novelty is fairly limited. This may help you to gauge the extent to which you are really in love with him, versus what he seems to have and the lifestyle that will bring to you.

A personal sense of security is important to a woman, but we will not all become rich and famous. You will find that wherever your heart is, so will be your treasure. Life is short and sometimes hard. Whether you appreciate it fully in the present or only glimpse the truth of it, and though it may seem painfully simple, it is the enduring things that will ultimately come to matter most to us and the fleeting things that fulfill the least. You can orient yourself now for a long-term bet on happiness by bearing this in mind and letting it inform your approach to finding the man of your dreams.

Ex-Wife Yet Again

Tamara was dating a doctor. He was a wonderful man who had unfortunate luck in love. He was twice divorced, and his last wife, Ann, complained that his obligations to extended family and six kids made him poorer than she expected. She would often say to him that she should have married a "richer doctor" instead. Needless to say, that marriage didn't last long. He came to expect that women were often shallow and was guarded in his future relationships, including with Tamara.

She avoided asking for expensive things and was effusively grateful for anything he did for her. She praised him, accepted him, and in all ways avoided complaining and negativity around him, and he eventually warmed up and proposed.

11. *He doesn't believe in marriage*

Many resent the notion that we must get permission from the state to formally unite in love, or to go our separate ways through divorce. The mature man will recognize that marriage is more than dating each other with a contract; it's a system that provides certainty and safety for the family. It's also an emotional incubator for both men and women. You can learn from each other and grow in an atmosphere where you are more likely to stay and not split up over any little thing. It provides more security for children who are dependent on parents physically, financially, and emotionally.

Marriage is the building block of civilization. When you marry, you make a commitment to stay together and work through whatever problems you encounter. Without this pledge, either of you can leave at any time as soon as something gets difficult or requires growth. This uncertainty promotes personal and cultural chaos. You have nothing stable to count on. When children are involved, it's even more complicated.

If you are dating a man who says he doesn't believe in marriage, you need to find out why. He might not have thought through to some of the many potential consequences. Or, he may be wanting a quick way out if it doesn't work.

Some believe that if they don't marry, their union has a better chance of enduring because everyone they know who has married has also divorced. According to the US Census Bureau, you have a far greater chance of staying together and building a meaningful life if you get married than if you don't.

When you understand the importance of marriage and live the principles of Fascinating Womanhood, you can help the man you love overcome any of these obstacles and find the rich, stable, and rewarding life you seek.

Inspiring a Proposal

To inspire a loving but reluctant man to want to marry you, you must help him feel you are indispensable to his life and happiness. That alone will usually overcome major objections or fear of marriage.

The solution lies in a combination of charm, femininity, acceptance, admiration, character development, and understanding men. How much you have internalized these qualities and made them a part of you will determine how successful you will be. In addition, you will want to create romantic atmosphere.

Don't sell yourself short or cheap by giving in to sex before developing the more important levels of intimacy and making a formal commitment together; it is high-risk behavior for both, but especially for women. Again, we tend to associate sex with romance. The chemistry as well as the intimacy of the act bonds us more quickly to the relationship than it does a man. We risk our hearts getting broken, unintended pregnancy, and emotional pain. As we have discussed earlier in this book, it's easier for him to have sex, even over a period of time, and then leave. Who wants to take a such a significant risk with something this important?

How to Tell If He's a Keeper

What makes a good man? How can you tell before you marry him?

Positives to look for:

1. *Does he have established healthy relationships?* Does he have close friends and good relationships with at least some of his family?

2. *Does he have a job, or is he in training or college and have his finances in order?* There can be emergencies but not perpetual fires to extinguish. He might have debt from college education, a home, or a car. Those things could indicate his ambition and willingness to take risks to get ahead. But if he buys impulsively without thought for the future and with an attitude of "I'll worry about that later," it could signal a dangerous lack of responsibility.

3. *Is he kind to others, especially strangers?* When we don't have to do what is right we really show our quality. In the case of strangers, there is less incentive to be kind. A man who shows kindness when he doesn't have to likely has great character.

4. *Is he thoughtful?* This can be expressed in countless ways, especially if he doesn't think you notice. Thoughtful men notice and remember important details about the people he's close to, such as remembering that you don't like fish or grabbing the coat you forgot when leaving a restaurant. Thoughtfulness may seem to revolve around small matters, but it's a big deal in the end.

5. *Is he humble?* When a man has humility, he shows acceptance and knowledge that he can learn from others and is not always right. He recognizes his own human

flaws but also his potential. Humility is the disposition to learn and the willingness to change.

6. *Is he a hard worker?* It's great to be married to a man with a good work ethic. Such men will tend to take responsibility where they find it, and they're reliable. A man who exclaims to all that he despises work and, if wealthy enough, would spend his life on a perpetual vacation, could be one who lacks character. People who try to get away with doing as little as possible can be difficult to live with, while it is almost always a a pleasure to be connected to those who are industrious.

7. *Does he have a kind attitude about children?* When a man is kind and goes out of his way with children, when children like and want to spend time with him, this indicates a valuable quality that is important to fatherhood.

   When we were growing up, my sisters and I used to try to introduce the boys we were dating to our youngest sister who was still a child. If she liked him right away, we knew he wasn't a bad guy. But the men she didn't like always turned out have serious issues. She was able to sense, often with one meeting, whether our dates were good guys or not.

8. *Is he honest?* We must all tailor our speech and occasionally withhold information due to natural limitations or relationship dynamics. An honest person seeks to empower and uplift others and will demonstrate trustworthiness to

you by communicating the most important facts, thoughts, and feelings of his life. An honest man is dependable and is perhaps most visible in his attention to punctuality and fulfilling promises to you and others.

9. *Does he have a sense of humor?* This quality can be overdone and abused. A good sense of humor is never cruel and helps make the stresses of life easier to bear. Masculine men use humor to diffuse tension, to delight, and to inspire. They use it to display cleverness and to invite praise, and it is a form of communication that can build intellectual and emotional intimacy. Men who can see the genuine comedy in everyday circumstances are easier to live with and tend to roll with the punches.

10. *Does he have a spiritual base?* Does he believe in something higher than himself? Whether you are religious or not, believing in principles and virtues that are greater than you promote a desire for transcendence.

It's important to know the man you are considering spending your life with. It's not enough to have a lot of fun together and a strong chemical attraction. Meet his friends and family. If you see a red flag, check it out. Pay attention to it. Don't dismiss it until you have ample reason to do so. Some suspicions should be dismissed for lack of grounds.

Suppose you were dating a man and you heard a rumor that he had been abusive in his past? Then, just as you were getting very alarmed, you discovered that an ex-girlfriend he broke up with was upset with him and had started a rumor by telling friends she was going to destroy him. The whole accusation may not have been true in the first place. She might have made it up out of spite. If you quit dating him too soon without investigating the facts, you might deeply regret it. You have to decide who to believe and who to trust. Give yourself time to really know him.

You might feel paranoid being so careful, but your future and sometimes even your life could depend on it. It's a big deal. Listen to intuition that says things like, "I feel weird about this," or "Something about him seems off." Dismiss your suspicions if you can find adequate reason, but don't be afraid give some credit to your instincts.

Sasha and Sam

Sasha was a single mother recovering from a failed marriage. She had 3 daughters she adored. After things settled down and her life became more stable, she found she was lonely and wanted to meet someone. One night she went with a friend to a club and met a charming man. She was flattered that Sam showed such interest in her. They started dating and he was polite and attentive. After a while, she brought him home to meet her children. He was kind to them and went out of his way to get their approval. Sasha thought it was odd that Sam didn't seem to have any friends and he said all his family had died. She dismissed her discomfort thinking she was just being paranoid and invited him to move in with her.

In the end, Sasha found out Sam had a criminal record and was a wanted pedophile in another state. His family had not died — they had disowned him. She became terrified for her girls. It ended safely for Sasha, but not before Sam had stolen all her money and racked up her credit cards. And when he found out she knew who he really was, he began to abuse her physically and even sexually. He was caught and put in prison, but the pain and anguish, as well as post-traumatic stress Sasha still suffers from, will take a long time to heal.

Though this example is somewhat extreme, these kinds of things happen when we don't pay enough attention to the red warning flags that often wave in front of us.

Sometimes warning signs are not clear and we don't see them until it's too late. There are clever men out there who can fool you unless you are careful.

Narcissism Run Amok

Dave was handsome and smart, and he made friends easily. His family spoke highly of him and so did his employers. He was charming and seemed sincere. Krista fell hard for him and was a year into the relationship before she realized how emotionally dangerous he was. He talked her into paying for several trips they went on together, saying he would pay her back, but he never did. She knew he displayed some narcissism but had no idea it was severe enough for her to be as wary as she should have been. They never married, but he ended up raping her and the debt she incurred from him took years to pay off. The emotional pain took longer.

Awareness greatly cuts down on devastating consequences. If you have fallen prey to a dead-end guy, don't be hard on yourself. It's impossible to predict every dangerous situation, but you can greatly improve your chances.

Men Who Are Controlling

In the beginning of a relationship, most controlling men will be reciprocal in giving and taking, but you will find him gradually changing over time. If he begins to demand more and more unreasonable control, it's time to set boundaries, or leave.

Saved Just in Time

A woman met a man at work who was funny, seemed nice and was very handsome. They started dating, and she thought it was going well. She had two children from her previous marriage. One day he announced he had purchased gym memberships for her and her kids. She felt uncomfortable about this because she didn't know him well enough. He didn't even talk to her about it. It seemed too much too soon.

If she accepted the gift, she would feel obligated to use the gym membership regularly. She told him she didn't feel good about his apparent generosity. The next day he came to her house with gym clothing for all the family. She told him she didn't feel good about the membership or the clothes. He got upset and left in a huff. The next day, she returned home from work to find he had broken into her house and had laid out all the clothes for her and her children.

When she confronted him with this criminal behavior, he got defensive and said he wanted to "surprise her." He surprised her alright, but not in a good way. She broke up with him immediately. She later researched him on the internet and found he was married to another woman in a different state.

Controlling, abusive men tend to prey on caring, sensitive women. No one else would put up with it. Once you accept one inappropriate behavior in a controlling person, it's even more difficult to set a limit the next time. Watch out for men who are inappropriately bold, loud, or obnoxious, with no apparent awareness of boundaries—men with no appropriate fear of consequences. If you have a creepy feeling, pay attention to it.

The Wine and Dine Ploy

It sounds great at first to be "wined and dined." Flowers all the time, romantic evenings with soft lighting and music. It pleases and excites our senses. Women need security and want to find love. Romantic gestures are fine if a man is sincere, but some men know how to turn on the charm to get what they want quicker, which usually involves sex.

It takes time to develop a true romantic relationship. Achieving it requires spending real time together, getting to know each other. Selfish and immature men are more likely to just seek physical pleasure. We prefer to think that when a man desires us, it's as a romantic companion, not just a play thing. This is where it's important to be able to discern if he is more an upstairs or downstairs guy (For a discussion of the Upstairs and Downstairs parts of the brain, see Chapter 9, Brain Matters).

It's not necessary to spend a lot of money to develop a relationship. In fact, doing something inexpensive might clarify how much money is a manipulative factor in the relationship. Is he trying to buy you? Is he happy doing simple things together as well as some that are costlier?   The fun things you do, spending time with each other doing ordinary stuff, like watching a movie together at home or going on a picnic, will help you get to know him as a person, to see who he really is.

If he is always sending flowers and telling you how beautiful you are, that's okay, but it's not critical. If he seems unwilling to take time to get to know you, to share his life with you, please be careful because he might be shallow. If your intuition sends uncomfortable signals about this, don't ignore it.

Let's say he is a person of little substance and his main goal is to sleep with you. He may use flattery like, "You're so beautiful" and "You're so hot" all the time or, "You turn me on." Could it mean he doesn't take you seriously? Of course, this doesn't mean if a man tells you you're beautiful, he's trying to get you into bed. It's too-much-too-soon, syrupy flattery you have to watch out for. Some men are charming only to get what they want, not because they are falling in love, but rather they are falling in lust.

How to Spot a Rat

There are a lot of good men out there. They protect us, love us, and can become our best friends. But some of them are rats and you should stay away from them.

How can you sort them out? It's harder to really get to know someone on the internet, but you will still get some early clues. Of course you will do yourself a favor by being careful, but you still need to keep something of an open mind and not see everything as a deal-breaker. No one is perfect, so we need to be women of character and compassion. In the end, spotting a rat correctly comes down to the degree of seriousness of any of the following warning signs.

Let's begin with a few simple deal-breakers:

1. *Criminals*

   Murderers, rapists, drug dealers, pimps, thieves, etc.

2. *Addicts with no interest in recovery*

   Alcohol, drugs, sex, theft, pornography

3. *Serial cheaters or men who insist on an open marriage*

4. *Verbal, physical, sexual abusers who have no respect for women*

The above list is pretty intense and most of us won't knowingly date or marry these sorts of men, but so many of us want to believe the best in a man and try to fix him. If he belongs to any of the categories above, you're in trouble and you should run fast.

Now let's take a look at a few things to watch out for but that aren't necessarily deal-breakers. Be careful and continue to look for more information if you see any of these traits:

1. *Is he superficial?* Though he might be charming, does he talk more about himself or shallow subjects (his car, clothes, jewelry, video games, overly focused on his looks or yours, etc.) than anything substantial?

2. *Is he often very critical of others such as colleagues, family, or friends?* Does he constantly talk about how stupid others are?

3. *Is he a self-promoter?* Does he talk a lot about how great he is, his accomplishments, and how much money he is going to make or has made? Men who focus mostly on themselves are much more likely to be narcissistic and self-centered.

4. *Is he unambitious or lazy?* Does he have life goals? Does he talk about his work, his education, friends and family, or does he talk more about video games or sports, and what fun thing he is going to do next? Recreation is good, but it could be a tipoff if it dominates his life and gets in the way of more important things.

5. *Is he more interested in truth or appearance?* When truth is a priority for a guy, he will seek it, speak it, and live it. People who prefer appearance don't care about the truth and are fine with fooling people and being fooled. They

will use presentation to justify whatever they wish and are often dishonest to themselves and others.

6. *Does he talk about personal growth?* Is he interested in doing what's right?

7. *Is he spiritual or interested in a Higher Power?* One can be spiritual but not necessarily religious. Spirituality has to do with the sense a person has of their place in the larger scheme of things. It concerns identity larger than oneself, or connectedness. Spirituality helps us escape our personal limitations, and therefore our egos before it allows us to contemplate and aspire to something greater — it provides you with a vision of what you might become.

8. *Does he talk graphically about sex?* This is a potential clue as to what is most important to him and what he thinks a relationship really is — a brief search for excitement.

9. *Is he willing to wait for sex after marriage?* There are many women today who assume that sex before marriage is a given. Men who use women or who have little substance seldom, if ever, will stay with a woman who is determined to wait until marriage to give herself fully to him. What does he do when you tell him it's too risky for you? Does he respect your feelings? Or does he try to shame you into giving in, or does he leave? This is something you need to know before beginning a serious relationship.

10. *Does he constantly flatter you and tell you how hot you are, but doesn't seem to respect you?*

11. *How does he treat those who serve him?* Some men don't think they need to be polite to those who "don't matter" — who aren't important to their business or private life. This is a warning sign.

12. *Is he addicted to anything?* If he is willing to change, you may still need to gauge his commitment and the severity of his addiction. People can be addicted to a lot of things, but some of the most serious categories are drugs, alcohol, and sex.

13. *Does he engage in high-risk behaviors* such as illegal activities of any kind. Any man who is willing to blatantly break the law is someone to watch out for because he has no respect for boundaries, societal norms, or values. This includes any commitments he makes to you.

14. *Does he seem comfortable with attitudes such as, "Men aren't meant to be monogamous?"* This should indicate to you that he is not loyal and is unlikely to commit to anything for long. It also shows that he doesn't appreciate the personal growth that marriage and real intimacy bring.

15. *How does he treat family, specifically children and pets?* Men who have disdain for children, who abuse kids or animals, have sociopathic tendencies. They are extremely high-risk people to get into relationships with.

16. *Does he try to borrow money* from you or want you to co-sign on a loan that could put you at financial risk?

Even though a superficial man might be charming, you become aware of warning signs as you get to know him and spend more time with him. If you are aware, he will let slip clues to his true character or nature no matter how he tries; especially when hungry, angry, lonely, tired, or under the influence of substances such as drugs or alcohol. This will display the degree to which his upstairs manages his downstairs, and this is a gauge of maturity and character.

Be cautious in your judgment of men who do not show deal-breaking characteristics. He may want to be a good guy but has low self-esteem or has been through a lot of trauma. Just remember, you can only change yourself.

Feminine power allows you to have astonishing *influence* on others, but it's influence, not overt control. What that means is, if you try to exert your feminine power in order to force change in another, it won't have the desired effect. Our greatest strength lies in our character and femininity, and we will be most successful in relationships when we set a powerful example and accept others as they are.

He might change, but don't plan on it because he might not. Remember, you are a feminine woman of immeasurable worth. There are many good men, the kind who are masculine, chivalrous, and want to protect you and be your hero—that's what you want. You can find the man of your dreams. Just be careful and concentrate on being the woman of *his* dreams as well. You need to avoid the sort of men who might disrespect, hurt, or abuse you. Avoid the rats.

In Summary:

- Timeless Fascinating Womanhood principles are helpful for both single and married women.
- You can prepare yourself to both attract and be attracted to the man of your dreams. It's not enough to just think about what kind of a man you want—you must be the kind of woman he is looking for and deserves.
- Understanding why men sometimes avoid or hesitate to get married will help you overcome his objections and inspire a proposal.
- Look for qualities in him that have lasting relationship potential to see if he's a keeper.
- Knowing the basics of how to spot a rat will save much heartache while you're trying to find the love of your life.
- There are good men out there who are kind, chivalrous and who want to protect us and to be our heroes!

With Love

My heart goes out to all the women of this world who are searching for answers and help with some of the most important questions in life. We all long for happiness and success in relationships. Some of you are up at night reading or on your computers, looking for something—anything—that will help improve your marriage, your love life, and your feeling of worth as a woman.

Reclaiming femininity, inspiring masculinity, and applying this knowledge to the creation of a lifelong love affair can have a profound effect on your life and on those of others. You will find a new sense of who you are, your value, and worth.

Women are amazing. We have given birth to every person ever born. We love our families, our neighbors, and our countries. We bring unique beauty to this earth. We are tireless in our search for ways to improve ourselves so that we will be better wives, mothers, and human beings. Know that you are valuable, no matter who you are or what challenges or limitations you face.

My sincere hope is that you will have a lifelong love affair with a man you love who adores you in return.

"What greater thing is there for two human souls than to feel that they are joined for life, to strengthen each other in all labor, to rest on each other in all sorrow, to minister to each other in all pain, to be one with each other in silent, unspeakable memories at the moment of the last parting."
~ George Eliot

About the Author

Dixie Andelin Forsyth has been happily married to her husband Robert Forsyth for 50 years and is the mother of 7 children and has numerous grandchildren. She is an accomplished artist who loves sculpture, making clocks, and trompe l'oeil. She also enjoys cooking, sewing, and creating a welcoming atmosphere in her home.

Dixie is the eldest daughter of Helen B. Andelin, author of the best selling books, Fascinating Womanhood; first published in 1963 as well as The Fascinating Girl and All About Raising Children. She has completed editing and revisions of all her mother's books and workbooks as per Helen's request prior to her passing in 2009.

As president of Fascinating Womanhood worldwide, she has established a successful YouTube channel featuring A Feminine Moment and does regular podcasts. She has also created a teaching program with certified teachers from countries around the world representing an inclusive group of cultures, races, and religions.

She can be found on the web at FascinatingWomanhood.com, Instagram, and on Facebook at TheRealFascinatingWomanhood.

CPSIA information can be obtained
at www.ICGtesting.com
Printed in the USA
FSHW020904121220
76842FS